Paul on Leadership

Servant Leadership in a Ministry of Transition

C. GENE WILKES

LIFEWAY PRESS
NASHVILLE, TENNESSEE

ISBN 0-6331-9531-6

This book is a resource in the Christian Growth Study Plan.
Course CG-1038
Dewey Decimal Classification Number: 303.3
Subject Heading: LEADERSHIP \ PAUL, APOSTLE \ CHURCH GROWTH

Printed in the United States of America

Leadership and Adult Publishing
LifeWay Church Resources
One LifeWay Plaza
Nashville, Tennessee 37234-0175

We believe the Bible has God for its author; salvation for its end; and truth,
without any mixture of error, for its matter and that all Scripture is totally true and
trustworthy. The 2000 statement of The Baptist Faith and Message is our doctrinal guideline.

CONTENTS

INTRODUCTION

God is reviving and reforming the church in America. Churches that have become aware of this reality and have decided to risk the status quo have begun to experience a new joy and purpose in being the church of Jesus Christ. Some leaders have chosen to create new models of church in order to be part of this movement. New wineskin churches like Saddleback Community Church in Orange County, California, and others have shown us how God can use new, intentional forms of church to bring fresh expressions of Christ's body. New models and methods continue to emerge as leaders and people respond to the call of God and the changing culture around them.

Some previously existing churches, however, began with the old wineskins of their churched culture, went into a season of winter to allow the old to die, and emerged like butterflies from their cocoons into entirely recreated beings. We have begun to hear stories of these successfully transitioned ministries; Flamingo Road in Fort Lauderdale, Florida, for example. These stories give us hope that we don't need to write off a church wrapped in the cocoon of its past. With patient servant leadership at the helm, churches who formerly sought to maintain their past have become mission-focused outposts in their ministry fields. These churches have gone through what I call "the ministry of transition," a process of changing whatever is necessary to become what God has called them to become.

I am writing out of a 10-plus-year journey to become what God called Legacy Church in Plano, Texas, to become—a mission outpost where every member is a missionary to his or her mission field. On this journey of transition, the lessons I have learned from the life of Jesus are captured in the workbook *Jesus on Leadership: Becoming a Servant Leader* (LifeWay) and the trade book *Jesus on Leadership* (Tyndale). There I shared how God brought me to my knees to wash the feet of those with whom I led and those with whom I shared soul-deep conflict. During those critical events I learned the power of *servant* in servant leadership. I still believe the truth that "dressed like a servant and acting like a slave, Jesus led," and that those who lead like Jesus will be willing to do the same. Servant leadership begins when God humbles his chosen leader to the reality that the mission of God is greater than the ego of the leader. I also continue to hold to the description of a servant leader as one who "serves the mission and leads by serving those on mission with him or her," which will be tested in this workbook.

I should not have been surprised that God had other lessons in store for me and his church as we continued to transition into the mission outpost he had called us to become. Through a series of crises that became the final steps of our transition, God revealed to me, both experientially and through His Word, the power of *leader* in servant leadership. Servant leadership begins with making oneself servant to the mission, but it can only continue when His servant is willing to stand as the leader to ensure God's mission is completed.

Paul on Leadership is filled with lessons I have learned from the transitional ministry of Paul, the apostle, a servant leader like his Lord, Jesus. The risen Christ captured the heart of Saul of Tarsus, who had succeeded in a centuries-old way of relating to God. Jesus transformed Paul's ministry from one of maintaining the ancient ways to joining the movement of God's Son as a servant leader in a ministry of transition. This biblical character models for you and me how servant leaders lead when God calls them to a ministry of transition.

I have created the following graphic for a ministry of transition that echoes Paul's ministry.

This diagram reflects the eight realities I have harvested from my study of Paul's ministry of transition in light of my own experiences. These are the realities you may experience as you follow Paul's example of servant leadership. They are timeless and transferable to the culture in which you find yourself.

As with *Jesus on Leadership,* I do not seek to provide the definitive word on how to carry out a ministry of transition. My desire is to enter the conversation about how to reach the mission fields in which we find ourselves and to allow the timeless realities preserved in Paul's ministry to guide us in the process.

A mission outpost is a church with a mission-field focus that equips and sends its members as missionaries into the world around them. A mission outpost is a "colony of heaven," "the called out ones," missionaries to their own culture. The journey from how you do church now to the ways in which God will use you to reach your community will be filled with great victories and painful losses. This is why I suggest you keep a journal during this season of transition. I will ask you to record prayers and thoughts throughout our time together, so, as you begin, designate a notebook or journal as your journal.

You will not go on this journey alone. You will also need other pilgrims who are willing to discover new realities with you. I will refer to your "mission outpost team" during this study. These are people who share your unsettled heart that something needs to change in order to join God in what He is doing to revive and reform the church. You can walk through this material alone, but I suggest that somewhere along the way you find a small group of fellow travelers to join you on this journey of transition. Neither Jesus nor Paul neglected the fellowship of others as they completed their missions.

This workbook is not intended to be a manual on church growth. I cannot guarantee you that if you do what we did your church will grow from one hundred to one thousand in three years. I can tell you, however, that if you will walk through the pages of this book with a trusted group of friends and leaders, you will soon discover God's desire for you and your church. Your pursuit of that divine desire will set you on the course of a ministry of transition to the future God has envisioned for you to become.

Acknowledgments

As leadership is not a solo sport, neither is writing. Chris Johnson and the team at LifeWay have made this piece a reality. I am just a writer without them. Ray Rust, my friend and mentor, gave me perspective from lifelong ministry and from one who is finishing well. I want to thank those who attended my conferences at Glorieta and Ridgecrest Conference Centers in the summer of 2003. Their responses, reactions, and encouragement helped me focus and refine the realities presented here.

Friends and ministry partners like Greg Sankey, Paul Turner, Eddie Hammett, Jay Abernathy, and Tom and Kris Koenigsberg served me in this project in tangible and intangible ways. Bill Easum and Lynn Anderson, servant leaders in ministries to churches in transition, gave me opportunities to test these ideas in broader arenas and gave me hope for what God is doing to revive and reform the church in North America.

I am indebted to the people who have made up the Legacy family throughout my ministry. They have embraced and rejected, tested and tolerated, rejoiced and wept over the advances and setbacks we shared while pursing the vision of becoming a mission outpost. I pray you are served by their experiences and lessons learned from them. I have been.

My wife, Kim, my best friend, partner in ministry, and my greatest critic and fan, continues to be "God's Spirit with a face" to me in many ways. I am blessed that my two daughters embrace Jesus' call on their lives and press to find fresh expressions of Christ's church in their personal journeys of faith. They, too, give me hope for the future church.

SERVING THE CHURCH IN TRANSITION

On our 15th wedding anniversary, I surprised my wife by sweeping her away to a favorite getaway—Jefferson, a small town in east Texas known for its historic bed-and-breakfasts. My wife loves antiques, so the town's restored homes and history made this the perfect gift for her. After checking into the famed Excelsior Hotel, we began to wander through the town and soon discovered how it gained its place in history.

We were surprised to find that by the late 1840s Jefferson had become the leading commercial and distribution center of Northeast Texas and the state's leading inland port. In the 1870s, Jefferson was second to Galveston in its volume of commerce and had a population of almost 7,500.[1] What had made it so prosperous, and what had happened to make it what it was today? Early inhabitants discovered steamboats could navigate Big Cypress Creek that ran through the town to Shreveport and on to Galveston. Cotton could be carried to the port, and goods from around the world could be floated upstream to the settlers of Texas and on to the western plains. Jefferson was the hub of business from the frontier and farms to the world.

We wondered, if things were so wonderful then, why is it a town of restored buildings and historical markers today? Why was it a tourist attraction rather than a center of commerce? As we poked around, we learned why Jefferson was no longer a vibrant business center.

Two things happened. The first the city could not have avoided, but the second could have kept them alive. The first event was the destruction of a natural dam, or rift, on the river above Shreveport in 1873. In an effort to make that part of the river

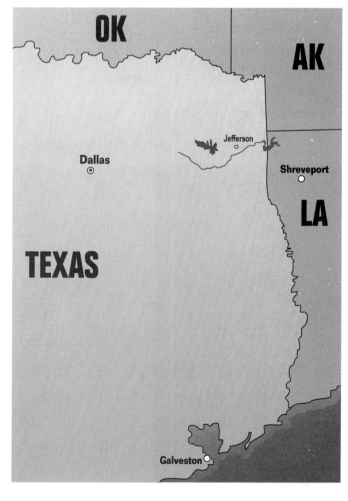

This week you will:

- Be challenged to consider change in order to reach your changing mission field.
- Be introduced to our main character Paul and the changes he had to face when God called him to take the Jesus story to the ethnics.
- Observe the elements of servant leadership in the ministry of Paul, the Apostle.
- See the pattern of how God worked in Paul's life to transition him from a life of religion to an adventure of faith with God.

navigable, the natural barrier was removed. The river was opened up. Mission accomplished. The river could handle more riverboats. A by-product of the rift removal, however, was that the level of the river lowered considerably downstream. Within months, steamboats could no longer make their way the length of the river to the Gulf. Progress upstream hindered continued growth downstream. The success of better navigation upstream literally spelled the death of Jefferson's river industry downstream.

The second event that hurried the end of Jefferson's vitality was its lazy attitude toward the railroad. City leaders had begun work to bring rail to town and eventually brought rail to the city, but it remained primarily dependent on the river for its livelihood. While the town worked on the docks, others completed the Texas and Pacific Railroad from Texarkana to Marshall, bypassing Jefferson. Soon trains replaced riverboats, and Dallas replaced Jefferson as the business center of North Texas. Jefferson missed its opportunity to survive by clinging to its proven method of business.

Progress upstream and dependence on one way of doing business turned Jefferson into a town caught in time—old buildings people visit to get away from modern life or to celebrate the past. Jefferson was for me a museum to missed opportunity.

The church in America today faces similar challenges and opportunities of a changing world in which to do its business of making disciples of Jesus. Like the people of Jefferson, church members and leaders must decide how they will respond to the new realities facing them.

Day 1

WHY CHANGE?

As I walked through the quaint, preserved town whose prime had long since come and gone, I thought of how many churches were like the town of Jefferson. How many churches' heydays were in the late 1800s or 1900s (or mid to late 1900s) and were no more than preserved buildings with historical markers in front where people came to remember the past or get away from it all. They are great places for weddings, anniversaries, and remembering the pasts of those departed, but they have little to do with the marketplace and the changing world around them.

My fear was that our church would become such a place if we let "progress upstream" or "dependence on doing what we've always done" take away our opportunity to be effective for God. I didn't want Legacy Drive Baptist Church to become another "museum to missed opportunity."

Jefferson was hit from progress elsewhere—changes in reality beyond its control. The same happens today, and you can either choose to scold those who brought that progress or find ways to throw lifelines to those drowning in the waves change created.

On the other hand, Jefferson missed its chance for survival when it depended solely on one way of doing business. If they simply had responded to a new way of moving goods while still moving the world by barges, they could have made the shift to the movement in culture.

Churches in America today face the same situations. Progress upstream challenges our influence in the marketplace. Our dependence on methods that played well half a century ago prevent us from seizing opportunities that can build bridges into the lives of those around us.

God is always maneuvering history for His purposes and to rescue the hearts of people. The church is the "business center" of God's work. We always have the opportunity to join God in what He is doing (build railroads, for example) or cling to what we have always done (float riverboats).

The church in the 21st century is poised before multiple possibilities to be effective as the body of Christ. The question is whether we will grasp those possibilities or turn our places of worship into bed and breakfasts for the soul.

What is the "progress upstream" that threatens the effectiveness of the church? Erwin McManus identifies six world realities that can cause either friction or traction for the church.[2] Those realities are radical migration; urbanization; population explosion; technology; a multicultural, pluralistic world; and what he calls "hypermodernism, the world of maybe." While these realities may seem far away and not affecting where you minister, they are truly factors in the changing world in which your church was planted.

Is Your Church Jefferson?

None of us would claim our church is like Jefferson. May I pause and say that I admire the people of Jefferson who have not let the town die completely but have rescued it from extinction by igniting the current bed-and-breakfast economy. To miss one opportunity is sad enough. To seize a second opportunity may allow you to stay alive and growing. This also applies to churches. We cannot throw up our hands and say that since we missed the train the first

Key Verse

I was made a servant of this gospel by the gift of God's grace that was given to me by the working of His power. This grace was given me—the least of all the saints!—to proclaim to the Gentiles the incalculable riches of the Messiah.
—Ephesians 3:7-8

time, we can't recover with another way of doing business. So let's begin your recovery by seizing the opportunity that is before you. First, let's assess the place you serve.

Here are some questions you can answer to get you started. Write your answers to each question in the margin.
- **What are you clinging to as a church that could be identified as the "riverboat syndrome," those things you refuse to change because they have served you so well in the past? Remember, I am not asking you to change your theology, only to consider how vested you are in your methodologies.**
- **What are the "railroad" churches in your community or a similar culture to yours—churches who seem to have seized a God-given opportunity and are reaching and training people as followers of Jesus?**
- **What are some "economies"—other than the way you've always done things—that may be ways to revive your church's influence and effectiveness?**

You may be thinking that I want you to toss out everything you have always done and start all over again. You couldn't be further from the truth. I join in the chorus of Alan Nelson and Gene Appel: "We . . . don't have a beef with the traditional, institutional church. . . . Our passion is to see these same churches [that changed our lives], possibly similar to the one you attend, continue to be kingdom-advancing churches for many years to come."[3]

My desire is to help you discover some current ways of thinking or seeing reality that may keep you from seizing the opportunity God has given you to continue to be a vibrant body of Christ in your mission field. I don't care about your buildings or constitution and bylaws—though these may be affected by your responses. I care that you participate in the unending story for the hearts of men and women.

Moving Beyond Jefferson

As we drove back to our mission field in suburban North Dallas after a wonderful time in Jefferson, I began to pray about how God wanted Legacy to carry out its unique mission to make disciples. As I began to seek, God led me to Kennon Callahan's book *Effective Church Leadership*.[4] He made three observations of realities the church had to face in the last decade of the 20th century. His words proved to be prophetic for my ministry.

Callahan's first observation was: "The day of the professional minister is over. The day of the missionary pastor has come."[5] A missionary pastor has a heart for reaching the lost around him as well as caring for and equipping believers who are part of the fellowship to join him in the mission field. Callahan started where it counted—with the leader. I was taken aback that here was a trusted observer telling me that the season in which my career as a degreed seminarian was over, and it really bothered me. But I had begun to experience this reality: churched people wanted me to be credentialed by an accredited institution; unchurched people just wanted to know if I staked my life on what I was telling them and how I could help them with their lives. Down deep, as much as I didn't want to admit it, I knew Callahan was right.

His second observation was: "The day of the churched culture is over. The day of the mission field had come."[6] The mission field geographically is the immediate locale around the central gathering and training place (mission outpost) of God's people. The mission field for each member of the church is that network of relationships God has orchestrated in a believer's life to serve, love, and share the grace of God in the name of Jesus. The difference

"The day of the professional minister is over. The day of the missionary pastor has come."

"The day of the churched culture is over. The day of the mission field had come."

between a mission-field-focused church and an institution-minded church is where you spend most of your money and where your best leaders invest their time. Are you spending more money on facilities than missions? Are your best leaders sitting on committees or starting ministries in the mission field?

This one was not hard for me to see. Gone are the days when everyone in the United States knows church language and Bible stories. I remember when a new Christian began attending one of our Bible fellowships. The story that day was about carrying the ark of the covenant through the wilderness. The guy leaned over to his wife and asked, "Why are they carrying a boat around in the desert?" His only recollection of the ark as a child was Noah's boat. She whispered back, "Not that one, dear, they're talking about the one in *Raiders of the Lost Ark*." "Oh," he said, and returned to listening to the lesson. It became clear to all in the room that those we had begun to reach did not swim in the same aquarium of faith we did growing up.

His third observation was: "The day of the local church is over. The day of the mission outpost has come."[7] A mission outpost is a group of people on mission with Christ to reach all peoples for His sake. These Christ followers, who share the same mission and vision, remain flexible structurally to respond to divine opportunities. They pursue people not yet in the kingdom while loving those on mission with them with the love of Christ. We get a glimpse of the first of these mission outposts in Acts 11 in Antioch. We will take a closer look at this church later as a model of a mission outpost.

Callahan had set this last one up with the other two. As I read those sentences for the first time, truth exploded in my heart and mind. "That's it!" my soul shouted. "That's what God wants Legacy to become, a mission outpost in this mission field." There were enough local churches in our community. What our community needed was a mission-driven, vision-drawn group of disciples who would do church as a mission outpost. I could begin to see myself as a missionary pastor on a mission field leading people in an outpost for the kingdom of God. My imagination began to paint pictures of what worship, small groups, and ministries would look like if our focus became reaching the indigenous people of our suburban mission field.

My religious heritage is Southern Baptist. One thing Southern Baptists have done effectively through the years is reaching people groups wherever they are for the kingdom of God. A network of mission outposts circles the globe to reach and teach people about the saving love of Christ Jesus. I wanted Legacy to be part of such a network in practice. I felt that God simply wanted us to do foreign missions at home! Our leaders and members needed to "think of themselves as missionaries learning the language and customs of a vastly different culture."[8] The world, our world of North Texas in particular, needed a mission outpost networked with other outposts who were intentionally reaching and training people for Christ.

What Next?

If these statements were true, I would have to begin to align our church and myself to be effective where God had planted us. This meant we had to change, and I have come to discover that while others like me thrive on change, most people are slow to embrace it.

Note that the need to change came from a changing world in which we are called to make disciples, not a desire to change. Servant leaders in churches today do not seek to bring change for change sake, but they are change agents. Why? God only calls a servant leader to lead when leadership to follow God into unexpected places is the next step for the church. Any

"The day of the local church is over. The day of the mission outpost has come."

Servant leaders in churches today do not seek to bring change for change sake, but they are change agents.

changes brought by servant leaders after Jesus' example and teachings come as a result of doing mission in their mission field. Like Paul, they do not seek to be the newest expression of church. Their goal is to embody the most authentic example of the body of Christ for that time and place. This is why much of this book is about transitioning ways of doing ministry and the issues involved in that process rather than offering a new model for you to implement in your church. It is about leaders with a servant's heart guiding followers of Jesus into the mission field of their neighborhoods and marketplaces.

That trip to Jefferson was just one step on a journey of following God's leadership for Legacy to be a mission outpost in our mission field. The first set of lessons I have learned on this journey was presented in *Jesus on Leadership*. As we have continued the path of discovery and transition at Legacy, I have learned other lessons. Many of these have come from the Apostle Paul's ministry. God used him to expand the Jesus movement beyond the Jewish faith to all peoples. I realized I could learn much from how God captured his heart and used him to transition a way of relating to God beyond traditions and religious culture to a faith in the living Christ wherever God would open the doors.

Here is the list of Callahan's three observations. Place a mark by the one that seems truest to the "progress upstream" in your culture. After you have made your choice, write a sentence or two in the margin, indicating why this particular reality is true in your mission field. Be prepared to share this with your mission outpost team at your next meeting.

- **"The day of the professional minister is over. The day of the missionary pastor has come."**
- **"The day of the churched culture is over. The day of the mission field has come."**
- **"The day of the local church is over. The day of the mission outpost has come."**

Christ's resilient church will continue to flourish and grow in any culture or environment. It is organic, vital, and will survive until its Creator returns to claim it for Himself.

One reason the church may not be growing where you are is because you may have fallen into keeping the past rather than following God into His future, or you have missed an opportunity to join God in fresh expressions of the body of Christ. The next part of this study will help you see how you can join the fresh movement of God through Christ's church.

ACTS OF THE SPIRIT

When an experience like my trip to Jefferson and reading of Callahan's thoughts crack the foundation of my world, I always head to the Scriptures to see if I can find anything there that can speak to what God seems to be doing in my life. Personal experience must always be weighed against divine revelation. I had observed that the movement of God in Christ Jesus clashed with the staid ways of religion in Jesus' days. I knew from previous reading that the same was true in the movement of God beyond the incarnational ministry of Jesus.

The book in the Bible called Acts of the Apostles could be named Acts of the Spirit. The story is not so much about what the apostles did as what the Spirit of God did through them—where and how the living Holy Spirit led them on the adventure of Christ's Great Commission. By sending His promised Spirit, Jesus empowered a small band of believers who staked their lives on the reality of Christ's resurrection. A small group of confused, discouraged people became world changers through the power of Christ's presence in their lives.

The Book of Acts is a chaotic tale of passionately devoted people who followed the Holy Spirit's leadership. It is as mysterious and revolutionary as any adventure novel! Few stories of human revolution have as many twists and turns and unpredictable outcomes as the story of those who brought freedom in Christ to the known world. America's revolution was about people fighting for freedom from another country. The church's history is about people laying down their lives so others can have eternal freedom through the One who laid down His life so all could live. This spirit of revolutionary freedom is the soul of the story called Acts.

The Great Commission in Acts

Acts is the Great Commission in action. Jesus' command for His disciples to be His witnesses for the entire world is the driving purpose throughout the events of the Acts story. This mission expanded the Jesus movement to include all people. The story of the acts of the Holy Spirit was set in motion by the commissioning call of Christ to His followers in order to continue His mission of redemption.

Read Acts 1:6-8, then write responses in the margin to the instructions below.
- **What is the context of Jesus' words to His followers?**
- **What question the disciples asked prompted Jesus' answer in verse 8?**
- **Write verse 8 in your words. Underline the main concepts in Jesus' promise.**

The context of Jesus' call to His disciples is His last days on earth after the resurrection before His ascension into heaven. The disciples wanted to know when the "kingdom" would be restored to Israel. They were still thinking in physical, earthly terms as to when Jesus would set up His ruling presence on earth. He told them after His resurrection, as He did before His death, that the timing of that was not for them to know, but it would happen when the Father determined it to be (see Matt. 24:36).

Jesus told His disciples they would receive the power necessary to do what He commanded them to do when His Holy Spirit came upon them in the

Key Verse
"But you will receive power when the Holy Spirit has come upon you, and you will be My witnesses in Jerusalem, in all Judea and Samaria, and to the ends of the earth."
—Acts 1:8

days ahead. When that happened, He promised they would become His witnesses in the city of Jerusalem, the surrounding area of Judea, the northern reaches of Samaria, and to the ends of the earth as they knew it.

1. Power

Three components of Jesus' call to His disciples to be His witnesses are important to our study. The first element of the call is the power that proceeded performance. We get our English word *dynamite* from the original word for *power* in this verse. This word is used 118 times in the New Testament, and a favorite word of Paul to denote such spiritual truths as the resurrection power of Christ (Phil. 3:10), the power that brings people to salvation (Rom. 1:16), and Christ's power that rules over all other powers and authorities (Eph. 1:19). This word is also used for miracles in the Gospels (Mark 6:5) and for spiritual forces that live and act in the spiritual realms, which Christ ultimately will destroy (1 Cor. 15:24). When Jesus promised that His disciples would receive power, He promised they would be empowered to carry out any aspect of the mission he called them to complete.

2. Witnesses

The source of this power, however, was not from the disciples themselves. Empowerment for Christ's mission call does not come from us but from the One who calls us. Jesus told His followers they would receive the spiritual power needed to complete His mission "when the Holy Spirit has come upon you." He spoke of the events that are described in Acts 2. The Day of Pentecost marked the third member of the Trinity's presence in the movement of God. The Holy Spirit empowered Jesus' followers to become bold witnesses. That same Spirit does so today for those on mission with Jesus.

The second component of Jesus' commission to His disciples was that they would be His "witnesses." We get our English word *martyr* from this Greek word. We often narrow the meaning of the word to those who died as a result of sharing their faith. However, the word originally had the meaning of a person who would testify or witness to a certain event or words. (See Matt. 18:16, for example.) Peter rightly called himself a witness to Christ's sufferings (see 1 Pet. 5:1), and Paul often called upon God to be his witness for his actions and thoughts (see Rom. 1:9). A witness is simply someone who will tell the truth about what he or she has experienced or knows. Jesus said His followers would be truth-tellers about what they saw and knew to be true about Jesus.

3. Influence

The third component of Jesus' promise to His disciples was the scope of their influence. Jesus told them they would be His witnesses in the city in which they found themselves, in their surrounding country, in areas at the edge of their travels, and to the parts of the world they may not have even visited. Jesus did not limit the impact of their witness. They would serve His mission in their hometown to the *terra incognita,* the unknown world. The scope of their mission is the same for servant leaders on mission with Christ today.

The scope of their influence is also one way to outline the story of Acts. Acts 2:1–8:3 records their witness in Jerusalem. Acts 8:4–12:25 tells about their testimony in Judea and Samaria. In Acts 13 through the end of the book, Dr. Luke recorded how the Word of God spread to "the ends of the earth."

You can observe the mission of making disciples expand from the Jewish capital city of Jerusalem to the world's capital city of Rome by reading the stories of the Holy Spirit's empowering work in disciples' lives.

Mission Invites Change

The Book of Acts tells the story of a movement of God, not how an institution was established. Christ's Holy Spirit ignited a grassroots movement that changed the world. It happened as a small group of people trusted Jesus as their Savior and the Christ, accepted the mission He gave them, and empowered by His Spirit, lived out that mission until their dying days. A call to mission was central to the life-changing stories you read about in this adventure book of God. When Christ-called mission and Spirit-filled power combined in people's lives, a spiritual reaction ignited that still starts fires in the hearts of people today.

The movement began with a call to mission. This mission was embodied in people, and the Spirit empowered those who gave their lives to the mission. All of this joined together to bring change in the lives of others and into the fabric of culture itself.

Everything that happened in Acts was completely new, never seen or experienced before in human history; and it all began in an upper room with hope-filled people praying and waiting for God to act (Acts 2:1-4). Jesus told His followers to go to Jerusalem and "wait for the Father's promise" (Acts 1:4; John 14–16). God sent His Spirit into that incubator of prayerful hearts. When God's Holy Spirit came at Pentecost, it became ground zero for the explosion of the Jesus movement around the globe.

Any examination of the church today should be seen in light of how God established and built the church out of that group of devoted followers of Jesus. The search is not for formulas or once-experienced, always-experienced events or practices. Our look in this book must answer the question, how does the living Holy Spirit of God lead and empower people on mission with Him?

If I were to make observations like Mr. Callahan regarding the realities in Acts, I could say:

"The day of the professional priest was over. The day of the missionary had come."

"The day of the Jewish religious culture was over. The day of the mission field had come."

"The day of the temple/synagogue was over. The day of the mission outpost had come."

These observations match Callahan's list because the shifts in how people related to God that took place as a result of God's new work among His people then are the same shifts in reality that are happening now. We should not be surprised that the tale of the acts of the Holy Spirit in those days sounds so familiar to those who are called on mission with Jesus today.

Return to the adapted list of Callahan's observations above and apply them to the Apostle Paul. Given what you know about his life, how did his life and ministry exhibit these observations? Write your opinion in the margin.

Each of these observations matches the life of our central character Saul of Tarsus turned Paul, the apostle. Through God's leadership in his life, he gave up his career as a professional religious leader, a Pharisee, to become a missionary, sent to the mission fields of his world. He left the familiarity of his Jewish religious culture and risked the frontier of the mission field. He moved from the base camp of the temple and synagogue to creating a network of mission outposts around the known world.

Paul, Servant Leader in a Ministry of Transition

Most of the Acts story is about God's leadership in Paul's life. Paul's leadership in the Jesus movement around the world and God's use of his pen to record truth for all people makes him a strategic character in understanding how God employs people to join him on the central mission of making

When Christ-called mission and Spirit-filled power combined in people's lives, a spiritual reaction ignited that still starts fires in the hearts of people today.

15

disciples of all people groups. In the Great Commission, the word commonly translated "nations" (Matt. 28:19) is *ethnos,* from which we get the word *ethnics,* the word I will use most frequently in this book to refer to taking the gospel to all people.

Paul is a key example for how leaders lead in the movement of God today, as servants of God first and as leaders who serve those who share the same calling and mission. His ministry built a bridge between the established religious past of Judaism to the fluid Spirit-led future of relating to God through a relationship with Jesus. He was a servant to the mission call of God on his life, and he constantly served those on mission with him. Paul built a bridge between the time-honored ways of relating to God and an unconventional, fresh way of knowing God. Paul was a servant leader who, in a time of transition, stood between the past and the future to tell his world about Christ.

A call to Christ-centered mission through the call of God first brings change to the individual. When God reveals the truth that your redeemed life is to be invested into the universal mission of making disciples of all ethnic groups, you must change. Personal, spiritual transformation precedes corporate, organizational transition. Paul brought change to the religious world of his day. That happened, however, after Christ transformed his heart, mind, and soul. If Paul is our example of servant leadership in leading a movement of Christ, we need to examine some of the key shifts in Paul's life and ministry. This is the next part of our study.

> **Look again at the three components of Jesus' call to His disciples—power, witness, and influence. Reflect on these components in your relationship with Jesus. Use the space provided in the margin to write your thoughts and/or prayers.**

Jesus said you would receive power when the Holy Spirit comes upon His followers. We know this to be true for all followers of Jesus when they put their trust in Him as forgiver and leader.

Do you have access to that power through your trust relationship with Jesus? If you do not, take time now to allow that relationship to begin.

Do you depend totally on the Spirit's power in your life to accomplish His purposes in you, or do you lean more upon your own efforts?

Are you a witness to Christ, a truth-teller in every situation of who Christ is and what He can do for others? Do your actions demonstrate Christ's love to others? Would you be willing to risk everything to stake the stand for Jesus?

What is the scope of your influence? Do you have an "ends of the earth" perception of what God can do with your witness of words and actions? Or do you see your influence only to those who show up in the church's buildings? Are you telling your Christ story to those in your home and hometown?

Let these questions either begin or restore what Jesus Christ has called you as His follower to do with your life.

Personal, spiritual transformation precedes corporate, organizational transition.

Day 3

A NEW WAY OF SEEING THINGS

Jesus' mission call can challenge everything you know about doing things with God. For me, serving as a professional minister with a local church in a churched culture was an entirely different world than leading as a missionary pastor in a mission outpost on a mission field! I was trained to be an academician in a teaching institution but had been handed the responsibility of leading people on mission. Managing in an institution in a stable culture is not the same as leading a wagon train across the western frontier. I wanted what God had called me and our church to become, but I didn't know how. I was stuck.

I knew God's call in my life was not unique. I had seen ministries and leaders bring new models of doing church onto the American landscape. The "innovative church movement" and "new paradigm" churches began to catch the attention of all who were interested in being effective for the kingdom. Through Christ's renewed call, I sensed my ministry, and I had been let in on what Christ was doing to revive and reform his bride, the church. I felt stuck, however—stuck in doing church the same way I had known it and unable to free myself and our people to build a bridge of transition from the hallowed past to the uncertain future.

Bill Easum gives a hint to some "unfreezing moves" to help churches follow Jesus into the mission field. "The key to unfreezing the church to be with Jesus on the mission field is to view our congregations and denominations as the roots and shoots of an 'organic movement' that goes far beyond mere organizational survival. Movements are different from institutions and behave much differently."[9]

Easum observes that movements function unlike institutions. (Keep your attention on Jesus as the leader of this movement and the church as those who follow Him as you read these observations.) Movements . . .

• Follow a leader. "Remove the leader, and the movement soon becomes an institution or religion."

• Embody the spirit of the founder.

• Are guided by mission rather than rules. "No longer is there only one right way to do something."

• Are mobile rather than static. "They are not tethered to place, property, and tradition."

• Depend on contextual people, "people who are tuned into the culture of their community."[10]

To become a missionary pastor leading people to do church as a mission outpost in a mission field meant some personal changes in me first. I could not lead the church to go to a place I had not first been myself.

In order to get a handle on what I may need to address, I looked again to the life of the Apostle Paul. Christ's call on his life demanded he make some changes in his life and ministry. We will look more deeply into the impact this call had on his life in later sessions, but for now let's observe some shifts in Paul's life that had to occur for him to follow Jesus into the mission field of the "ends of the earth."

Key Verse

So he reasoned in the synagogue with the Jews and with those who worshiped God, and in the marketplace every day with those who happened to be there.

—Acts 17:17

Shifts in Paul's Faith and Ministry

Paul wrestled with major shifts in how he related to God, his thinking about God, and how he did ministry. These shifts give a hint to some shifts that may occur in your life and church as you follow Jesus into your mission field.

Read Galatians 2:8-9. What was the shift in how he perceived the way to salvation? Write your thoughts in the margin.

Read Acts 13:44-46 and Ephesians 3:6. What was the shift in the apostle's target group? Write your thoughts in the margin.

Paul's foundation for being made right with God shifted from law to grace. Revealed to him by God, people no longer had to keep the rules to receive God's favor. God's grace in his Son, Christ Jesus, comes to all who trust Him. His letters to the Galatians, Romans, and Ephesians centered on the fundamental truth that being made right with God was "by grace through faith" alone. Christ's revelation changed the rules for how one was accepted by Holy God.

Paul first led on mission among his own people, the Jews. He reasoned in the synagogues and among Jewish followers of the Messiah. He began where he was most comfortable, with those who shared his heritage and culture. Christ's call, however, challenged him to shift his focus to those who were not members of the Old Covenant and whose culture was different from his. On his first trip into the mission field (Acts 13-14), he moved his primary target for the gospel from his own people to indigenous ethnic groups, the Gentiles. (The word *Gentile* meant anyone who was not a Jew, much as the word *barbarian* to the Greeks meant anyone who was not a Greek.)

Read Acts 14:23 and Titus 1:5. What was the shift in Paul's perception of who should lead among God's people? Whom did he count on to lead in the movement?

Paul was a trained Pharisee, a professional priest among the Israelites. He filled the role of the representative of God to the people. He satisfied all the requirements to be recognized as a religious leader among his people. Once on mission with Christ, however, he did not depend on professionally trained leaders to lead among the people of God. While some professional priests like him became Christ followers, he primarily appointed spiritually gifted, untrained pastors/elders to lead among the new followers of Jesus. Rather than trying to make leaders adapt themselves to his formalized training, he raised up indigenous leaders who learned from their mentors. His leadership base shifted from professionals like himself to leaders who were raised up within the movement. We'll look more closely at Paul's personal perception of himself as a leader in week 6.

Read Acts 17:17. Identify a shift in Paul's strategy to reach people.

Paul's strategy was to set up shop in the marketplace rather than wait for people to come to the local place of worship. His heritage and training had taught him to tend to the sheep who gathered on the Sabbath in places designated for activity about God. Jesus' call to the mission field, however, pulled Paul out of the established places of worship into the marketplace. He learned to rub shoulders with the lost in the marketplace and "speak to whoever came by." His evangelism strategy shifted from reaching others in the local place of worship to spending most of his ministry time in the marketplace.

Read Acts 5:42 and Acts 20:20. What was a shift in Paul's base of operations?

Read Acts 1:8 again and Acts 28:30-31. What was a shift in Paul's span of influence? Where did the mission start? Where was it at the end of the Acts story?

In the worldview of Saul of Tarsus, the temple in Jerusalem was the base of operations for the work of God in the world. In the mission-driven world of Paul the apostle, the base of operations shifted to house churches planted among the various groups he sought to reach for Christ. Rather than pilgrimages to the holy city, followers of Jesus were called to cluster in homes where they lived as the mission outpost for the movement of God in Christ Jesus. This network of churches in homes and contact points in the marketplace became the communication and relational network of God's people.

The span of Paul's mission grew from a local area to an international scope. He was trained to do the work of God in a central locale to which the faithful gathered regularly and supported obediently. As he followed the leadership of the Spirit, on the other hand, he shifted his span of influence from his hometown assignment as a Pharisee to the center of the known world, Rome. The unhindered sharing of the gospel in Rome through Christ's servant leader, Paul, signaled the unending story for every group of people who will see their influence in Christ as global.

Read Ephesians 2:14-16 and Galatians 3:27-29. What was a shift in the goal of Paul's ministry? What changed about the goal of his life's work?

Finally, the goal of Paul's life mission shifted from reaching and serving one nation, the Jews, to reaching and leading all people who confess that Jesus is Lord—a holy nation, a people belonging to God (1 Pet. 2:9). God's revelation that all people were one in Christ Jesus and that He was building them into a living dwelling place of His presence changed Paul's goal in life to serve the one nation of Israel. God changed the sent one's goal from serving one nation under God to reaching all the people who became one in Christ Jesus.

God has called you in Christ Jesus to make disciples of all people groups. Like Paul, you and your church may need to make some shifts in focus, strategy, and other areas to get on mission with Christ. The shifts Paul had to make may be applicable to you and your church. Take a moment to review the shifts in Paul's ministry and compare them to how you are living out the Great Commission call on you and your church. Place a check mark by the shifts you feel may need to take place in your life. Then return and circle those that need addressing in your church's life. Be prepared to share your thoughts with your mission outpost team.
❑ **Foundation for being made right with God: keeping the rules or offering grace?**
❑ **Target group: people just like you or other people groups?**
❑ **Leadership in the movement: imported, trained professionals alone or raised up pastors/elders?**
❑ **Strategy for reaching your mission field: gathering in a local place**

of worship or setting up shop in the marketplace and opening homes in neighborhoods?
- ❑ **Base of operations: church buildings or house churches?**
- ❑ **Span of effort: neighborhood church that serves the local area or mission outpost with global impact?**
- ❑ **The goal of your life's work: correct one nation or be part of one people in Christ?**

The call to mission will challenge every aspect of your personal life and the life of your church. Begin now to pray for God's leadership first in your relationship with him your obedience to your place in the mission of redemption. Pray also for those you worship and do mission with that together you can be about God's purposes for you.

Day 4

PAUL AS A SERVANT LEADER

Ken Blanchard, coauthor of *The One-Minute Manager* and many other influential books in business, is a servant leader. His life and writings demonstrate it. His life-changing encounter with Christ came through the witness of his friends. One, Phil Hodges, was the cofounder of the Center for FaithWalk Leadership with Ken. Another was Bob Buford, the founder of Leadership Network; and the third was Bill Hybels, the senior pastor of Willow Creek Community Church. God used each one's witness to lead Ken to a relationship with Christ.

Ken wondered in light of his newly found trust in Christ about the meaning of all that he had done before trusting Christ. He writes: "As my perspective of faith changed, so did my views on leadership change. I realized that Christians have more in Jesus than just a great spiritual leader; we have a practical and effective leadership model for all organizations, for all people, for all situations. The more I read the Bible, the more I realized that Jesus did everything I'd ever taught or written about over the years—and He did it perfectly. He is simply the greatest leadership model for all time."[12]

Blanchard rightly acknowledged that Jesus is the best model for leadership for all people, especially for those who lead in Jesus' movement to rescue the world! Blanchard's summary statement and the book that follows it describe Jesus as a servant leader after whom all leaders should pattern their lives.

A similar insight is the basis for my previous work on servant leadership, *Jesus on Leadership.* There I offered Jesus' model of servant leadership as the primary model for leadership in home and business. I observed in the ministry of Jesus four basic elements that create the chemical reaction of servant leadership. Those elements are mission, vision, equip, and team.[13]

These four aspects of servant leadership answer the question: How can I lead as a servant? A servant leader is first a servant to the *mission* and leads people to the *vision* or end picture of that mission. A leader serves those on mission with him or her by *equipping* them to do the mission and by building a *team* that will carry on the mission beyond his or her leadership. Servant leaders are servants to the mission first—all else flows from that.

In light of God's call on my life to lead our church to become a mission outpost in this mission field, I asked, "Was Paul a servant leader? Are the elements of Jesus' example of leadership apparent in his ministry?" If Paul was an example of a servant leader in the Spirit-led movement of redemption to all people, we must examine whether his leadership model fits that of the One who called him.

Mission

The beginning of servant leadership is becoming servant to the mission call of God on your life. Blanchard and Hodges described two possible realities that will result without a clear mission or purpose: "If everyone does not understand your purpose or is not excited and passionate about it, your organization will begin to lose its way. . . . One of the reasons organizations are bureaucratic is because no one knows what the organization is supposed to be doing. What is your purpose or business? What business are you in that excites people?"[14]

Your church will "begin to lose its way" or become "bureaucratic" without a clear mission or purpose. Mission, which comes through God's call, is the beginning of servant leadership and the reason people invest in what God is doing through your leadership.

Saul of Tarsus became Paul, the apostle, because he became servant to the mission to carry the good news of Jesus to all people groups.

Two examples illustrate this point:

Read Acts 9:15. What did God say was the mission he had for Paul (then Saul)?

Read Ephesians 3:2, 6-7. What was Paul's message in verse 6? What did he say he had become to that message in verse 7?

God's mission for Paul was "to carry my name before Gentiles, kings, and the sons of Israel" (Acts 9:15). In his letter to the Christ followers in Ephesus, he described the same mission when he wrote, "This mystery is that through the gospel the Gentiles are heirs together with Israel, members together of one body, and sharers together in the promise in Christ Jesus" (Eph. 3:6, NIV). In addition, we know he had become a servant to that mission when he wrote in the next sentence, "I became a servant of this gospel by the gift of God's grace given me through the working of his power" (v. 7, NIV). The word for servant here is *diakonos,* the word from which we get our English word *deacon,* which means "to wait on tables."

Earlier in that chapter Paul used the phrase "the stewardship of God's grace which was given to me for you" (v. 2, NASB). The word for *stewardship* in this verse was the common word for a "house manager," a trusted slave given the care of the master's home and affairs. Paul understood God's call on his life was to "manage the affairs of God's grace" so others could know Him.

Paul described the mission for all Christ followers. "Now all these things are from God, who reconciled us to Himself through Christ, and *gave us the ministry of reconciliation,* namely, that God was in Christ reconciling the world to Himself, not counting their trespasses against them, and He has committed to us the word of reconciliation" (2 Cor. 5:18-19, NASB, author's italics). *Ministry* in this passage is the same word for *servant* in Ephesians 3:7 (NIV). According to Paul, we are all servants, or ministers, to the mission of reconciliation through Christ Jesus.

Paul lived a mission-driven life. He was driven to get up every morning and work deep into the night—sometimes all night—because he believed to the core of his being that what Christ called him to do was why he was created. He believed that part of God's grace in his life for salvation was played out in his service to the mission God called him to do (Eph. 3:8). His status as a Pharisee was laid aside, even demeaned, in order to present himself as a servant of Christ. He humbled himself to the mission and never sought a place in society again.

The Mission and Your Church

Much has been written in the past decade about the importance of knowing your church's God-given mission.[15] While it may seem overworked, mission remains the answer to the question, Why are we here? or, What business are we in? Let me give you a hint before you feel like you may be the only church leader who has not developed a mission statement. You and I share the same universal mission if we are disciples of Jesus Christ. Our Leader made clear before His ascension back to the Father. We are to "make disciples of all people" (Matt. 28:19), and we are to be His "witnesses" to the ends of the earth.

You do not need to assemble a mission-statement task force to come up with a mission unique to your church. Jesus gave it to you, and if you are a servant leader called by Him to lead, then your mission is the same as those eleven disciples who first received the Great Commission. You can state it uniquely for your people if you sense the basic words of Scripture are not clear enough, but you have no need to find another reason to do what you do. The challenge, of course, is to make sure the mission drives everything you do.

Vision

For me, "vision is what the mission looks like when it is complete."[16] Vision answers the missional question, If your church were continually to make Christ followers of all groups (or a targeted group), what would it look like? Jesus' vision for His mission as Suffering Servant Messiah was the kingdom of God, here on earth and in eternity (Isa. 53:11; Luke 4:16-20). You could say that Christ's mission call to make disciples will look like Revelation 7:9-10 when people from every nation, tribe, and tongue stand before the throne of Christ and worship Him.

The answer to this question is driven by God's unique picture for your ministry. It often comes from the context of your mission field. God defines your mission. The mission field plays a major part in discerning God's unique vision for your church.

At Legacy we acknowledge we are a unique expression of the body of Christ in this mission field. We compare ourselves to no one. We criticize no one, and we cooperate with any fellowship or church that is on the same mission we are on. Another example is a church in California. Erwin MacManus leads a church in the urban mission field of Los Angles. If they make disciples of those in their mission field, it will be a "mosaic" of people from many language groups worshiping and serving God together.

Paul clearly served the mission call of God in his life, but did he offer a compelling vision that captured the hearts of people like his mentor Jesus?

Read Ephesians 2:14-18. What did Paul say Jesus did to bring all people groups together into the body of Christ?

Read Ephesians 2:19-22. What was the picture Paul painted for his readers? What was the compelling image that people would want to embrace?

If you are a servant leader called by Him to lead, then your mission is the same as those eleven disciples who stood on the side of the hill the day He returned to heaven.

The apostle had a clear, compelling vision of who people were and how they would live together if they trusted what Jesus did for them in His death and resurrection. In Ephesians 2, he wrote that Jesus, "destroyed the barrier, the dividing wall of hostility, . . . and in this one body to reconcile both of them to God through the cross, by which he put to death their hostility" (vv. 14-16, NIV). Paul painted a picture of those who were "foreigners and aliens" (v. 19, NIV) to the grace of God, and that "in him you too are being built together to become a dwelling in which God lives by his Spirit" (v. 22, NIV). That's a compelling vision! Who would not want to move from being foreigners to the love of God to fellow citizens with other Christians? Who would not want to be part of a group whom God was building into a "dwelling in which God lives by his Spirit"? Paul presented a compelling vision to those he led.

Paul lived a vision-drawn life. The picture of all ethnic groups standing united before the throne of God in heaven tugged at the apostle's heart daily. He longed to see what God had revealed to him. This vision drew him to complete the clear mission Christ gave him to complete.

I had the privilege of visiting the Southern Baptist Convention in Cochran, Alberta, Canada. LifeWay had invited several church leaders from across the country to talk about spiritual transformation as the foundation for any discipleship model. We experienced a genuine fellowship as each of the participants told his or her story, and we sought ways to be faithful to God's call on our lives.

As part of that dialogue, I presented the four elements of servant leadership. At the end of the discussion about mission and vision, Geary Taillon, then president of the Canadian Southern Baptist Convention, said, "I have always seen it as 'focus plus passion equals courage.'" I agreed and tied his insight to mission and vision. "It is the focus of mission and the passion of vision that gives a servant leader the courage to lead." We agreed, and I have never forgotten Geary's insight that day. A mission-driven, vision-drawn life is the source of courage for a servant leader.

The Vision and Your Church

I like Bill Hybels' definition of *vision*. "Vision is a picture of the future that produces passion."[17] What picture of the future of your church produces passion among those who are on mission with you? If that is not clear and compelling, now is the time to get your task force together. While all God-honoring, Christ-centered churches share the same mission, each body of Christ is given the gift of becoming a unique expression of that mission in their mission fields. God uses the diversity of expression like diversity of personalities to attract people to Him. Just as your temperament is attractive to some and unappealing to others, your church's personality as the body of Christ draws some and sends others seeking God in other places. Vision describes your unique personality as the body of Christ.

George Barna defines a leader as "someone who effectively motivates, mobilizes resources, and directs people toward the fulfillment of a jointly embraced vision."[18] The unifying thread of the elements of this definition, according to Barna, is the "pursuit of the fulfillment of a common vision." Vision is what draws people passionately into the future. The leader's job is to articulate, own, and personify that future.

Discovering God's vision for your church can be tricky. This is not a manual to help you know God's picture for your future, but it can be a starting place for what God wants your church to become in order to reach the people groups in your mission field.

Start a vision quest by answering the question, If we allowed God to use us to make disciples in this mission field for the next five (or 10 or 20) years, what would we look like? Stay focused on people's changed lives, not the number of buildings or size of budgets. Be prepared to share your thoughts with your mission outpost team when you get together next.

Day 5

PAUL THE EQUIPPER AND TEAM BUILDER

Key Verse

Tychicus, a loved brother, a faithful servant, and a fellow slave in the Lord, will tell you all the news about me.
—Colossians 4:7

Tom is one in my band of brothers. We have served in leadership together. We have shared the victories and defeats of leading a people on mission with Christ. Tom was raised in California and is wild at heart. He lifts weights in his 30s and swam with his brothers off the coast of California to be near sharks when he was in his 20s.

Tom also has a passion to influence the lives of young men in his world. He has mentored them on the premises of our property, but his favorite place for influencing young men is in his garage. Tom likes being with guys his own age, but he said he had a passion to "reach guys at a younger age before they get stuck in their ways." He knew too well from personal experience how men's lives can be derailed if certain habits and relationships are not addressed early on.

Authors Bruce Bickel and Stan Jantz captured Tom's strategy for reaching young men this way: "So Tom decided to combine his passion for mentoring men with his passion for lifting weights. He put the word out that his garage would be open three nights a week for guys to come lift for an hour or so. Tom would instruct them, lift with them, and then afterwards they would 'cool down' and talk. It wasn't long before the guys came and lifted and talked and it wasn't long before their discussions turned to serious matters, like life and relationships and God."[19]

Tom is a servant leader on mission to make disciples. He chooses to carry out his mission of mentoring and equipping in his garage as well as in a room on the church's property. I know firsthand that life change happened through those times of lifting weights and talking. The authors said they talked with a couple of dads who love that their sons are lifting at Tom's house. "They agreed that Tom was a great role model, because he was showing them how to build spiritual as well as physical muscles."[20] Sounds a little like Paul's strategy to me.

Take a moment to describe someone like Tom that you know mentors and equips others for ministry in their home or marketplace. What would your church be like if more people followed the example of the person you described?

A nagging question for true leaders is, How do leaders serve? Leading is often portrayed as the strongest leading the strong. Weak people get trampled in the process. If you are a servant leader, however, service to those you lead is core to how you lead. Jesus modeled this powerfully—although paradoxically—the night He washed the feet of His disciples (John 13:3-17). Dressed like a servant, acting like a slave, He led.

Paul followed the example of his Lord and equipped those on mission with him and built ministry teams to ensure the mission to reach all peoples continued in his absence.

Equip

Paul trained those he invited to join him on the mission to the ethnics. Here are some examples of how he did it.

Read Philippians 1:1. What name do you recognize along with Paul's name? How does he describe them both?

Read 1 Timothy 1:18. What did Paul say he was writing to Timothy? Why did he say he was writing them?

Paul chose an apprentice named Timothy to equip in order to carry out the shared mission of taking the good news of Jesus to all people. Paul chose Timothy as one of his companions on his second missionary journey (Acts 16:1-2). When Paul wrote his letter to his friends in Philippi, he recognized Timothy and called himself and his young partner "servants." The word here is *doulos*. Both had become servants to the mission to all people groups. Remember Jesus' teaching on leadership? He said, "And whoever wishes to be first among you shall be your slave" (Matt. 20:27, NASB). Paul considered himself a slave of Jesus Christ, and according to Jesus' requirements for leadership in the kingdom, this qualified him for leadership.

Two of the 13 letters of Paul in the New Testament are letters of instruction to Timothy. He wrote instructions to equip the young church leader to be a servant leader to those on mission with him. The mentor said he wrote his apprentice, "so that by following them you may fight the good fight, holding on to faith and a good conscience" (1 Tim. 1:18-19, NIV). Paul served Timothy who was on mission with him by equipping him to serve the mission where God planted him. We also have a letter that gave Titus instruction for ministry.

Paul lived an instructional life. Paul was a teacher/trainer. He invested his life in others so that they could participate in the God-given mission of making disciples. He equipped people in two primary ways: he taught them the truths of the mission, and he trained them in the skills of the mission. All 13 of his letters contain instructions about the person of Christ, how Christ reconciled all people, and the implications of that new relationship in everyday living. You can outline most of Paul's letters this way: greeting, theology, application of that theology, and farewell. These brief explanations for who Christ is and what that means to people's everyday lives make up God's revelation to people on mission since Jesus walked on the earth. (His pattern is also a good model for preaching and teaching.)

Paul also trained his followers by giving them the skills to do ministry. The obvious evidence of Paul's equipping comes from his letters to Timothy. Paul's instructions gave Timothy skills to use in his ministry of making disciples.

Paul also instructed his young apprentice, Titus. He trained him well enough to be confident to leave him on the island of Crete to "straighten out what was left unfinished and appoint elders in every town, as I *directed* you" (Titus 1:5, NIV, author's italics). The word *directed* means "to give detailed instructions as to what must be done."[21] Instruction is part of how you equip someone you serve to complete the mission.

Read Titus 3:1-11. List in the margin some of the practical and theological instructions Paul gave Titus.

Paul, the apostle, was Paul, the equipper. He took the time and energy to train those on mission with him to do the work of mission, specifically to the ethnics.

Your Ministry of Equipping Others

If you consider yourself a servant leader, you must check yourself against those you are training on mission. Several months ago a "duh" reality hit me. You know, one of those times you look at yourself in the mirror and say, "You are dense, aren't you! How did you not see that before?" Then you hit yourself on the forehead with the palm of your hand and say, "Duh."

Well, my last duh experience was the realization that while I was training church members in our core mission competencies to share Christ, I was not training the staff! Here were more than 20 people who came together every day to carry out the mission of Legacy, and I had not taken the time recently to train them in our core skills. Soon after that reality check, we began to meet weekly specifically to train them to share their faith. Yes, we had gone through the training before but not with this particular configuration of staff. Which brings up the truth that equipping is ongoing: You are never done with equipping people for the mission until Christ returns!

Are you training others to join you on mission to make disciples? Write the names in the margin along with the skills you are training them to do.

Now list those you have invited to join you on mission who have not received training either directly from you or through another equipper. Beside each name, write the skill he or she needs to master to be most effective.

Equipping is not optional. To invite people to join you on mission and to give them a place on the team but never to train them for their position of servant leadership is neither fair to them nor helpful to the team. Mission outposts are training centers, and those who lead them must be continually equipping its members for mission.

Team

A second way servant leaders lead by serving those on mission with them is to build a team. I've learned that "leading a team is the highest expression of servant leadership."[22] This is so because a team leader exemplifies the realities of servant leadership. A servant leader who leads a team:
- is humble.
- is not a position seeker.
- gives up personal rights to find greatness in service to team members.
- risks because he trusts God is in control of his life, takes up Jesus' towel of servanthood and "dressed like a servant, acting like a slave, leads."
- shares responsibility and authority to meet a greater need.
- multiplies his leadership by empowering others to lead.

To lead a team on mission is to maximize the people resources God has placed around you and minimizes your weaknesses as an individual leader. I love John Maxwell's first teamwork thought, "You may be good—but you're not that good!"[23] No authentic servant leader leads on mission without a team. The God-given task is too big. Only ego-centered, delusional people go it alone.

Leading a team is the highest expression of servant leadership.

We have tried to capture the behavior-driving core values of Legacy in our permanent documents that lead our ministry. One of those reads, "Servant leadership demonstrated in team ministry is the most effective way to lead people on mission." We have learned that solo leadership is limiting and destructive to the leader. We have also seen how servant-led teams can be used by God to make significant differences in people's lives and ministry.

Paul led in team. Let's look at his ministry for evidence of his example.

Read Colossians 4:7, 10-15. In the margin write the names of all whom Paul mentions in those verses.

Read Romans 16:3, 9, 21. Whom did Paul call "fellow workers"?

Read any of Paul's letters, and you will find a list of people at the end of each one. Most of these people were partners in ministry. They were members of his ministry team that he trained and depended on to complete their shared mission. Like Jesus, who entrusted His mission of redemption to His disciples, so Paul shared the effectiveness of his God-given mission with this team. His favorite expression for these team members is "fellow workers." In his letter to Colossians, he mentions familiar names like Mark, the cousin of Barnabas, and Dr. Luke. If you dig deeper into the team Paul built, you recognize men like Tychicus and Onesimus. From his ministry in Rome, you know Priscilla and Aquila and Timothy. These were not acquaintances on his Christmas card mailing list. These were people with whom he experienced heartache, trouble, pain, and victory day after day. They were people who gave their lives to God's call to take the good news of Jesus to all peoples.

Paul lived a team-shared life. The biblical model of leadership among God's people is servant leadership in relationship with others. We call that a team. Evidence of Paul's team-shared life comes from his description of Tychicus mentioned in his letters to the Ephesians (6:1), to Titus (3:12), and to the Colossians (4:7). In Colossians 4:7, he writes that Tychicus "a loved brother, a faithful servant, and a fellow slave in the Lord, will tell you all the news about me." Paul trusted this team member with an accurate description of himself and his ministry. He called him a brother, one who shared the adoption of sonship through faith in Christ. Tychicus was a "faithful servant." The word for *servant* here is *diakonos,* the source of our word *deacon.* Paul considered this team member a "fellow slave in the Lord." The word for *slave* came from the word for one who had no rights or privileges, a *doulos.*

To Paul, Tychicus was a brother, a servant, and a slave in the mission to all ethnic groups. Now that's a team member! In giving their lives to Christ and making themselves servants to the mission, they had become like brothers.

Servant leaders have names of people like Tychicus written on their hearts. These people share the scars of ministry but smile with you knowing God used even the tough times to accomplish His purposes through you. They also share the rip-roaring victories that demonstrate God's awesome power in people's lives.

Take a moment to write the name(s) of the person(s) who is a Tychicus in your life. After you write his or her name, write a short paragraph as to why he or she is like Tychicus was to Paul.

If you desire to be a servant leader after the example of Paul, you must be an equipper and a team builder. These are key elements to being a servant

Servant leadership demonstrated in team ministry is the most effective way to lead people on mission.

leader who leads people through the adventure of transition. Paul, the one sent by God to carry the good news of Jesus to all people, embodied the servant leadership model of Jesus, his rescuer and leader. His servant leadership on the mission field of the world reflects each element of Jesus' leadership.

If God has called you to join Him on mission to make disciples of all people, I invite you to examine the servant leadership model of Jesus and His servant Paul. In doing so, you can discover how God would have you lead in your mission outpost in your mission field to expand the kingdom of God.

Looking Ahead

The primary biblical material for this study is Acts 9–21. Take time to read these chapters in one sitting as you would a historical novel. You may want to read this part of the story in language like Eugene Peterson's *The Message* or J. B. Phillip's translation of the New Testament. Take notes in the margin or in a journal as you read.

Here is an overview of the path we will follow through the Book of Acts to harvest the realities of servant leadership from the ministry of Paul. The overview creates a progression of how God generally calls, prepares, and uses a servant leader to carry out his mission for his or her life.

1. The call to join Christ on mission (Acts 9:1-31)
2. Preparation for the mission (Acts 9:20-30; Gal. 2:1; the silent years of Paul's ministry)
3. Seeing/experiencing the vision (Acts 11:19-30)
4. Sending/launching the missionary beyond the mission outpost (Acts 13:1-3)
5. Opposition and conflict to God's new work (Acts 13:4–15)
6. Shared leadership for the expanding mission (Acts 16)
7. Message and character, the foundations for godly leadership (Paul's letters)
8. Finishing well and the unending story of Christ's salvation work (Acts 28:30-31)

Our realities of servant leadership will come from the seedbed of this portion of the Acts story. Careful study of Paul's life and ministry in this context will help us see how God developed him into a servant leader for His purposes.

A Word to the Reader: Please do not feel forced to move ahead. Take the time needed to process and pray about what God's Spirit is revealing in your heart about where God wants to lead your church. Begin to pray now for a humble and teachable spirit as you take the next steps. If you fall behind the prescribed time to complete the study, don't worry. Responding to the Spirit's lead in your life is more important than finishing a study on time.

1. "Jefferson, TX," The Handbook of Texas Online. http://www.tsha.utexas.edu/handbook/online/articles/view/JJ/hgj2.html (Accessed 7 July 2002).

2. Erwin Raphael McManus, *An Unstoppable Force* (Loveland, CO: Group, 2001), 43-60.

3. Alan Nelson and Gene Appel, *How to Change Your Church Without Killing It* (Nashville: Word Publishing, 2000), 1.

4. Kennon Callahan, *Effective Church Leadership* (New York: Harper & Row, 1990; Indianapolis, IN: Jossey-Bass, 1997).

5. Ibid., 3.

6. Ibid., 13.

7. Ibid., 22.

8. Nelson and Appel, *How to Change Your Church,* 9.

9. Bill Easum, *Unfreezing Moves* (Nashville: Abingdon Press, 2001), 18.

10. Ibid., 19-22.

11. Erwin Raphael McManus, *Uprising: a Revolution of the Soul* (Nashville: Thomas Nelson, 2003), 46.

12. Ken Blanchard and Phil Hodges, *The Servant Leader* (Nashville: J. Countryman, 2003), 10.

13. C. Gene Wilkes, *Jesus on Leadership* (Nashville: LifeWay, 1996; Carol Stream, IL: Tyndale House Publishers, 1998).

14. Blanchard and Hodges, *The Servant Leader,* 46-47.

15. The most influential piece on this topic among churches is Rick Warren, *The Purpose-Driven Church* (Grand Rapids: Zondervan, 1995).

16. Wilkes, *Jesus on Leadership* (Tyndale), 20.

17. Bill Hybels, *Courageous Leadership* (Grand Rapids: Zondervan, 2002), 32.

18. George Barna, *The Second Coming of the Church* (Nashville: Word Publishing, 1998), 106.

19. Bruce Bickel and Stan Jantz, "Love Teaches" in *Stories We Heard About Love* (Nashville: J. Countryman, 2001), 105-14.

20. Ibid., 113.

21. Louw and Nida, *Greek Lexicon,* 33.325.

22. Wilkes, *Jesus on Leadership* (LifeWay), 217.

23. John Maxwell, *The 17 Indisputable Laws of Teamwork* (Nashville: Thomas Nelson, 2001), 12.

CALL AND PREPARATION FOR MISSION

This week you will:

- Observe God's call for Paul to carry Jesus to the rest of the world.
- Discover what calling means to you and how being on mission can happen in your life.
- Learn how God prepares you to begin the journey of faith motivated by His call.
- Think about how you can prepare your church to begin the journey of following Jesus to make disciples of all peoples.

Doug is a retired Navy chaplain. He serves as a volunteer chaplain for his city's police and fire departments. Doug is an ordained minister who has served on church staffs as pastor, business administrator, and minister of education. He resigned from his last church position because the pastor wanted all of the staff to have the same denominational affiliation. Doug was not one of them, and while the separation was equitable, he found himself over 50 and for the first time without a job or place in ministry as he had known it.

Doug and his wife patiently waited for God to lead them to a place to provide for his family and use his experience in ministry. They assumed another church job would open up and he would finish living out his calling on a local church staff. God had other plans.

While prayerfully seeking God's leadership, Doug was introduced to Marketplace Ministries, a company founded by Gil Stickland, another retired military man, that provides chaplains to companies. Now, rather than going to the office in a local church, Doug travels, serving employees of the various companies who have asked for a chaplain in the marketplace.[1] Once called to a ministry mostly within the walls of church buildings, Doug now carries the love of Christ into the open frontier where people spend most of their days.

This session is about calling. We will explore God's calling on Paul's life and connect what we can see from it with God's calling on your church and life. Like Paul and Doug, don't assume you know the outcome of God's call for you to join Him in making disciples of all peoples. Jesus has a way of surprising us with His intentions, but that is part of the joy of following Him.

God's call on your life and your church's life is the beginning of an adventure you cannot pre-script. Active obedience to God's call is more like a "journey without maps" than following a strategic plan. You cannot predict where God may lead you, but you happily give up your game plan to discover the vistas you would never see if you stayed on the plains of certainty.

LEADING IN THE WRONG DIRECTION

Philip Yancey confesses to be a changed man. Somewhere along life's journey God revealed to him an entirely new way of relating to God and others. It was so radically different from his childhood through young adult experience that it completely changed his life. His confession recorded in his book *What's So Amazing About Grace?* reveals the change in how he experienced God: "I think back to who I was—resentful, wound tight with anger, a single hardened link in a long chain of ungrace learned from family and church. Now I am trying in my own small way to pipe the tune of grace. I do so because I know, more surely than I know anything, that any pang of healing or forgiveness or goodness I have ever felt comes solely from the grace of God. I yearn for the church to become a nourishing culture of that grace."[2]

Something changed in Yancey's life that led him past the "ungrace" of his perceptions of God to an entirely new relationship with God through grace in Christ Jesus. His book is a call to grace by a man being healed from the wounds of a religion of ungrace.

You and I cannot escape the influence of family and the values culture imposes on us in our formative years. Josh McDowell wrote, "What we experience in our human relationships, especially during childhood, significantly affects how we perceive and experience our relationship with God."[3] Most often without intervention by God, we are left to act out the part handed to us from the previous generation.

You and I are often bound by the traditions that trained us. Change is hard to experience the longer we live within the boundaries of our past. A life bound to family, tradition, and the expectations of both is not necessarily a bad thing. That life, left unexamined, however, can prevent followers of Jesus from experiencing the fresh expression of God's work. If holding to the status quo becomes more valuable than following Jesus, we risk the missed opportunity of experiencing God in eternally significant ways.

What are some ideas, ways of doing church or beliefs about God that have changed from your childhood to now? Write them in the margin and be prepared to share them with your mission outpost team the next time you gather.

Make a list of each team member's list for the group. Ask, "Are these common ideas we as a church hold on to?"

Servant leaders may serve the wrong mission if all they do is lead others in the worn paths of their pasts. Culture, religion, and family, like templates for molten metals, can become inflexible molds to a servant leader's passion to serve God. This problem is not a new one.

Harnessed by the Past

Saul of Tarsus grew up in an institution of society which had begun as a movement of God. What started as the adventure of a ragtag band of escapees

Key Verse

Falling to the ground, he heard a voice saying to him, "Saul, Saul, why are you persecuting Me?"

"Who are You, Lord?" He asked.

"I am Jesus, whom you are persecuting," He replied. "But get up and go into the city, and you will be told what you must do."

—Acts 9:4-6

Servant leaders may serve the wrong mission if all they do is lead others in the worn paths of their pasts.

31

from Egypt was now woven into the fabric of everyday life. Saul could not avoid the influence of the brand of Judaism on his life. Like a tropical fish trapped in an aquarium, Saul swam in his religion unaware of the larger ocean of God's work. Something had to happen outside his experience to displace him from where he had settled down to live out his faith in God. That displacement was the encounter with Jesus on the road to Damascus.

How had Saul's life become limited to the faith of his culture? God continued the covenant movement with Israel when he chose Abraham and his descendants to be God's chosen people. That movement of faith began as a wild journey from the Ur of Chaldeans to the unmarked land of God's promise. That journey continued through Isaac and Jacob. Jacob, renamed Israel, bore sons who soon found themselves at the feet of their brother Joseph in Egypt. Centuries later God told the people of Israel to drop what they were doing and follow Moses into the desert. After a 40-year saga to raise up a generation who trusted God without reservation, the people entered the promised land under Joshua's leadership.

The people settled among the locals, and the slow, seductive process of disobedience began to work its way into the hearts of the people. What began as a wild adventure became domesticated in the days of the kings, exile, and the eventual return to the promised land. Yes, there were times of revival when God breathed fresh wind of the Spirit into the people's lives, and there was always the remnant God kept his eye on (2 Kings 19:30-31). But the adventure was over. Settling into a predictable pattern of religion became the status quo.

By Jesus' and Paul's day, the movement of God had become an institution of society. Attention had turned from following God to managing an institution. The adventure of faith had climbed into a hammock of religion.

God, the Father—Lion of Judah—sent Jesus, the Son, to call His people from their stale religion and rejoin Him on the wild-eyed movement to reconcile all people to Himself. Those who want to return to the adventure of following God may find themselves in the midst of a group who have traded their hiking boots for slippers. They will soon know the danger of trying to revive the spirit of pioneers among settlers. A living room in suburbia is more comfortable than a hostel on a mountain trail, and we know from Jesus' life and ministry that conflict followed Him as He sought to introduce a renewed relationship with God into a centuries-old religion about God. All those who seek to follow Jesus too many times find themselves locked in conflict with those who prefer predictable religion over chaotic adventure.

Where do you prefer to live out your relationship with God? Mark a spot on the continuum between "adventure" and "hammock" to describe your preference. Be honest.

Adventure   **Hammock**

Saul of Tarsus became a Pharisee in the Old Covenant. He had become a servant to the mission of organized religion. Being a Pharisee signaled an all-out commitment to the core beliefs and values of his faith. Paul obtained the highest echelon of leadership among his people, and achieving such status ensured him prestige, security, and influence. Paul had climbed the ladder of religious success, but he was not on mission with God. Although he was convinced that he was furthering the work of God, he actually was, in his own words, "kicking against the goads" of God (see Acts 26:14).

Servant leaders can passionately serve the mission of their choice and still be planets away from God's purpose for their lives. As you choose the obvious pattern for life handed to you, be careful not to miss the sacred journey God has called you to join.

What does a life look like lived out in the narrow passages of the past? Brent Curtis and John Eldridge wrote: "The central belief of our times is that there is no story, nothing hangs together, all we have are bits and pieces, the random days of our lives. Tragedy still brings us to tears and heroism still lifts our hearts, but there is no context for any of it. Life is just a sequence of images and emotions without rhyme or reason."[4]

Without a purpose, a sense of calling beyond our own inventions, or the invitation to join God on the adventure of faith, we find ourselves wandering in a wilderness of meaninglessness or limply living out the life our chosen career path has fixed for us. Every day is a reaction to events and emails rather than a response to God's promptings. God's call is the reality that gives us the opportunity to join God on the journey.

Pause again and mark where you place yourself on the continuum between "limply living life" and "called on a journey with God." Be honest, don't let the "right answers" of your past determine your answer. Be prepared to share your feelings with your mission outpost team.

Limply Living Life   **Called on a Journey with God**

You can be living in the seemingly predetermined path for your life and even be seen as bringing new concepts to the table but be outside the alignment of God's purpose for your life. Take Paul for example. We tend to see the Pharisees only as legalists and keepers of the status quo. While this is true from the perspective of following Jesus' new-wineskin faith, oddly enough the rival sect of Sadducees saw the Pharisees as "dangerous innovators—modernists, in fact."[5] While we may see the Pharisees as staid traditionalists, Paul's contemporaries saw his religious group as innovators.

You can be perceived as an innovator within your business or ministry and still miss the leadership of God in your life. It is not your reputation as an innovator that makes a difference in the Jesus movement. Being on mission with God is the goal. Innovation follows mission. Innovation will come when God calls you on mission to serve the people on mission with you and those in your mission field.

The Call That Changed Everything

What changes a life limply lived to a life of adventure with God? For Saul of Tarsus, it was God breaking into his life and calling him to a higher purpose for his life.

Read Paul's description of his heritage in Philippians 3:5-6. How did he describe himself?

Read Acts 7:58; 8:1, 3. How does the writer of Acts describe Paul (Saul) in this context?

Saul's resume read well among his contemporaries. He had the pedigree and degrees to boast if he chose to do so. He was well respected and followed

Servant leaders can passionately serve the mission of their choice and still be planets away from God's purpose for their lives.

the path of his handed-down religion to the letter. Once he achieved his place in the religious community, Saul, the Pharisee, used every power and authority at his disposal to destroy those who trusted Jesus as the Messiah. His passionate loyalty to the past and traditions of his faith established him as a defender of the faith.

Clinging to his understanding of how people were to relate to God through the law and its interpretation, he saw the followers of the Nazarene not as threats to his religion or position but as those who dishonored God. His motivation was not necessarily personal but, as far as he knew, exactly what God wanted him to do. We will see in sessions to come that those who oppose change or the fresh work of God's Spirit are not always defending themselves. They are fighting for their perception of God and His work in the world. Resistance to new expressions of God's movement among His people is not always based on personal bias alone.

Paul, however, stood outside the movement of the Spirit of God which had begun in Jesus. So he led in efforts to destroy this "heretical sect." His zeal for preserving the law of God drove him to remove anything resembling the message that Jesus was Messiah.

However, something changed his life direction. Read Acts 9:1-9. What happened as Paul traveled to Damascus to change his life's calling from keeping religious tradition to pursuing an adventure with God?

Christ's call through Ananias, a humble servant of Jesus, for Paul "to carry my name before the Gentiles and their kings and before the people of Israel" (Acts 9:15, NIV) changed Paul's mission in life. The dramatic events on the road to Damascus combined with the days of solitude created a place of hearing in his restless heart. After three days of spiritual incubation, he no longer sought to destroy the work of God in Christ Jesus. He joined the fellowship of suffering he helped create! God captured his heart in a way expressly chosen by God to bridle his wild heart, and Paul responded by committing to a mission that would be God's call for him, not his chosen way of life.

This call to go to the ethnics transformed his life from a keeper of religion to a missionary for Christ. He was no longer to maintain the institutions of tradition; he now was to make the mission call of God on his life the *why* for all he did and said.

George Barna defines a Christian leader as "someone who is called by God to lead and possess virtuous character and effectively motivates, mobilizes resources, and directs people toward the fulfillment of a jointly embraced vision from God."[6] Leadership among God's people begins with calling.

We will look more closely at the nature of God's calling to join Him on mission in the next section. Before you leave this section, stop for a moment and examine your own life and life direction. Place a check by the statements that reflect your understanding of why you do what you do now. When you have completed this list, write a prayer to God expressing your sense of His leadership in your life at this time.

❏ **My life could be characterized by simply following the path laid out for me by others.**
❏ **I have a sense that God is invading my life in order to redirect what I am doing with my life.**

❑ I am living out the adventurous journey God has planned for me.

❑ I am somewhere between an unhealthy restlessness about what God wants for my life and the revealed intentions of God for my life.

❑ I know how Paul felt. God crashed into my life and changed why I was alive and what I was to do with my life.

❑ I am trying to figure out what God wants me to do for Him, but I am curious about this concept of call.

❑ My church has a clear sense of God's call for what He wants us to do for Him in our mission field.

❑ I am not sure we know as a church what God's call for us really is.

Write your prayer to God in the margin, in your journal, or on a separate page.

Day 2

A LIFE ON MISSION

I like to run with two groups of people. One group runs on trails, and the other runs on roads. The trail runners call the road runners "streeties." While I prefer trails, I spend most of my time running with the streeties; there are more of them, and it is easier to find streets to run on in the barren terrain of North Dallas than on natural dirt trails.

One group I run with meets and runs almost every Saturday morning around White Rock Lake in Dallas. A member of the group is named Jennifer, and she works for a consulting firm. She is also a Christian who sees her job as a way to further the work of God in people's lives. She told me about an opportunity she had to invite a coworker who did not know Jesus to her church and to join her small group. I told her how cool it was for her to seize every opportunity to lead others to Christ. She said, "Yes, it is. I guess I am a missionary with a corporate sponsor!"

"A missionary with a corporate sponsor" is an ideal picture of a life captured by the call of God. A yes to Christ's call to "follow me" is a yes to a life immersed in the adventure of being part of God's redemptive purposes for all of creation—no matter who compensates you. Of course, Jennifer honors the employee guidelines of her company and works hard to complete her assignments in ethical and God-honoring ways; but, like a doctor with the cure for the most deadly of all diseases, she graciously offers the antidote to those who need it.

Often the path of work assignments becomes the next steps God uses for His redemptive purposes. Like Paul who went to the market centers of his world on mission with Christ, so Jennifer perceives every data center and IT department a divine assignment with eternal implications. Missionaries see life that way.

Do you see yourself as "a missionary with a corporate sponsor"? Or do you see your daily activity as something separate from God's call on your life to follow Him? Do your church's mission trips have more meaning than your daily trip into the marketplace, neighborhood, or school? Be prepared to share your answers with your mission outpost group.

Key Verse

A person should consider us in this way: as servants of Christ and managers of God's mysteries.

—1 Corinthians 4:1

Captured by God's Call

God's redirection of Paul's life through a clear calling leads us to our first reality of servant leadership in a ministry of transition from the life of Paul:

Reality 1: Servant leaders find their mission when God's call captures their heart (see Acts 9).

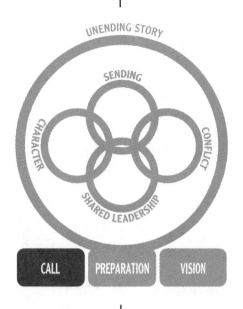

Calling is the event, or series of promptings, in which you find God's ultimate direction and purpose for your life.[7] I wrote in *My Identity in Christ,* "Your response to God's call to follow Him is the single most transforming event in your life—all else flows from it."[8] Call will become the gyroscope of life direction. Os Guinness put it this way, "The Puritans lived as if they had swallowed gyroscopes; we modern Christians live as if we have swallowed Gallup polls."[9] The mission call of God in the leader's life is the instrument that keeps him or her on course. Without it the leader is left to choose his or her own mission to serve.

Reggie McNeal emphasized the importance of call when he wrote: "Women and men who have similarly received a life-changing call [like Paul] consistently live out the same truth. The call provides them with their life direction. It informs their decisions by reorienting their priorities and establishing a new set of core values. The call provides a content that becomes their life message. They would not be who they were without it. During times of great testing in the leader's life, the call serves as an internal-navigation beacon of hope and reassurance."[10]

This call is not an encounter with God we produce for ourselves. Calling is realized through a combination of God's leading and the leader's willing response to those leadings. Leaders are sometimes like the film character in *Bruce Almighty* played by Jim Carey who barreled down the road of life crying out for God to speak to him while he passed signs on the side of the road and in trucks that turn in front of him with directions to prevent a crash. We too easily miss the leading of God when our attention is focused more on our own perceptions of how God speaks than becoming aware of His promptings around us.

Calling captures you. You don't capture it. Paul, our example in this study, never insisted it was he who found Christ. He confessed that his obsession to reach all people for Christ was because "Christ Jesus took hold of me" (Phil. 3:12, NIV). Paul insisted throughout his ministry that the source of his mission was revelation, not collaboration with others (Gal. 1:12). He also wrote, "For this reason I, Paul, the prisoner of Christ Jesus for the sake of you Gentiles . . . that by revelation there was made known to me the mystery, as I wrote before in brief" (Eph. 3:1,3, NASB).

A Different Way of Knowing

Revelation is how a Christian knows God ultimately. It is God's move toward people to show His person, ways, and reality. Paul staked his authority on the reality that God revealed His mission to him, not on his conviction that it was what God wanted him to do.

We, however, live in a world where how people know truth is centered in the reasoning of the individual. This is a tenet of our postmodern culture. A postmodern person may confess, for example:

Reality 1: Servant leaders find their mission when God's call captures their heart.

36

My reasoned conviction about things is superior to the outdated perception that God revealed Himself in the Bible. Isn't the Bible just one group of people's reasoned convictions about God anyway? Their world was held up by pillars, and they murdered others because they believed God told them to do that. They said Jesus is the only way to God. The God I know wouldn't tell someone to kill someone else, and it doesn't make sense if God wanted everyone to love Him, He would only let people come to Him through Jesus. What about the people who never heard of Jesus? Revelation is an outdated method of knowing the truth; therefore, I will pursue my own path of understanding.

Contrary to the postmodern mind-set, God's revelation is timeless and transcends all cultures and reasoning by people. God reveals ultimate truth about Himself and our reality through His living Holy Spirit and His chosen leaders who spoke and wrote His revealed truth for all people. Without the revelation of God's purpose for his life, Paul would have continued in his personal "reasoned conviction" about what was right and wrong.

Is God's call always as dramatic as God's call on Paul's life? Not necessarily. Paul's temperament, personal convictions, and his embedded lifestyle in his religion necessitated such a dramatic encounter with Jesus. Other people did not need as traumatic an event to redirect their lives. Remember Jesus' personal, warm redirect of Peter's life after his disciple had denied Him (John 21). Either way, by falling to the ground in a moment or through a relational conversation, the end result is a heart captured by God. Once captured by the loving and purposeful God, a pliable heart can be set in the direction of eternal purposes.

Calling Affects Everything

The biblical concept of calling affects every area of life for the one who says yes to God's call. For too long, many Christians have distorted the biblical idea of calling by separating life into sacred and secular categories. In too many Christian circles, career has replaced calling as one's purpose in life or, worse, separated them as two different career opportunities. However, a significant difference exists between career as offered in our society and calling as described in Scripture.

John Ortberg describes a difference between call and career: "A call, which is something I do for God, is replaced by a career, which threatens to become my god. A career is something I choose for myself; a calling is something I receive. A career is something I do for myself; a calling is something I do for God. A career promises status, money or power; a calling generally promises difficulty and even some suffering—and the opportunity to be used by God. A career is about upward mobility; a calling generally leads to downward mobility."[11]

Without a biblical basis for calling, we can slip into believing our personal pursuits for wealth and security equal God's desire for our lives. Calling is seldom about changing careers. It is more often about allowing God to refocus what you do or why you do it.

Ed Silvoso refers to calling that enters the marketplace as an "anointing for business." He wrote: "To be anointed for business is to be set aside by God for service in the marketplace. Once anointed, we are to use our job as a ministry vehicle to transform the marketplace so that the gospel will be preached to, and heard by, every creature in our sphere of influence. The same principle applies in all areas of the marketplace: business, education and government."[12]

Either way, by being knocked off your horse in a moment or through a slow realization over years, the end result is a heart captured by God.

Silvoso argues that "the central role of the Christian is in the market-place."[13] God's call sends them outside the walls of the church to do business God's way and to be used by God to change the world in which they work.

The Apostle Paul instructed Christians not to create dividing walls between their faith walk and what they did every day. He wrote, "Whatever you do, work at it with all your heart, as working for the Lord, not for men, since you know that you will receive an inheritance from the Lord as a reward. It is the Lord Christ you are serving" (Col. 3:23-24, NIV). He was not referring to religious activity when he wrote these words. His instructions are in the context of everyday work life. Followers of Jesus are to do their jobs as "for the Lord." The word for *serving* here is the same word Jesus used to describe leaders when he said, "If you want to be first, you must become slave of all" (see Mark 10:44).

The Apostle Paul is a biblical example of someone God prepared before he was called to a specific task. His training as a Pharisee and birth into a Jewish family with Roman citizenship served to be the platform for God's using him to bring the good news of Jesus to the entire world. God simply redirected all that was in Paul's life to His purposes rather than for Paul's own purposes.

I believe Ken Blanchard's confession of how God worked in his life prior to his trust response to God's call on his life is similar to how God prepared Paul prior to his call to go to the ethnics. Blanchard wrote that after he met Christ he realized that everything he had written about leadership Jesus had done! His books *Leadership by the Book*[14] and *The Servant Leader*[15] are tools for learning to lead like Jesus. Blanchard did not change his career as a consultant and writer for the marketplace. He simply allowed God to "redeem" them for His purposes. Don't overlook what God has done and is doing in your life and your church to prepare you to carry out His call.

The Change Call Makes

Read 1 Corinthians 4:1. Write in the margin the key words that Paul used to describe himself.
Now read Romans 15:20.[16] **How did Paul describe God's work in his life? What did he say was his "ambition" (NIV) or "aim" (HCSB)?**

I presented the realities of servant leadership from the life of Jesus before a group of leaders in innovative or "new paradigm" churches. Most of them stared blankly at me as I taught. In the middle of the presentation, a leader injected that servant leadership was not palatable in his world. "Godly ambition" was what drove him in his ministry. I stammered a little and told him I was not sure there was such a thing, but I would consider his position. Since that encounter, I have come to the conclusion that although it sounds like an oxymoron, "godly ambition" is a reality for those who have made themselves servants to God's call on their lives. Erwin McManus reminds us:

> It's important to note that ambition itself is not wrong. In fact the Bible never speaks of ambition itself as negative. Ambition is a God-given motivation. One of the great tragedies among many followers of Christ is the loss of ambition after coming to faith. They have become convinced that any personal ambition is dishonoring to God. . . . Ambition is not the problem; it's selfish ambition from which we need to be freed. . . . Ironically, we have been better at destroying ambition than we have been at eliminating selfishness.[17]

Paul's words at the end of Romans make the case for godly ambition and that it is a good thing. The original word for *ambition* in Romans 15 literally means, "to befriend honor" (my interpretation of the compound Greek word *philo* + *timeomai*). Ambition is friendship with honor. Paul wrote that his greatest desire was "to preach the gospel where Christ was not known, so that I would not be building on someone else's foundation" (v. 20, NIV). He loved the honor of being one called to tell the world about Jesus. Servant leaders find their highest honor in living out the mission call of God with their lives.

Paul knew the downside of ambition, too. He ambitiously pursued position and power his entire life prior to God's call to take Jesus to the ethnics. He warned followers of Jesus to "do nothing out of selfish ambition or vain conceit, but in humility consider others better than yourselves" (Phil. 2:3, NIV). He then went on to point to Jesus' humility as their example.

Patrick Lencioni in *The Five Temptations of a CEO*, describes the first temptation of company leaders as "choosing status over results."[18] The mythical janitor/mentor of the story taught the young CEO that too many leaders seek to advance or guard their status rather than giving their lives for results that benefit the company. He concluded, "In fact, great CEOs should be almost overwhelmed by the need to achieve something. That is what drives them. Achievement. Not ego."[19] Servant leaders always put the achievement of the organization or church above their status. They are able to do this because they have made themselves servant to the mission, not their advancement within an organization.

> **Saul's ambition changed from achieving honor for himself to pleasing God. You can tell the heart of a servant leader by the source of his joy. John Eldridge asks, "When you strip away everything that you get recognition for, what's left?" That's a good question. Why don't you answer if for yourself now? Write your thoughts in the margin.**

Paul's ambition was to live out God's call on his life. That desire came from God's calling on his life. This refocused his ambition so that his only boast was in the cross of Christ alone. He confessed, "May I never boast except in the cross of our Lord Jesus Christ, through which the world has been crucified to me, and I to the world" (Gal. 6:14, NIV).

> **How do you discover whether God's mission for your life has captured your heart? Here are some hints that mission, the why of all you do and say, guides your life. Read each statement. Mark the statements that are truest of where you are on your journey with God at this time. The statements are singular for personal reflection. When you gather with your mission outpost team, read them as plural for your church. Be prepared to share your thoughts with your team at your next gathering.**

- ❑ **My heart tells me that I am to be a missionary in this mission field.**
- ❑ **I am willing to do whatever it takes to make God's calling happen.**
- ❑ **"Sacred" and "secular" are not separate categories when I consider living out God's calling on my life.**
- ❑ **I am living out God's calling rather than seeking to fulfill others' expectations of me.**
- ❑ **Obedience to the call rules over personal ambition in matters of calling.**
- ❑ **Nothing matters to me or my church more than the mission call of God.**

Servant leaders find their highest honor in living out the mission call of God with their lives.

PERSONAL PREPARATION

Key Verse

But when God, who from my mother's womb set me apart and called me by His grace, was pleased to reveal His Son in me, so that I could preach Him among the Gentiles, I did not immediately consult anyone. I did not go up to Jerusalem to those who had become apostles before me; instead I went to Arabia and came back to Damascus.
—Galatians 1:15-17

Being called by God for mission is almost always followed by a season of preparation by God for that mission. Realigning your life to the mission call of God is not as easy as putting a bag of unpopped popcorn in the microwave and cooking it on high for three minutes. Preparation for call is more often like the season of winter in nature. It seems there is no purposeful activity in the cold, dark days of winter, but Parker Palmer, described one gift of winter: "Despite all appearances, of course, nature is not dead in winter—it has gone underground to renew itself and prepare for spring. Winter is a time when we are admonished and even inclined, to do the same for ourselves."[20] The season of winter prepares us for the spring of our calling.

Jesus taught the same reality that unless a kernel of wheat falls to the ground and dies, it remains only a single seed. But if it dies, it produces many seeds (John 12:14). Preparation for mission, the season of dying, precedes the season of new life and abundance.

Reflect on where you and your church are in preparing for God's mission call on your life. Have you entered a season of winter or dying to the old ways in order to experience a springtime of growth? What are your fears about a season of winter? What is it about "falling into the ground and dying" that may prevent you or your church from being responsive to God's call? Be prepared to share your responses with your mission outpost team.

A Kernel of Wheat Dying

We often forget that Saul of Tarsus fell off the biblical scene for more than a decade after his call on the road to Damascus and before he emerged in Antioch with Barnabas. This was his season of "a kernel of wheat dying." In order for him to produce "many seeds," his past and his preconceptions about God had to fall into the ground and die.

Read the Key Verses again. Add to them the following verses, Galatians 1:17–2:1. After you have read the passage, write out the places and length of time Paul detailed when he wrote to the Galatians.

Paul's original intent for spelling out this time line was to establish that what he was saying and doing was not as a representative of any person or group but that he was called through revelation. As we examine his time line, however, we learn that he spent years alone and separate from the influence of even the leaders of the Jesus movement in Jerusalem.

Paul was called by Christ outside of Damascus. His life was threatened by his peers in that city, and he fled to Arabia. After some time in the desert regions there, he returned to Damascus (v. 17). Three years after returning to his original mission field, he did go to Jerusalem and met with Peter and James, the "former apostles" (vv. 18-20). He then went to the areas of Syria and Cilicia and stayed well away from the churches to the south in Judea (vv. 21-24).

Chapter 2 of Galatians begins with the announcement that after 14 years he went again to Jerusalem with Barnabas. Many scholars believe Paul was describing the time between his conversion and his trip to Jerusalem recorded in Acts 15. Others believe this was time from his call and the "famine visit" to Jerusalem described in Acts 11. Either way you interpret the data, it still reveals there was a long period of time between his call and when we see him in public view.

The questions we want to ask related to this testimony of Paul are: What happened during those silent years? What went on in his mind and life that prepared him for his public ministry in Antioch told about in Acts 11? We can only speculate about what really happened in his heart and life, but we see a new man, a changed man, emerge on the other side of those years. One thing we know for certain is that he had to wrestle through all of the shifts in how he related to God and did ministry as a result of his call (see week 1, day 3).

As a review, return to that section of this workbook and reread one of the passages that describe one of the major issues Paul had to work through in light of his new relationship with Christ and the resulting mission he was to complete. Write in your own words what that struggle to make the shift must have been like for Paul.

We can also determine from some of his writings some of the key issues of faith he had to get straight before he could take the good news of Jesus to all people. For an example, read Galatians 3:24. (The context is Galatians 3:19-26.) What was Paul's conclusion about why God revealed the law to His people? Write your answer in the margin.

Saul of Tarsus, the "Pharisee of Pharisees," had to answer the question, What about the law now that God has revealed that people are made right with Him through trusting Jesus to be their Savior? Saul, the religious leader, had spent his adult life defending the law as the way people were made right before Holy God. In these days of silent dying—his ministry's winter—he came to the conclusion, guided by the Holy Spirit, that the purpose of the law was like that of a guardian, leading children to a teacher. The law's requirements led people to realize that their only hope for being right with God was by some way other than keeping all the rules. The kernel of wheat, justification by works, had to fall into the ground and die so the many seeds, justification by grace, could multiply in the lives of millions.

Passionate leaders sometime jump into change quickly. Any downtime seems a waste or delay in reaching their goals. Winter looks like a waste. Spring and summer are the seasons of choice for the catalytic leader. God, however, often leads his servant leaders through times of character preparation before placing them on the front lines of transition. Take King David, for example. King Saul pursued him in caves and deserts for 25 years before he was crowned king. Remember Joseph with the coat of many colors? God allowed him to be thrown into cisterns and prison cells before he became the number two world leader. Moses, the great deliverer of Israel, tended sheep for 40 years before God sent him into Pharaoh's palace to demand, "Let my people go."

Even Jesus of Nazareth, the Son of God, experienced his own silent years from age 12 to 30. Upon His emergence in public, God sent Him into the wilderness for 40 days to be tested by His adversary. God prepares those He chooses.

The kernel of wheat, justification by works, had to fall into the ground and die so the many seeds, justification by grace, could multiply in the lives of millions.

These out-of-the-way assignments in perspective can be seen as preparation for the greater influence God has prepared for you. Reggie McNeal observed: "God uses a preparation model for developing leaders, not a planning model. . . . Leaders of great legacy look back over their lives and see that in every ministry assignment, God was preparing them for the next. Trusting God with their destiny, they wound up with influence over much."[21]

Just because you are not seen does not mean you are not being used or not being prepared. God can use quiet days and restless nights to build your character while helping you see His clear call for your life.

Preparing for Mission

This review of how God prepared Saul of Tarsus between his call and public ministry leads us to our second reality for servant leaders on mission with Christ.

Reality 2: Servant leaders allow God to prepare them for mission (see Gal. 2).

This may seem too obvious to highlight as an enduring reality of servant leadership, but it is essential to being servant to God's mission for your life. Servant leaders are not prefabricated on some assembly line somewhere. They are not self-made men and women who declare themselves ready for leading. Servant leaders on mission with Jesus allow God to use any locale, method, or circumstance to mold them into the leader God desires them to become.

Several areas of the servant leader's life become targets for change as part of God's preparation for their leadership. God targets the heart, how one thinks, and the leader's audience of approval during times of preparation.

God takes aim first at the heart of the leader. When God's call to mission captures the servant leader's heart, a shift in loyalties must take place. Who calls the shots and where ultimate loyalties lie are the bull's-eyes of God's work in the leader. When that change is made to Christ as leader, no longer does ego edge God out of the center of decision making and character. Christ takes His rightful place as leader in the heart. Only then can the leader be a servant leader.

Read Galatians 2:20. Substitute the word "ego" for the word "I" in the first part of the verse. Describe what God has done with Paul's ego. What are some implications for your life if this were to become your confession? Write your answers in the margin.

Ken Blanchard reminds us that God changes the heart where ego is central and "edging God out" to a heart that is Christ centered and "exalting God only."[22]

What are some heart issues God may address if you will allow Him to prepare you to be a servant leader? What are some matters of the heart God has already spent time addressing in your life? Write your thoughts/comments in the sidebar or in your journal.

Servant leaders who lead in transition must allow themselves to break free from traditional thinking in order to think biblically.

Reality 2: Servant leaders allow God to prepare them for mission.

A second area God addresses in times of preparation is how the leader thinks about or sees ways of carrying out God's call. Servant leaders who lead in transition must allow themselves to break free from traditional thinking in order to think biblically. This is not an easy task. We are all influenced by how we have been taught to think and see reality. The way things have always been can reel us in from chasing new expressions of faith. Do not overlook the work Paul had to allow God to do in his thinking to get him out of the temple and into the mission field. God had to deconstruct and rebuild his faith in order to use him. You, too, must allow God to challenge everything you have thought about how to do church. Some you will keep. Others you will cast aside like boxes of memorabilia stored in your attic at home.

To think biblically is to take the events and teachings in Scripture at face value and to seek timeless, transcultural truths and apply them to where and when God has called you. I often ask myself, "Is what I am doing consistent with the whole revelation of Scripture?" and, "Can this truth be applied in any culture anywhere at any time?" These two questions help me challenge existing methods while opening my heart to fresh ways God would use us to reach more people effectively.

Peeling back the layers of tradition and habit in our methods is careful work. The leader must go through this exercise before he or she can lead a group of people through it. The practices of preparation in the next session will help you through this process.

On first reading of this area of God's preparation in your life, make a short list of some items you may need to change from thinking about traditionally to seeing through a biblical matrix.

A third area God targets for change in the season of winter is where the leader seeks his or her approval. Or to ask it another way: To whom are you playing? Who is your audience?

Paul experienced this when he left the fraternity of the faithful to join the fellowship of the saints. He suffered some bad press from those with whom he formerly served. Those who opposed him often came in behind his time spent with people, and they tried to convince them he was wrong. You may know these as the Judaizers, Jews who were convinced one must become a Jew to be a follower of Jesus. They opposed the new gospel of Jesus as the only way to be right before Holy God. They fought Paul's message and its implications wherever he went. How did he cope with this constant opposition? He was convinced he lived to please the God who sent him, not those who wanted things to stay the same.

Read Galatians 1:10. Whom did Paul seek to please? What was his proof that he was pleasing the right one?

Paul made clear that he did not seek others' approval. He did not live his life to gain others' applause. He sought the approval of God alone, and he gladly wore the title "servant of Christ." This conviction allowed him to stay true to his call and survive opposition.

A servant leader in a ministry of transition must make the choice Paul did, or he will find himself playing to the audience of his peers rather than pleasing the One who called him. Make no mistake; this can be emotionally wrenching and could cost you your career—but set you on the journey of your calling. Standing firm to make a necessary change while your peers challenge and even attack you is no fun. Only when God is your audience of one and He alone is your source of approval can you survive and even flourish in those times.

Who is your audience? Really. To whom do you play for approval? Take some time to listen to your heart, and record your impressions in the sidebar or in your journal.

Journal for the Journey

August 3, 1995—I had just let a staff member go, and we had failed at raising enough money to build a new worship center. Confusion and uncertainty were the meal of the day. My prayer that day, "Father, thank You for this place you have put me by Your providence. Help me to hear You and know Your heart. Master of my life, discipline my pride as You are doing now so that Your work—not mine—will be accomplished. There are too many important decisions to be made that require Your work not mine. May I say with my aggressive, goal-oriented, often overzealous brother Paul, 'Ego has been crucified with Christ, and ego no longer lives, but Christ lives.' May I also know with him that 'when ego is weak, You are strong.'"

SPIRITUAL EXERCISES OF PREPARATION

In our final stages of change, the church faced tangible transitions. One of those was updating the church constitution, which had not been updated since 1984. The church was also ready to be called by another name and to accelerate our small-group ministry. I knew it would be a challenging year.

I had just returned from running a marathon at which I had received several T-shirts. I often use objects to signal an important season with our leadership team. So, with the memories of my last marathon in my mind (and legs), I gave each member of the leadership team a logo T-shirt from the race.

I said that we had been running well to finish the race laid out before us and that we were nearing the end of that race. However, in a marathon, the race does not really begin until mile 20, the mile at which your body has used up all of its stored energy. That is also the time your training is tested most. It is easy to cruise through the first 18 or so miles if you have trained adequately. But the last 6.2 miles tell whether you took shortcuts on your training runs.

As I passed out the T-shirts, I said, "Get ready. This next leg of our race is a tough one. We are at mile 20, and the real race is about to start." I reminded them of how well they had run up to that point. "We will need one another to finish well. Let's sign our names to one another's T-shirt as a commitment that we will finish this race together." Everyone in the room signed the T-shirt of everyone else. We prayed together and asked God to use us in the days and months ahead. The team did finish that leg of the race. Everyone completed the race, and we received the prize of finishing well what God had called us to complete. I still have that T-shirt in my office. It reminds me of both the aches and the pains and the joys of victory that faithful persistence brings.

You may be or may have been on a team that shared something to signify their commitment to one another and to the mission they had been given to complete. Write a description of that symbol and what it meant to you and your team. What symbols could you use with your present team to show your shared commitment to one another and the assignment given to you? Write in the margin. Be prepared to share what you write with your mission outpost team at your next gathering.

Exercises to Prepare You for Mission

Preparation for mission is not passive. Like an athlete training for her next race or a master musician for his next concert, servant leaders make room for God's transforming presence in their lives by training themselves in the ways of God. When Paul wrote to his apprentice Timothy instructing him how to lead on mission, he told him to "train yourself in godliness" (1 Tim. 4:7). Why godliness? Because, Paul said, physical training has limited benefit for the body that will pass away; but godliness, a life patterned after God, is beneficial because it holds promise for both our present and the life to come.

The Greek word for train in this verse is the root word from which we get

Key Verse

Train yourself in godliness, for, the training of the body has a limited benefit, but godliness is beneficial in every way, since it holds promise for the present life and also for the life to come.
—*1 Timothy 4:7b-8*

our English word *gymnasium*. The Greeks and Romans, like Americans, put a high value on knowledge and physical training. Most major cities in the ancient world had a gymnasium, which was the center for physical and intellectual learning for upper-class boys. Even Jerusalem had a gymnasium in the days of Jesus and Paul. Boys were trained in the sports of wrestling, swimming, and running. They were also trained in reading, music, and math. The gym eventually became a public place of both physical and intellectual training for all citizens of the city.

Paul captured the metaphor of training in the gym for spiritual training. Just as athletes trained for certain sporting events, followers of Jesus should train for certain ministry events. Just as people would gather to gain knowledge in the public gym, so God's people gather in the mission outpost to learn of God's character and His purposes. One ministry event a servant leader must train for is the marathon of transitioning a people to be on mission with Christ in the mission field.

The church as a gymnasium, a community gathering place for physical and intellectual training, is a valid image for a church on mission. Your vision for your mission outpost may include building or opening a life training center for your community that combines physical activities with literacy training or discussions on current ethical issues from a biblical perspective.

What are the exercises of godliness that God, your Coach, can use to prepare you to play well in the sporting event of His call on your life? The people of God have recognized several staple spiritual exercises that enhance a relationship with God. A review of some of these time-honored exercises will be helpful as you constantly allow God to prepare your heart, soul, mind, and strength to love God and carry out His mission for your life.

Here are some spiritual exercises that you as the change leader can put into your routine to prepare you for your ministry of transition. They are also exercises you can lead your mission outpost team to do together, like a "team in training" program.

The exercise of listening prayer—Paul depended on prayer to find the strength and insight to lead. He called his readers to put on the armor of God in order to stand firm against the schemes of the evil one. We tend to stop before the end of that passage and miss his call to prayer. He wrote, "With every prayer and request, pray at all times in the Spirit, and stay alert in this, with all perseverance and intercession for all the saints" (Eph. 6:18). The servant leader prays at all times in relationship with the Spirit of the One who called her. Paul challenged his readers to keep an attentive ear to the Spirit, persevere in ministry and to pray for those on mission with them.

Paul also asked for the Ephesians to pray for him. Servant leaders humbly ask others to pray for them. Notice his prayer was not to get him out of jail but to speak boldly where he was chained. He was happy to be called the "ambassador in chains" (Eph. 6:20).

Michael Slaughter, chief dreamer of Ginghamsburg Church, confessed, "I'm unlearning the approach to prayer marked by one-way talking or reciting self-directed wish lists. I'm moving to the kind of radical prayer that senses the will of God and does it."[23]

Take 20 minutes for listening prayer within the next two days. Write what you hear from God in your mission outpost journal.

The exercises of service and giving—Servant leadership is strengthened through acts of service to others. To proclaim you are a servant leader and

Servant leadership is strengthened through acts of service to others.

never to dress like a servant and act like a slave while leading is to nullify any spoken messages about this value. People will not embrace the core value of servant leadership until the leader is a servant. Paul's favorite description of himself was "a slave of Christ Jesus" (Rom. 1:1). He not only introduced himself in that manner, but he also validated his position in Christ and among his fellow Christ followers by his actions (2 Thess. 3:7-9).

Giving is evidence that the servant leader has relinquished ownership of his or her possessions and status. Since the statement "God owns it, and I manage it," is true, the servant leader is set free to invest resources in people and projects that yield eternal value. Giving indicates that God has begun to change the leader's heart into the likeness of his Son's heart.

Is there anyone you refuse to serve? Is there anything you would not be willing to give in order to accomplish the mission God has given you? The answers to these questions can reveal the true nature of your heart.

The exercise of community—Some leaders see themselves as loners. Servant leaders are never alone. God never intended for you to be in a ministry of transition by yourself. You need a community of encouragement, a band of brothers or sisters to share your victories and defeats. A biblical word for community is fellowship, *koinonia*. In this fellowship of servants, Paul found strength and encouragement. He remembered when Peter, James, and John offered Barnabas and him the "right hand of fellowship" and encouraged them in their mission to the ethnics (Gal. 2:9).

Living in authentic community with others on mission with you is essential to your ability to finish the race laid out for you. This corps will provide care in times when healing is necessary from injury on the field of change. They can also hold you accountable for your spiritual development, and they can monitor whether you are leading out of humility or pride. This community of partners on mission can celebrate like no others the baby steps and the quantum leaps you experience. They will also feel more deeply the hurts others can inflict upon you. I wish I could sit around with Paul and his team after events like the Ephesus riot (Acts 19:23-41). His friends prevented him from speaking in an arena where he must have been itching to preach Jesus.

List in the margin the names of those who are your "community" upon whom you can depend when the riots happen.

The exercise of active waiting—Leaders by nature are impatient. They want to see results, and they drive others to produce them. Servant leaders accept the reality that their efforts alone cannot create the ultimate changes to accomplish what God has shown them without God's help. Exercising active waiting can help the impatient leader.

One fruit of the Spirit is patience (Gal. 5:22). The word for *patience* can also be translated "long-suffering." I like to describe this character trait of the Holy Spirit as "patient endurance." The exercise of active waiting is trusting God's seasons of change. God produces the fruit of transition in His timing, not ours. We learn to be active in our waiting like "the farmer waits for the precious fruit of the earth and is patient with it until it receives the early and the late rains" (Jas. 5:7).

The farmer does the hard work of cultivating, planting, and keeping weeds out of the field, but ultimately it is out of his control whether rains come or conditions are best for growth. I've seen a hailstorm destroy a wheat field in less than 20 minutes, and the farmer lost his income for a year. I have also watched as the combines reap acre after acre of golden grain, and the

Some leaders see themselves as loners. Servant leaders are never alone.

farmer paid off all his debts. In both cases the farmer does his work, but he must wait for the outcome which is out of his control. Leading in a ministry of transition is often the same. Servant leaders actively engage the work of planting and cultivating, but ultimately they confess with Paul, "But God gave the growth" (1 Cor. 3:6).

What are the things you are patiently waiting to happen? Prayerfully write that list in your journal and ask God to strengthen the gift of His Spirit, patience.

The exercise of confession—*Confession* literally means "to say the same thing."[24] Confession is not informing God or someone about something he or she did not know. Confession is agreeing that what you both know you did has certain consequences in relationships with God and others. Confession makes accountability possible.

Sometimes I'd rather run a long run on a hot day than confess the implications of what I have done in front of the congregation or across the table from a friend. Confession is hard because it drives at the heart of our pride, but it is essential if we are serving in team and modeling leadership like Jesus. You must lift the weight of confession in order to live a life of character. Confession is the foundation for integrity. People will not follow those they do not trust. They will follow those they know are honest about their shortcomings and authentic about their struggles.

Paul taught that we are to carry the burden of one another's sin in order to restore us to the fellowship of followers on mission with Jesus (Gal. 6:1-3). Confession is possible when combined with community. For there you will feel safe enough to speak and sure enough that you will still be accepted when you expose what is in your heart.

This is a tough exercise because you must have someone you trust to share your heart. If you do not have that person or group, pray for God to guide you to them. If you do have such a partner, go to them this week and thank them for how they serve you.

The exercises of spiritual leadership and submission—Every servant leader needs a mentor, a guide, someone who is farther down the road. Getting advice is different from folding it into your life. In order to benefit from a mentor, you must not only be ready to hear the advice; you must also be willing to do it. Paul reminded his readers that submission to one another is a core value for living in community with others (Eph. 5:21). This spiritual exercise is difficult because it reaches to the core of your heart struggle: ego. Only when Christ rules on your heart's throne can you truly submit to the leadership of another.

This gentle process begins when you bend your knee to Christ as Savior. It continues when you submit to His leadership, and it becomes real when you allow another person to guide you. Our pride tells us we can do it alone and that others have nothing to offer us in the pursuit of mission. Genuine humility allows us to submit to another and to accept leadership in our own lives.

J. Robert Clinton advised an inquiring young man about what he should do to pursue his desire to go to China as a missionary. He wanted to stop his training and begin work in the foreign country. Clinton wrote him, "Perhaps the key issue in all of this is submission. Are you willing to submit to God's purposes right now for you? Anyone can submit to something he or she wants. Submission is tested only when the thing is not desired."[25]

> **Getting advice is different from folding it into your life. In order to benefit from a mentor, you must not only be ready to hear the advice; you must also be willing to do it.**

Like confession, this exercise is a heart builder. Whom can you truly submit to when you need correction or direction in your life?

The exercise of private and public worship—Rick Warren reminds us, "Worship is not a part of your life; it is your life."[26] Servant leaders who follow Jesus on mission put God first, praise who God is, and celebrate God's mighty acts in all they do. God is the focus of their thoughts, and God's pleasure is what they seek. Everything from leading team gatherings to casting vision is an act of worship. They proclaim with Paul that they do "everything for God's glory" (1 Cor. 10:31). The matrix of their actions is the presence of God. They gladly gather with others on mission to hear what God has done in people's lives and together sing praises to His greatness. Public messages become stories of victory in the face of defeat and encouragement to continue on the path because "God is for you!" (see Rom. 8:31).

Worship is neither traditional nor contemporary. It is not hymns or choruses. It is not drums or organ. Worship is the servant leader's expression of his love relationship with the God who rescued him from the "dominion of darkness and brought [him] into the kingdom of the Son he loves" (Col. 1:13, NIV) and who called him out for this grand mission of making disciples.

Servant leaders who live a lifestyle of worship model the joy of pleasing the One who called them. Describe for your mission outpost team ways you live a lifestyle of worship. Record your description in your journal.

SEEING THE MISSION FIELD

"I don't have any friends who aren't Christians. All my friends go to church."

When I heard this church member's confession, I knew why he didn't grasp my messages on seeing people as Jesus sees them. He had come to me to complain that my messages were no longer "touching" him as they had when he first came to the church. He wondered why my interests seemed to have turned from helping him grow to talking about the people who weren't yet at the church. I tried to explain that a sign of Christian maturity was a love for the lost—not knowing the latest end-times theory or embedded Bible code.

"But those kinds of things help me grow in my faith," he responded.

I tried to give a gentle reply, "No, what will help your faith grow is to love a lost person as Jesus would and to invest your life in him until he bends his knee to Christ. Then spend the rest of your relationship with him helping him live a changed life for Jesus."

He stared at me like I had just told him to start a company and take it public in six months. He had no point of reference for what I had just said. He was trapped in a world he did not know how to get out of. It was all he knew, and until something or someone dislodged him from that world, he would go on thinking church was for him and those like him. All I could do was encourage him to leave his church world and enter the mission field of his friends and coworkers.

Too many Christians have become such a part of the Christian subculture that they are no longer part of the counterculture Jesus brought when he announced the "kingdom of heaven is at hand." Too many so-called disciples of Jesus have set aside the adventure of mission for the latest Christian bestseller and hottest radio host.

Tradition and Zeal

Moving beyond Jefferson, and the comfort of the status quo, requires that you see the mission field as God sees it. Saul of Tarsus was trapped in the subculture of Judaism before Jesus stopped him in his tracks. Until that attitude adjustment, he had an "insider/outsider" mentality toward people. Those on the inside were the chosen. At minimum those on the outside were not to be touched; if necessary they were to be eliminated.

He confessed to the Galatians, "For you have heard about my former way of life in Judaism: I persecuted God's church to an extreme degree and tried to destroy it" (Gal. 1:13). Saul was passionate about chasing down those who were not part of the religious experience he had grown up in. He wanted the heretics and blasphemers destroyed. If they didn't fit into his perceived picture of religion, they were not allowed in.

He confessed his motivation for his actions when we wrote, "I advanced in Judaism beyond many contemporaries among my people, because I was extremely zealous for the traditions of my ancestors" (Gal. 1:14). We chide Saul of Tarsus for his zeal for tradition, and we excuse his violent behavior because now he is on our side. But his fervor and behavior toward those who did not believe as he did are not much different from the way some church members feel about others who are not like them.

Most church members are too polite to attack openly someone they don't want in their church. Manners matter even to the meanest member. Public appearance is the mark of a good Pharisee. Most church members, like Saul of Tarsus, would preserve tradition rather than reach out to people. They simply ignore outsiders on their weekly paths to the church's facilities. They maintain the past rather than pursue God's future by resisting any change for the purpose of reaching those who are different.

Tradition (the way we have always done it) and zeal to prevent outsiders from being in the group still prevent some followers of Jesus from seeing the mission field as God does. Holding to tradition and zeal for the status quo are the two lenses through which many disciples of Jesus see the world. Yet the lenses are the wrong ones because they defuse the light and distort the images. Jesus reminds us, "If your eyes are bad, your whole body will be full of darkness" (Matt. 6:23, NIV).

Seeing the Mission Field

Read Matthew 9:37-38. How does Jesus describe the mission field?

Jesus saw the mission field as an abundant harvest (Matt. 9:37). All that was required was workers who would help in the harvest. No prejudice allowed; only a willingness to be part of God's soul harvest when He moved.

Read the key verse for this session, Romans 1:16. Who was eligible for the power released in a trusting relationship with Jesus? Write your answer here.

The resurrected Jesus revealed to Paul that the power of the gospel was for "everyone who believes" (Rom. 1:16). No ethnic, religious, or social distinctions separated those who trusted Jesus as Lord from joining the fellowship of believers. The work of the church, then, according to Hauerwas and Willimon, is to be "a place where God is forming a family out of strangers."[27]

I tell people that to make disciples does not mean starting with Christians and making them better. Making disciples means starting with the lost and hurting, then leading them to a love relationship with Jesus, and walking alongside them as they grow into the likeness of the Son. The Great Commission insists we begin with the raw material of a heart without Jesus in order to produce devoted followers of Him.

Brian McLaren, who calls for a church on the other side of all we know so far, says it this way: "The church on the other side must increasingly begin with 'rawer' raw material. The goal is not to turn a nominal Catholic into a back-slapping Baptist, or a backwoods Pentecostal into a refined Episcopalian, or a constipated Presbyterian into an extroverted charismatic. No, not for the new church. There the challenge will be to turn a secular atheist (or secular nominalist for that matter) into an enthusiastic student of the wisdom and ways of Jesus Christ."[28]

When we see the mission field filled with those who need a relationship with the risen Lord rather than as "enemies of the cross," a term Paul used of his religious opponents (Phil. 3:18), we can begin to adjust our practices to reach and embrace those whom our Lord sent us to love.

In your own words, or those of some you have heard, describe your church's overall attitude toward those in the mission field. Are they simply unseen by the church? Are they seen as obstacles to what the church is doing? Are they

the focus of all you are doing as a church? Be prepared to share your answers with your mission outpost team when it gathers next.

Preparing Your Church for Transition

We will see in the next session that change does not come easily for most people. However, the mission call of God on the leader means a mission call on the people. This truth begs the question, "How do you prepare people to do the challenging work of transitioning from local church to mission outpost? How do you move beyond Jefferson?"

Let's look at how God prepared the first on-mission disciples to prepare to go into the world. Change began in the Book of Acts when a small band of believers huddled in a room waiting on the Lord.

Read Luke 24:49. What were Jesus' instructions to His followers?
Read Acts 1:4, 14. What did Jesus promise them? What did they do while they waited for His promise to become reality?

Jesus told His followers to "wait in the city until you have been clothed with power from on high" (see Luke 24:49). We know Jesus was referring to the first-time pouring out of His Spirit to establish the church. But the instructions may also be true for your church today. Waiting on God to act is the beginning of change in your church. Dan Southerland confessed he hates to wait like the rest of us, but he concluded that "the difference in a home run and a foul ball is timing. Sometimes we have to wait—even though we hate doing it."[29]

The little band of Christ followers heeded their leader's instructions and waited in Jerusalem. They did not know what they were waiting for, but they waited. It was not a passive waiting, however. They did two things while they waited: they prayed and they recognized the leaders among them. Luke tells us that "all these [gathered there] were continually united in prayer" (Acts 1:14). To prepare your church to transition from being a local church to doing church as a mission outpost, you must have intentional times of listening prayer as a body.

Also while they waited, they sought to replace Judas as a leader commissioned by Jesus. This leader, Peter said, must have been with Jesus from the time of the "baptism of John until the day He was taken up from [them]" (Acts 1:22). This leader from among the waiting and praying group must also be willing to join them on mission "to become a witness of His resurrection with us." This leader must have been with Jesus and on mission with His commissioned disciples. The lot of leadership fell to Matthais. To prepare your church for transition, you must make sure everyone in leadership has "been with Jesus" and shares with the other leaders the mission of being a witness to the resurrection of Jesus.

If you were to follow the example of those early believers, you would set aside intentional times for listening prayer as a church. You would also take time to assess the hearts of your leaders to know their relationship with Jesus and their willingness to be a witness to His resurrection.

5 Questions Your Church Must Answer
The answers to these questions will tell you whether you are ready to begin the adventure of becoming a mission outpost. Take some time to assess your own readiness and your church's readiness. Be prepared to share your answers with your mission outpost team when you gather next.

Waiting on God to act is the beginning of change in your church.

1. **Why has God placed us in this mission field?** The answer to this question is your purpose or mission.
2. **If we say we know why we are here, is everything we do currently contributing to that reason for being on mission? If so, how are we enhancing that ministry's effectiveness? If not, are we willing to change or remove the things that are not contributing to our mission?** The answers to these questions guide your initial decisions for change.
3. **What is God's picture of what we should become? Can we paint that picture in 25 words or less or in a drawing or picture?** The answers to these questions provide a simple picture of your future. This God-inspired image is what you transition toward.
4. **Has the core leadership prayerfully accepted the mission as God's call on the church body as a whole? If so, are they willing to put into practice the implications of that call? If not, what issues need to be addressed before there is agreement about the implications of the call?** The answers to these questions will help you discover who will be the leaders of the transition and those you need to continue to serve as you lead them into God's future for your church.
5. **What essential changes do we need to make to become what God has called us to be?** The answers to this question begin the detailed process of strategic decision-making to become what God has called you to do and become.

God prepares those whom He calls. Take as much time as you need on this session to allow God to prepare you as the leader and your church to launch into the waters of transition. Don't let a "finish in six weeks" mentality keep you from experiencing this season of preparation. Read ahead to know what is next. Know, however, that you may spend extended time in this session when you finally begin the actual journey of change.

In our next session we will obverse how God shows the servant leader the vision before those He leads and how he or she knows when to expand the mission by intentionally sending other leaders out into the mission field.

1. The story about Doug and Marketplace Ministries was aired on Fox News Network, 19 and 21 June 2003. http://www.foxnews.com/story/0,2933,89886,00.html.

2. Philip Yancey, *What's So Amazing About Grace?* (Grand Rapids: Zondervan, 2002), 42.

3. Josh McDowell, Bob Hostetler, and David H. Bellis, *Beyond Belief to Convictions* (Carol Stream, IL: Tyndale, 2002), 107.

4. Brent Curtis and John Eldridge, *The Sacred Romance* (Nashville: Thomas Nelson Publishers, 1997), 41.

5. F. F. Bruce, *Paul: Apostle of the Heart Set Free* (Grand Rapids: Eerdmans, 1997), 47.

6. George Barna, *The Second Coming of the Church* (Nashville: Word Publishing, 1998), 107

7. I know there is an ongoing debate whether God has one plan for each life. I write with the conviction that God does have an ultimate call for each individual life, to have a relationship with Him through His Son, Jesus Christ, and to join Him in His redemptive movement for all people. How that is played out in each life is the joy of the individual's participation in that calling.

8. C. Gene Wilkes, *My Identity in Christ* (Nashville: LifeWay Press, 1999), 29, 40.

9. Os Guinness, *The Call: Finding and Fulfilling the Central Purpose of your Life* (Nashville: Word Publishing, 1998).

10. Reggie McNeal, *A Work of Heart* (Indianapolis, IN: Jossey-Bass, 2000), 41, prepublication edition.

11. John Ortberg, *If You Want to Walk on Water, You Have to Get out of the Boat* (Grand Rapids: Zondervan, 2001), 71.

12. Ed Silvoso, *Anointed for Business* (Ventura, CA: Regal, 2002), 33.

13. Ibid., 23.

14. Ken Blanchard, Phil Hodges, and Bill Hybels, *Leadership by the Book* (New York: William Morrow, 1999).

15. Ken Blanchard and Phil Hodges, *The Servant Leader* (Nashville: J. Countryman, 2003).

16. In 2 Corinthians 5:9 Paul acknowledges his "ambition" is to please God.

17. Erwin McManus, *Uprising: A Revolution of the Soul* (Nashville: Thomas Nelson, 2003), 27.

18. Patrick Lencioni, *Five Temptations of a CEO* (Indianapolis, IN: Jossey-Bass, 1998), 27, 124.

19. Ibid., 30.

20. Parker Palmer, "There Is a Season," in *Let Your Life Speak* (Indianapolis, IN: Jossey-Bass, 2000), 101.

21. McNeal, *A Work of Heart,* 45

22. Blanchard, "How to 'Altar' my Leadership EGO," *The Servant Leader,* 26; see also: "12 Steps to FaithWalk Leadership," in Blanchard, Hodges, and Hybels, *Leadership by the Book,* 104-5.

23. Michael Slaughter, *unLearning Church* (Loveland, CO: Group, 2002), 156.

24. For example, *confess* in 1 John 1:9 can be interpreted this way.

25. J. Robert Clinton, *The Making of a Leader* (Colorado Springs: Navpress, 1988), 35.

26. Rick Warren, *The Purpose Driven Life* (Grand Rapids: Zondervan, 2002), 66.

27. Stanley Hauerwas and William H. Willimon, *Resident Aliens* (Nashville: Abingdon, 1989), 83.

28. Brian D. McLaren, *The Church on the Other Side* (Grand Rapids: Zondervan, 2000), 32.

29. Dan Southerland, *Transitioning: Leading Your Church Through Change* (Grand Rapids: Zondervan, 1999), 39.

SEEING THE VISION AND EXPANDING THE MISSION

I called my wife from an airport after a weeklong conference to confirm my arrival and see what was planned for the weekend. When she answered, she was elated about something. She began, "You'll never guess what happened last night! I stayed up until 5:00 a.m. talking with Dustin [not his real name] online!"

Two things you need to know about my wife: (1) She's a night owl, and (2) God has called her to minister to high school students. Staying up to the early hours of the morning is nothing new in the summer months when she is not teaching. Although 5:00 a.m. was a new summer record, that was not really startling information. Something else had happened to put such joy in her already animated voice.

My wife's calling is reaching out to students that are not connected to others or Jesus. I knew she had been going by Dustin's house on Sunday morning and bringing him to our worship and student ministry. She had become acquainted with his situation through our daughter's friendship with him and others in his group. He had expressed interest in connecting to the church but didn't know how. Kim offered to bring him to where other Christian students gathered. She had done this for several weeks, and Dustin had become comfortable with the group.

Like my daughters, Kim had become pretty adept at instant messaging. If you hope to connect to students in a connected world, you will learn to instant message. She often spent long hours online with students, and many nightlong conversations would turn into early-morning chats. On this particular night, the conversation turned to faith. Dustin also was connected to another youth worker at the same time he was messaging Kim. When the topic turned to faith, in tandem Kim and the youth worker began to lead Dustin to the information he needed to know and begin to trust Christ. They sent him to a Web site that clearly presented the plan of salvation. They would answer questions when he returned. The online conversation continued until Dustin typed that he had committed to be a follower of Jesus! Later the student worker sent a series of lessons for new Christians, which Dustin completed in a week while on vacation with his family!

When I finished talking to Kim, I realized I had just heard for the first

This week you will:
- Examine the characteristics of change and how people respond to it.
- Observe, in a model, how vision becomes reality.
- Examine some possible transitions you may face in ministry.
- Learn six principles of transitioning a ministry.
- Discover ways to expand the mission God has called you to complete.

time about instant-messaging evangelism. IM, Web-based information, relationships extended through cyberspace—things had changed since I was first trained in Evangelism Explosion many years ago. Yet the result is the same: one who was lost was found and now on a journey of faith with others leading him face-to-face and through cyberspace!

How one shares the gospel to a connected generation has transitioned. It is still based on relationship and introducing people to the person of Jesus, but how you communicate in relationship and how you introduce people to Jesus has taken on forms we could not imagine 20 years ago.

The Apostle Paul's entire ministry was on the road between a Christianity founded in Judaism and a faith for all people—whatever their ethnic or religious background. We are part of that same ministry. This session is about transition—how the church responds to God's call to make disciples of all people in this century and in the context of each mission field.

Day 1

VISION IS REALIZED IN A MODEL

Key Verse

And the disciples were first called Christians in Antioch.

—Acts 11:26

Vision answers the questions, What are we becoming? And where are we going? Every vision must have concrete expression, or it will remain only a dream. The Hubble Telescope was a drawing before it could be launched into space. The Chicago architect Daniel Burnham (1864–1912) advised other designers to "make no little plans. They have no magic to stir men's blood and probably themselves will not be realized. Make big plans; aim high in hope and work, remembering that a noble, logical diagram once recorded will never die, but long after we are gone will be a living thing, asserting itself with ever-growing insistency."[1]

Vision is the servant leader's "big plans" that are recorded in the "noble, logical diagram" and last as "a living thing, asserting itself with ever-growing insistency." The realization of that vision comes in the form of visible models that serve the mission. God had called Legacy Church to become a mission outpost in our mission field. But what did that vision look like?

You Can Learn from Others

Seeing the vision is difficult at times, even for the leader(s) to whom God has revealed it. How do you "see" buildings that model the vision, a network of vital small groups, ministry teams led by servant leaders, and authentic, God-honoring worship when they are only a "noble, logical diagram" on a paper napkin from your last breakfast with a friend? One way to do this is by sending teams to teaching churches and learn from their best practices.

Dan Southerland shares the key truth to expose key leaders to "model churches."[2] "It is nothing short of sheer genius to figure out ways to expose your leaders to a model church. If a picture is worth a thousand words, then a living model is worth a million." The church where Southerland pastors, Flamingo Road Church in Fort Lauderdale, Florida, is a model church for many.

At Legacy we have used several model churches to help our ministry teams and leaders see how our vision may function when we begin to realize that vision. Notice I said *may function*. When we go to model churches, we seek to find the principles that drive the practices and ask, "How would we do this to be more effective in our mission field?" You must contextualize any practice or principle for your mission field. No two are alike.

Too many leaders have gone to conferences at model churches and have brought home their methods to be implemented in an environment with an entirely different set of values and conditions. What is effective in the suburbs of southern California may do little to realize God's vision on the plains of Kansas. But, if you can dig under the veneer of their practices to see the core values and vision that drive them, then you can come home to Kansas and prayerfully consider ways God may have you build bridges in your mission field.

Name some model churches your team can learn from. What are some areas your team may want to explore with a model church? Would a visit be beneficial? What are some overriding reasons to go to a model church to discover what God is doing there?

A Biblical Model for a Mission Outpost

Legacy's vision to become a mission outpost needed a biblical model. We could never be on mission with God without seeking direction from how God has worked in the past. The Book of Acts is not a how-to manual for doing church. It is, however, a clear picture of how different groups of people expressed the presence of God in their lives and how they reached their mission fields. In our effort to describe what a biblically functioning mission outpost looked like, I discovered 10 hallmark characteristics of the church in Antioch of Syria that became guiding principles for us. Acts 11:19-31 and Acts 13:1-3 describe God's work there.

The Antioch Phenomenon illustrates how one group of believers experienced the life-changing presence of Christ in their lives. The church experienced several major seismic shifts as it grew and invited in all who responded to the message of Christ. Antioch is a biblical model of a mission outpost for the movement of God in Jesus Christ.

I believe Paul experienced the reality of God's mission call on his life in Antioch as he saw people from all walks of life and parts of the world becoming united in Christ. This became a tangible representation of what God called him to do on the road to Damascus. His two-year ministry there let him see firsthand how a church made up of ethnics looked and functioned.

Seeing the Vision

God often provides leaders a picture and experience of the vision prior to their leading others to it. In the church at Antioch, Paul saw the vision and experienced ministry to the ethnics. Later God called him to plant churches in other places, using Antioch as a model. This leads us to our third reality of servant leadership in a ministry of transition from the ministry of Paul.

For the servant leader to lead others to the vision God has revealed, he or she must see it first. This "seeing" may come from a time of prayer, a season of seeking God, or an event in which God reveals himself. For example, we know that the God-given vision for Paul's life was to go to the ethnics to proclaim that "Jesus is Lord." The implications of this call were not fully realized until Barnabas brought him to Antioch in Syria to participate in what God

> **The Book of Acts is not a how-to manual for doing church. It is, however, a clear picture of how different groups of people expressed the presence of God in their lives and how they reached their mission fields.**

was doing there. I believe that when Paul saw the church gathered there, his heart whispered, "This is it!"

Reality 3: Servant leaders see and experience the vision before those they will lead (see Acts 11).

Antioch was the launching pad of Paul's worldwide mission to bring the gospel of Jesus to all people. What happened in the church that became foundational experiences for Paul and his ministry? What can be translated into your mission field today? Maybe God has graced you with this picture from biblical history for you to get a glimpse of what He has in store for you and your ministry.

The Antioch Mission Outpost Model

Here are six key characteristics of the mission outpost that formed in Antioch of Syria.[3] These have led to my working definition of a *mission outpost,* "a church with a mission-field focus that equips and sends its members as missionaries into the world around them." After each characteristic evaluate your church by responding to the statement about the value. Be prepared to share your responses with your mission outpost team.

1. Our church is intentionally mission driven (Acts 11:19). In reality, the church at Antioch was not formed intentionally. The Bible tells us that the Christians from Jerusalem were scattered because of the death of Stephen. Although Jesus told them they would be his witnesses in Samaria, it took persecution to drive them into the mission field. Fear, not faith, sent them into the mission field. Some of Jesus' Jewish followers settled in Antioch and most likely took up residence in the community of other Jews in the city. Luke noted that these refugees from persecution initially spoke the message of Jesus "to no one except Jews."

Like many Christians who have grown up in church, these followers of Jesus felt comfortable speaking about Jesus only to those who understood their religious language and ways. Churches plateau because members speak the message of Jesus only to those who believe as they do. To be effective in your mission field, you want to be unlike the church in Antioch in its beginnings. While some churches form effectively because of a negative circumstance like a church split, the better way to form is intentionally to realize the mission God has called you to compete in that mission field.

True or False "My church is intentionally mission driven. All we do serves our mission to make disciples of all people." If your response is true, state the evidence of that truth. If your response is false, describe how this is so.

2. Members "speak" to lost people (Acts 11:20). A certain number of those who came from Jerusalem were Hellenistic followers of Jesus. We know a large number of that community came to trust Jesus as their Leader by the events described in Acts 6:1-3. Luke said some of them were from Cyprus and Cyrene, communities outside the religious bubble of Jerusalem. The unique characteristic of this group was that they began to speak about Jesus to those outside the Jewish community. While this may seem insignificant, their willingness to speak to those not in the religious world they knew resulted in a significant number of Greek-speaking ethnics trusting Jesus is the Son of God.

A people who are a mission outpost will at a minimum speak to lost people about Jesus. This small fact separates missionaries in the marketplace from church members who consider the church to be their own. Some churches cannot transition to a mission outpost because they are not comfortable speaking to anyone except those like themselves.

On a scale of 1 to 10, rate your church's willingness to speak to lost people as evidence of their desire to share the message of Jesus with people unlike themselves. Record your answer in the margin.

3. Church leaders encourage others to join in ministry (Acts 11:25). When the church at Jerusalem heard that the hand of God was on the church at Antioch and many new believers were added to the church, they sent Barnabas to check it out. When Barnabas saw the large number of pagans trusting Jesus as Lord of their lives, he knew he had a challenge. His Jewish brothers knew and understood the Old Covenant and its promise of a Messiah. They knew the laws of God and the history of God with His people. The Greek-speaking ethnics, on the other hand, had no clue about these things. How would he meet this need? He remembered a fiery, young Pharisee who taught like no other. He heard him explain in detail from Scripture how Jesus was the Messiah. He had heard of him in Damascus and had stood up for the reckless defender of Jesus in Jerusalem (Acts 9:27). Barnabas inquired about Saul's whereabouts and went to Tarsus to bring him to Antioch to teach the things of God to these new ethnic followers of Jesus.

Mission outposts always have a need for others to join them in ministry. When they begin to reach their mission field, the need to mature new believers grows with each new family member. A characteristic of a biblically functioning mission outpost is that leaders see a need and recruit others to help meet that need. Mission outpost servant leaders are always encouraging others to join them in ministry.

True or False "People are continually recruited to join us in our ministry of making disciples, to serve the needs of those brought into the family of God through the work of God's Spirit." Circle your answer and write a brief description of why you answered as you did.

4. Our church trains believers to become maturing disciples of Christ (Acts 11:26a). Barnabas and Saul taught the believers in Antioch for a full year. Imagine large numbers of people coming into your church with no knowledge of the Bible and from pagan religions with varied beliefs and practices. The task was huge, and the two servant leaders patiently taught the foundations of the faith to those who longed to know.

After this period of consistent training, Luke tells us the disciples were first known as "Christians" in Antioch. Some commentators believe this was a self-designation by the followers of Christ in order to demonstrate their identity.[4] Others have suggested it was a name given by the community to describe the new religious sect.[5] I believe it was a designation by those on the outside who watched the lives of those in the church change as they sought to live like Jesus. Life change was the result of Spirit-guided teaching, and the community in which Jesus' followers lived took notice.

How well does your church train believers to become maturing disciples of Christ? Circle the description that best describes your church.

Not Very Well	OK	Very Well

Do you believe your church's members have a positive reputation as Christians in your community? Ask a store owner in your neighborhood, not the chairman of deacons.

5. Our church gives to those in need (Acts 11:27-30). When a prophet came to Antioch and told of a coming famine in Jerusalem, the ethnic Christians collected an offering to meet the need. The standard for each gift was "each of the disciples, according to his ability, determined to send relief to the brothers who lived in Judea" (v. 29). This group of Christ followers reflected the generous heart of their Savior.

Mission outposts, after the model of the one in Antioch, generously give to the needs of the larger Christian community. They also respond to the needs of those outside the church as a witness to Jesus. These outposts of grace do not keep all their funds for themselves. They share their resources to build the kingdom of God worldwide and to meet the needs of those who live in their mission field.

Rate your church's generosity toward sharing with other churches and meeting needs of those in your community. Explain your answer.

Not Very Generous	Generous	Very Generous

6. Our church sends members on mission (Acts13:1-3). We will see in more detail later in this session that the Antioch mission outpost expanded its influence by sending members out to tell the world about Jesus. The Christ followers in Antioch knew they were part of a global movement of God to bring the gospel of Jesus to all people. They wanted their world to know what they had experienced by a heart change.

Mission outposts send missionaries into their immediate mission field, but they also send those on mission to the "ends of the earth." One sign that your church operates like a mission outpost is the number of members who are sent on mission beyond their immediate mission field.

True or False "My church sends a proportionate number of our members out on mission to tell others about Jesus through their actions and words." Support you answer.

The church in Antioch is a picture of a mission outpost. With that church as a model, describe what your church would look like if the people and leaders began to act out God's call on their lives like the people in Antioch did. Be aware of the mission field God has planted you in. You may want to refer back to earlier exercises about who's in your mission field and the example of Paul's mission-driven life. Write your picture in the space below or in your journal. Be prepared to share your thoughts with your mission outpost team when you gather next.

> Mission outposts send missionaries into their immediate mission field, but they also send those on mission to the "ends of the earth."

TRANSITION, THE ROAD BETWEEN NOW AND THEN

Having seen the reality God has called you to become, the servant leader must step out and initiate the actual process of transition. The process starts with the decision to finish what you begin and to understand how people may respond to your decision to lead.

Mike (not his real name) called me because a friend of his had told him I might understand what he was going through. Mike had been at his church for five and a half years. He had led them through a relocation and transition to a more contemporary style of worship. They had changed demographics, moving from an aging downtown situation to one that was young and wealthy. A great move sociologically, but most of the members who moved with him really did not fit the new culture. He had led the church not only to move physically and to change their worship style, but he had reduced the number of standing committees to two and focused the deacons more on ministry than on maintenance.

"Gene," he said, "those closest to me say I have a 32-year-old mind in a 57-year-old body. The church likes what we have done to get them to where they are, but I am beginning to see there is still so much more to do to make this church effective in its community." I told him I knew exactly what he was talking about. I wasn't sure he was ready to hear that he probably had another five years of transition still ahead of him.

Then he said, "I'm at a crossroads. I feel like I have to roll up my sleeves and finish this thing, or it's time for me to release it to someone else." Again I knew precisely the decision he had to make.

A ministry of transition from a local church to a mission outpost deeply affects everything about how you do church. It takes longer than a two-year tenure to envision, lead, and serve those you lead toward that vision. It is more than changing from a hierarchical organization to a flatter one. The transition I am speaking of is more like working to become healthy—an experience I discovered firsthand 10 years ago when diagnosed with heart disease. We must always keep in the forefront that we are talking about the living body of Christ when we speak of change.

The church is organized, but it is living. You, however, can't lay down 10 organizational rules of change on the church any more than you could have given me 10 physical laws of health and expected me to become healthy by hearing the list. Real work of change is involved. You must always be aware of the people who will be affected by the transition and know that without a doubt God will participate in this adventure if you will allow him to do so. What God may be calling you and your church to do is not a simple exercise in organizational shifts. It is how you live your lives as the gathered and scattered church of the Lord Jesus Christ.

> Transition is the path between where you are now and what God would have you become.

Transition Is Part of Life

Transition is the path between where you are now and what God would have you become. It is not a mechanical process any more than replacing 100 percent of your body's cells every seven years is mechanical. Transition is part of life.

- The transition between childhood and adulthood is adolescence.
- The transition between an acorn and an oak tree is a sapling.
- The transition between dating and marriage is engagement.
- The transition between your old self and your completed new self in Christ is sanctification.
- The transition between captivity and the promised land was 40 years in the wilderness.

Transition is the road to life. It implies health and growth toward maturity.

Transition is the road to life. It implies health and growth toward maturity. To stay the same is to be dead. Leading others down the path of transition in the direction of revealed vision is the work of servant leadership.

What are some transitions you have experienced in your personal, family, or business life? Pick one and describe it to your mission outpost team when you gather next. Describe how that season of transition affected you emotionally, spiritually, or physically. Have you experienced any transitions in your church that have affected you? If so, share them with your team.

Change or Transition?

Transition is different from change. Transition is deeper and more like the metamorphosis of a caterpillar to a butterfly than voting to change the name of your church before you've embraced your core values.

Read 2 Corinthians 5:17. What is the description of one who is "in Christ"? What is the consequence of being in that new state of relationship with God? Write your answers in the margin.

Being "in Christ" means becoming a new creation. God forgives you, reformats your heart's hard drive, and loads entirely new software as your operating system. This begins the transition of your life from living as you did to living as a new creation in Christ. Changes are made as a result of the fundamental transition that takes place in your heart.

The difference between change and transition is described in the book *A New Kind of Christian*. The teacher Neo befriends a discouraged pastor and invites him to attend a meeting where he addresses a group of college students. In response to the question, "Don't all generations think of themselves as the most important generation, when all the biggest changes in history are taking place?" Neo answers:

Let's say I'm making an omelet. I mix the eggs with a little milk and put them on the griddle. A good omelet is cooked slowly, so I keep stirring the egg with my fork as it cooks, slowly stirring, stirring, stirring. Like this. But at some point, something happens. The egg that has been changing from raw to cooked and rather suddenly transitions from a liquid to a solid. At that point, if I keep stirring with the fork, I will ruin the omelet. The tool that succeeded in helping me bring the omelet to this point now threatens to destroy it. The tool that I need now is not a fork but rather a spatula, so the omelet can be gently folded and then served, like this. Here's what I'm trying to say tonight: yes, all ages are ages of change, but not all ages involve transition. You young men and women happen to have been born at a time of transition.[6]

62

Soon after *A New Kind of Christian* was published, I shared this passage with a group of church leaders. One of the participants smiled after I finished and quipped that most conflicts in the church swirl around whether you use a fork or a spatula to make the omelet. He was right. In church we tend to spend more time arguing over which utensils to use in making the omelet than whether the church is appetizing to those hungering for the things of God.

You and I live in an age of transition, a "hinge" in history in which the future seems fuzzier than ever. The opportunity is great, but the challenge is as great also—and filled with conflict and opposition.

Nelson and Appel described the transition process this way: "Transition starts with an ending—and ends with a beginning. In the middle is a very precarious area between old reality and new reality called the Neutral Zone."[7] This neutral zone is where the success or failure of the changes is decided—much like the success of a sprint relay team is decided in the exchange of the baton from one runner to another. I have to agree with the description of "precarious" for this zone. In these uncharted waters of transition, people decide to give up the past and embrace the new, or they decide in the other direction. This neutral zone is not so neutral because this is where people react or respond to change.

While this time can be filled with conflict, it can also produce different kinds of growth opportunities. Nelson and Appel observe: "The pruning that God does to make us more productive for his kingdom often happens within our churches as we confront issues of power, control, selfishness, letting go of the past, releasing personal ministry preferences, and mourning the loss of comfort zones. Far too many churches get so consumed with getting through the transitions that they fail to capitalize on the inherent personal growth within them."[8]

The time of transition is not lost time. God often prunes the church and humbles the leaders in order to position both for the future He has prepared for them.

What growth opportunities have you experienced in times of transition as a person, as a leader, as a church? Be prepared to share with your mission outpost team how these images help you.

How People React to Change

Ken Blanchard and Phil Hodge have written "The Seven Reactions People Have to Change—and Ways Leaders Can Ease the Transition."[9] All seven reactions and suggestions for leaders ring true for the ministry of transition I have experienced. I will comment on their insights to help you identify how people may react to your proposed "endings" and "beginnings" and ways in which you can respond to those reactions.

As you read through this section of the workbook, make notes on your own experiences related to either reactions to change or how you have responded to it. If you are preparing for change, you may want to make notes on which reactions people may have and/or which responses you need to prepare for as you walk through change.

1. "People will feel awkward, ill at ease and self-conscious when confronted with change." Change proposed by a leader forces people to go where they would not normally go on their own. Like a child who has mastered walking and running, learning to ride a bike without training wheels challenges her basic skills and threatens her self-confidence.

Blanchard and Hodge suggest the leader should "tell people what to expect." You do this in order to help people overcome awkward feelings. I tried as many times as possible to paint the picture of our future. (I still do.) I also tried to explain how others had been through the same changes and felt exactly how they are feeling. Describing "next steps" is helpful too.

2. "People will feel alone even if everyone else is going through the same change." People process change through their own personal experiences. They deal with change as it affects them personally, not how it affects the whole. The sense of being alone in change grows out of their personal losses and challenges.

Blanchard and Hodge tell the leader to "structure activities that create involvement. Encourage individuals to share ideas and to work together to help each other through change." Transition in the church is best done in community. One tactic we have used throughout change has been gathering groups for times of sharing and listening. We have done this in larger groups as in our TouchPoint Gatherings, and we have done this in smaller groups throughout our small-group organization. When people know they have been heard and have a part in the solution to their concerns, they are more likely to follow you through the transition.

3. "People will think first about what they have to give up." Loss of security is one of our deepest fears. For example, when you propose meeting in small groups off campus, the first thought to those who have been in Sunday School classes their whole Christian life will be the loss of what happens that hour every Sunday rather than the opportunities meeting in homes and offices throughout the week will bring.

Blanchard and Hodge invite the leader not to "try to sell the benefits of the change effort initially. Let people mourn their perceived losses. Listen to them." Part of leading in a ministry of transition is being a pastor to those who grieve the loss change brings. Plan purposeful times to hear the hearts of those you lead while being empathetic to their sense of loss. The authors are right. People don't care about your enthusiasm about the new until they know you have empathy for their loss of the old.

4. "People will think they can only handle so much change at once." A friend came into my office and said, "Everything in my life is changing. I don't want my church to change too."[10] People are forced to juggle changes in how they communicate and work through their stages of life and constantly changing relationships with others. The change you offer them in order to be more effective in reaching and maturing people in Christ may seem too much to add to their already filled plates. Remember that, unlike you, they have not given their full-time attention to future opportunities.

Blanchard and Hodge guide the leader to "set priorities on which changes to make, and go for the long run." As we began to see the volume of changes necessary to become a mission outpost in our mission field, we knew we had to prioritize where we would invest our resources and efforts. For example, before we tackled changes to our constitution and bylaws, we chose to focus on changes in our worship experience because it is our "front door" to reaching people. "Go for the long run" is the authors' best practical advice in a ministry of transition. I suggest you post those words where you can see them everyday.

5. "People will be concerned that they don't have enough resources (time, money, skills, etc.) to implement the change." A scarcity mentality can overcome both

When people know they have been heard and have a part in the solution to their concerns, they are more likely to follow you through the transition.

leaders and followers when changes begin to happen. Vision always demands resources greater than the present state, so this concern is real to those who face the change. People vote with their feet and their pocketbooks no matter what 51 percent said at the last business meeting. Loss of people and financial resources cause people genuine concern as you face the future.

Blanchard and Hodge tell servant leaders to "encourage creative problem solving." Bill Hybels said during the 2003 Willow Creek Leadership Summit that "leaders love problems." Problem solving is what leaders do, and they love doing it! Facing the reality of fewer resources calls for creative problem solving by the leader and those he leads as part of the leadership challenge in a ministry of transition.

6. "People will be at different levels of readiness for any particular change." I have discovered that people are wired differently to react to change. Some of it is their temperament. Some of it is conditioned responses. Whatever the case, you cannot view the church as a homogeneous group who will respond in the same way to your proposals.

Blanchard and Hodge suggest you "don't label or pick on people. Recognize that some people are risk-takers and others take longer to feel secure. Someone who's an early adopter of one type of change might balk at another type of change." My tendency as a change agent is to write people off as weak or selfish because they won't embrace the changes I have proposed. Neither assumption is necessarily true. People respond differently to change as they respond differently to items on a restaurant menu. A close friend summarized his reason for leaving Legacy to attend another church in town was "I prefer orange, and you are serving raspberry. It's as simple as that." It wasn't, but that is how he articulated it. It came down to simple preferences in style; he was convinced our friendship could continue even if he and his family joined another church. I knew otherwise.

7. "If pressure is taken off, people will revert to old behaviors." Homeostasis is the natural "process by which an organism maintains constant internal conditions in the face of a varying external environment." That truth in nature is also true about people and how they react to change. Since we prefer things to stay the same, we naturally resist any challenges to our "natural state." This is too often true when church becomes a static institution and its keepers have things operating the way they want them to operate.

Blanchard and Hodge encourage the servant leader to "keep people focused on maintaining the change and managing the journey." Servant leaders keep pressure on the group to change much like a parent keeps pressure on a child to overcome his fear of the dark. The art of servant leadership is knowing when to put pressure on people to change and when to pull off to the side of the road for rest and recreation. Once you start down the path of transition, you cannot look back. Remember Jesus' words, "No one who puts his hand to the plow and looks back is fit for the kingdom of God" (Luke 9:62).

Journal for the Journey

January 28, 2002—The day before I had cast the vision for our new ministry to children, "Adventure Club," and suggested that the church should be called by another name so others would call Him by name. Both initiatives met resistance. This was my prayer on Monday morning.

"O God, You have called me to birth a fresh expression of Your body. I feel I have been obedient to that call, but I continue to wonder when all the pieces will be in place. You have given me glimpses of Your vision and Your provision. I have hope, but it is so hard. Kim and I asked this morning, 'When will it get easy?' I know it never will as long as we are in the spiritual struggle to birth a fresh work of Yours.

"Thank You for always being present, always giving me assurance when I need it and evidence of Your power and love. I am not complaining—just needing a little encouragement today. I will trust Your timing. You are God, and I am not. Blessed be Your name. I am honored to be called Yours.

"Oh, by the way, tell St. Paul to quit rolling his eyes. I know I've known nothing compared to what You asked him to do! Tell him I'll reserve some time with him when I get there to hear what *thilipsis* really means."

Day 3

⚬⚬⚬

SHIFTS IN MINISTRY YOU MAY FACE

I sat in a closet-turned-office that was furnished with discarded furniture and listened as a young worship leader told her story. She had been transferred with her husband into the city, and they believed God had led them to the church. She joined the choir but longed for a more relevant worship experience. She had gone to the pastor with some others and requested they begin a worship service for the younger members of the church and community. He agreed after some time spent going through the bureaucratic maze to get permission for the experiment.

She was made the worship leader, put on staff part-time, and given permission for the group to meet at 8:30 on Sunday morning. The group could meet where the church gathered for its meals and times of fellowship. They were given hand-me-down equipment with no enhancements to the room. She gathered a team, planned the gatherings, and soon a group began to gel. The only problem was that over a two-year period the group in the basement at the earlier hour began to rival the size of the group that gathered in the over one-hundred-year-old sanctuary that had always met at 11:00. She began to be accused of "splitting the church" and ruining the effectiveness of what had gone on so long in the "church" hour.

As I listened, I knew she had been called to this ministry and that God was using the new thing that was happening in the basement to challenge the status quo. A younger population in the city needed what was being offered by this ministry. The larger church and its leaders had the opportunity to make some shifts in how they did things to meet the needs of others in their mission field.

She is no longer serving at that church, and the church has regrouped into one service at the later hour in the stained-glass sanctuary. Opportunity missed. Status quo maintained.

Many churches experience what this church did when faced with a new opportunity to reach people and build up the church. The ideas are great, the initial success is invigorating, but when it comes to making multiple shifts in how you do things, many leaders and churches fail.

This part of the book will address shifts in ministry you may face while following Jesus' call into the mission field. The list is not complete but representative of realities many churches face.

You may have turned to this portion of this resource first because you want to know what you need to change to get where you want to be. What we have done at Legacy, and what other churches have pursued, cannot be the list of changes you need to make to transition your church. I can only tell you the things we had to address to get from where we were to where we believed God wanted us to be.

You will deal with some of the same issues, but you will need to address some that are not mentioned here. The key is to know your current reality and to see the end picture you trust God has painted for you to embody. Anything you are about to change must be about becoming more effective in making disciples in your mission field and moving along the path toward the vision God has given you.

What needs to change if you are no longer going to function as a local church but as a mission outpost? Here are seven shifts we made and continue to make at Legacy.

1. We moved from "singing songs about God to singing songs to God."[11] Worship is the focus of transitioning from a local church to a mission outpost for two significant reasons.

The first is that the expression of worship in a mission outpost on a mission field is different from that of a local church in a churched culture. A local church atmosphere tends to perpetuate the traditions that appeal to those who are familiar with that expression of worship. Mission outposts, on the other hand, seek to present the good news in the sounds, instrumentation and arts of those in the mission field. This principle suggests a blend of time-honored praise to God and contemporary expressions of the gospel message. William Easum offers that worship needs to be indigenous to the people you are trying to reach.[12]

This practice of indigenous worship has been part of mission strategy in foreign fields for some time. Legacy supports a missionary to Albania who recently began producing Christian worship music for the people in the mountains who have their own form of music and praise to God. Music of and by the natives is part of how the message and praise of God is translated into people's lives. We are blessed in America to have Christian music in any major genre of music in our culture. Head-banging teens to classical devotees can find a style of music to guide them into the presence of God.

The second reason for transitioning worship is that God is, I believe, reviving and reforming the church for a new season of its purpose in the world. God is doing this either to prepare us for Christ's return or to prepare us to be His people in a hostile world—particularly in America. Evidence of this revival around the world is authentic, heartfelt worship. As one member put it, "Our focus in worship has grown increasingly more intimate as we sing songs *to* God and not just *about* Him." Dan Southerland described their transition in worship as "from traditional to extremely contemporary."[13]

Worship is the lighting rod of transition in American church culture. God's mission call on your church to glorify Him and to reach your mission field should be the primary reasons for making changes in form and style of worship. We made this shift over a period of eight years. We added a third service, which was mission driven, in 1992. Two years later we decided to offer only one worship style. From that time on we sought to find our expression of worship as God's people and be consistent with it. Each decision brought questions from the churched among us. Our last season of questioning came when we moved into a new facility, the Legacy Center, in January 1999. This time the venue of worship changed. We moved from three services in a small pew-filled, stained-glass worship center to a multipurpose-styled convention center. The form and function of our current building more fully allows us to offer our expression of worship to God to our community in forms that are contemporary and relevant.

As we remained true to our form of worship and communication of the gospel, however, longtime churched people again had to decide to join us on mission in this venue or seek the refuge of more familiar surroundings. Our goal was to provide a safe place for those in our mission field to experience the love of God and to participate in authentic worship. The good news is that those we are seeking to reach are responding.

How has your church responded to the opportunity to worship God in the language and musical style of your mission field?

2. We moved from programs to ministry and spiritual transformation. Traditional church mentality insists leaders manage programs for those in the church. Mission outposts minister to those in the mission field. We have moved from church programs to ministry-oriented activities. We have moved from discipleship as a program to being the main thing we do as a church. We try not to compartmentalize our ministries but to coordinate them so all we do serves our mission to make disciples.

We have also transitioned from having traditional "fellowship/church-wide events" for the churched to offering outreach "opportunity events" such as marketplace luncheons, holiday dinners with friends, skills and drills basketball camps, and community-wide concerts. We also moved from having a conventional weekly church program to offering ministry opportunities like small groups for mothers with teenagers, English as a second language, divorce recovery support groups, and infertility support groups. Accountability groups have surfaced as men seek to hold themselves accountable in their growth as followers of Jesus. Women's small groups do Bible studies and facilitate topics like weight loss and lifestyle issues.

The role and purpose of staff have changed through transition in this area of ministry. The purpose of staff at Legacy is "to equip people to carry out the mission of Legacy Church by building relationships and modeling servant leadership." Staff ministers are not hired to manage programs. This has been a difficult transition for staff who were trained to manage an organization rather than to equip people for ministry. We evaluate our ministry directors based on the number of people involved in their ministries, not simply the number of people attending events. We calendar and budget events based on their effectiveness to do mission rather than because we did them last year.

Evaluate your church as driven by programs and scheduling of events or as being driven by ways in which you can meet the needs of your mission field and members.

3. We moved from fellowship with disciples to making disciples. As long as we were primarily attracting those who transferred from other churches, we did not need to change anything about how we received new members or how we helped them find a place to belong and serve in the church. Longtime church members knew how a local church worked, and they found their way in according to how they did it in their last church. When I came to Legacy,

The purpose of staff at Legacy is "to equip people to carry out the mission of Legacy Church by building relationships and modeling servant leadership."

we received people during an invitation, asked them to sit on the front row and complete an information card, and then I presented them to the church for membership. When we began to reach new believers and those returning to church after some time away, we had to make major changes in how we assimilated people into our community of faith.

We currently offer a Membership Workshop on Sunday mornings for those desiring membership. We offer this on the first two Sundays of the month, and it is the first step of intentional discipleship at Legacy. Here we practice "truth in advertising" about who we are, what we expect of ourselves, and the next steps to join us on mission. As part of the workshop, team members assist the new members with completing a spiritual gifts inventory and a ministry profile. This information is passed on to ministry directors and team leaders who recruit the new members to ministry. Those completing the workshop become members when they sign a covenant of membership.

One hot topic of change in some churches is the use of an invitation to facilitate people's response to the message. This is a matter of preference for the local church, not a core doctrine, so address it as you do any other traditional practice to assess its effectiveness. I discovered that many who were not reaching their lost friends and leading them to Christ leaned on the pastor's effectiveness to "draw the net" during this time as their evangelistic efforts. Not offering an invitation meant they had to do the work of an evangelist, which every believer is called to do, but they would rather not go there. Many innovative churches, including Legacy, offer multiple options for how a person can join the church—including invitation, response card, new member class, and individual appointment with staff member or pastor. Remember, in the Bible one's public confession of trust in Jesus was baptism. We believe that remains true today.

I have only addressed the threshold of becoming a maturing follower of Jesus for many churches. There must be a variety of entry points for people to follow Jesus and grow as His disciple. Beyond those entry points must be a variety of ways in which people can worship, reach, connect, grow, and serve as evidence of their relationship with Christ. Disciple-making is the benchmark for all structures in the church.

How are you intentionally helping people grow as disciples? Is there a clear path people can follow to grow? If asked, can you diagram or describe it?

4. We moved from tenure and office to giftedness and service as the basis for ministry and leadership. I like to call this "from Uncle Bill to Mission Field Mike." Uncle Bill is synonymous with tenured members who see their place in ministry on the "power committees"—for example, the personnel and finance committees. Mission Field Mike represents those who are reached by the ministry of the mission outpost and who are mentored and released into leadership.

Too many local churches have inflexible organizational charts, and the same leaders recycle through terms of service. Leadership focuses on "holding an office" or "chairing a committee." Those who have been there the longest and who are the most connected to the core families of the church get the power jobs. This paradigm of church leadership prevents a church from doing mission because people pay more attention to getting people "elected" and filling organizational charts than making disciples. It also gives the false impression that if you sit on a committee and make decisions for others you have somehow done your part of making disciples. No misconception is further from the truth!

Mission outposts, on the other hand, are flexible in structure in order to meet needs or goals related to the mission. Leaders lead teams and are chosen for their giftedness and passion for the ministry in which they find themselves. Tenure of membership is a minor consideration for those desiring to join in ministry.[14]

Electing people to offices and holding chairmanships is no longer part of the Legacy culture. We seek to find people who are passionate about our mission and their ministry that serves the mission. We release spiritually gifted people to do ministry. We launch new ministries as leaders step forward to serve. Our organizational chart is seldom the same from year to year. Our ministry directors and leadership teams equip and hold people accountable to what they are commissioned to do.

This transition began several years ago when we introduced the reality of spiritual gifts to our church. What began as a Sunday evening lesson became the impetus for discovering and releasing new ministries in our church. I do not have the space here to describe the implications of spiritual giftedness as the basis for ministry and leadership. I have recorded some of that in the workbook *Jesus on Leadership*.[15] The move from tenure and status to spiritual gifts and passion has created more ministries and people in ministry than any other cultural change we have made.

What is the basis for ministry leadership in your church? How do you discover and develop leaders to carry out your mission to make disciples?
We will look at three more possible transitions you may face, but as you complete this part, go back through your assessments and prioritize which transitions are most needed to be addressed at your church now. Write your number one priority in the margin.

Day 4

TRANSITIONING 101

Key Verse

For as many of you as have been baptized into Christ have put on Christ. There is no Jew or Greek, slave or free, male or female; for you are all one in Christ Jesus.
—Galatians 3:27-28

God showed Paul through revealed truth a picture of what the church could look like when people's hearts are changed. "In Christ Jesus" all ethnic, social, religious, and gender barriers among God's people are removed. Having seen that reality and knowing the culture in which he lived, the apostle had to decide whether he would allow the barriers to remain or address them in the power of the gospel. He chose to address them, and we are the beneficiaries of his bold witness.

He called people to remain in the situation in which Christ found them but to see it from a different perspective. For example, he showed both slaves and free that being bought with the price of Jesus' death changed their status before God and others. "For he who is called by the Lord as a slave is the Lord's freedman. Likewise he who is called as a freedman is Christ's slave" (1 Cor. 7:22). Since that is true, the church as God's gathered people had to transition to this new reality for all to see. Transitioning is driven by changed lives, not changing organizations.

Transitioning happens when God reveals to you what His church should look like and you decide to risk pursuing that vision. Just as Paul could do nothing but preach this good news and engage people where they lived, servant leaders captured by God's vision can do little more than constantly be about leading the church toward that vision.

Here are three more transitions you may face because you are a new people in Christ.

5. *We moved from congregation-led to team-led decision-making.* One of the most difficult transitions for us was as we moved from being a congregational-led church to becoming a team-led church. The tradition of our church, as with most Baptist churches, was democratic decision-making. The reason for this shift was not to take power from the people and make the pastor the primary decision maker in the church. What really drove this change was our need to make decisions faster and more effectively. As new ministries surfaced in response to need and giftedness, we could not wait for the slow process of getting approval from the whole body in the usual process of regularly scheduled business meetings.

This shift happened subtly and without vote. I did not stand up one day and say, "I make a motion we no longer vote on things as a whole church. All in favor say 'Amen.'" We simply began to give more authority to what we called our core teams. We quietly became a team-led church. When asked, "When did we vote on that?" we answered, "The finance team made that decision," or, "The personnel team led by Gene made that call." As we continued, we put more and more weight on the decisions of those teams. Of course, the leaders and members of those teams needed to be mentored about the mission, vision, and core values so they could truly support and encourage completion of those things. Alignment of values and vision in the core teams was essential to becoming an effective team-led church. This process can be akin to what Leonard Sweet describes as moving "from standing committees to moving teams."[16]

My role as decision maker has changed through this transition. We have always been a pastor-led church, but how I share my leadership has changed throughout the years. During the shift from being congregational led to team led, I was too often the sole target of opposition or criticism. I soon saw the need for shared leadership. I began to share more and more leadership with our staff. The church, however, was soon wondering if Gene, the deacon team leaders, core teams, or staff ministers were calling the shots. (I told you this was not a well-crafted process!)

We ultimately put into place a church leadership team to serve alongside me as the leaders of our church. This team and I share the primary leadership responsibilities of the church. The other teams take their lead from this team. This decision, as you would expect, has brought on its own set of issues. The culmination of this process was updating our constitution and bylaws.

Legacy is a leadership team-led mission outpost today. The leadership team and I are accountable to the church for its vision, mission, and core values, and we have agreed to hold the church accountable to those same things.

How are decisions made in your church? The model is not the issue. What counts is whether a decision-making process is in place that can facilitate the mission and adequately share authority to empower others to do their part of the mission.

6. *We moved from doing church missions to sending the church on mission.* Brian McLaren foresees missions "on the other side" this way: "Every church a mission organization. Every Christian a missionary. Every mission agency

Transitioning is driven by changed lives, not changing organizations.

a facilitator of the work of the church. Every neighborhood a mission field. We can hope that Christianity will be as inconceivable apart from mission as fire from burning."[17]

If we said we would become a mission outpost, we had to act like one when it came to sending members on mission. In a broad stroke this meant a shift from writing one check to denominational agencies to doing hands-on missions. This has taken many forms over the years. With people and finances we have sponsored church plants. Currently, a house church joins us when we gather for worship, and we are sponsoring a Gen X church start, a church meeting in a movie theater built primarily on a ministry to children, and a Chinese-speaking fellowship meeting in the high school down the street from our facilities. We have partnered with the local crisis pregnancy clinic and Habitat for Humanity chapter to meet needs in our community.

We have recently embraced the strategy of "servant evangelism" popularized by Steve Sojorn at Vineyard Community Church in Cincinnati.[18] To "demonstrate God's love in a practical way," we have practiced free coffee giveaways at local coffee shops and given out change so people in a local fast-food drive-through could upsize their order. These intentional acts of kindness give our people simple ways to see where they live every day as their mission field.

One example of being a mission outpost in a mission field is our English as a second language ministry. This ministry began by offering ESL classes on Sunday afternoon. More than two hundred internationals gathered in our buildings for fellowship and to learn English. We gave each participant a Bible in his or her first language as we taught them our language and customs. We soon discovered the world had come to our backyard!

We have invited a couple to join our staff from mainland China to coordinate our international ministries. Their motto is, "You can be an international missionary without leaving your hometown." The ministry now offers services to the professional community, college students, and stay-at-home-moms. This ministry partners with the Chinese-speaking fellowship we are sponsoring for those who prefer to worship with others who speak their same language.

We are still writing checks to mission agencies, but more members are involved in missions than ever before.

In what ways are you leading your people into the mission field? Do you spend your time raising money for funds for faceless people, or do you ask people to invest in high-impact projects locally and globally where you can describe what their money is doing?

7. We moved from gathering at the church to scattering into neighborhoods. Larry Crabb describes the church as "a community of people on a journey to God."[19] I like that picture of God's people. It suggests relationship and movement toward God. A church on mission is like that. Dan Southerland wrote that one of their major transitions from a program-driven church to a purpose-driven church is to move "from a traditional Sunday School plan to a relational, participation-oriented small group approach."[20] For several decades the "small group movement" has challenged the conventional ways in which to gather people to be the church. This has caused confusion, conflict, and confrontation in many churches. The issue, however, is not, what is the only way? The question is, what is the most effective way to gather people in meaningful relationships in your mission field? This has allowed for a variety of ways to organize people around this function of the church.

At Legacy we have changed how and where our people gather in groups. We have kept some groups on Sunday mornings. We have done this because of the vital children and student ministries at that time, and we want the entire family to have an opportunity to grow and connect on Sunday morning if they desire. Our primary method of experiencing authentic community, however, is in our LifeGroups, small groups that meet anytime, anyplace, and anywhere. As I write, I am on my way to pray with a small group that meets every Thursday for lunch in a company break room.

How do you group people to experience authentic relationships? Are these grouping constructed to allow for personal growth and for their members to experience authentic community?

Now that you have seen the "what" of transition, let's take some time to look at the "how." These principles are not the last word on how a servant leader leads in a ministry of transition, but they can be benchmarks to evaluate your effectiveness in becoming a mission outpost.

Six Principles of Transition[21]

Here are six principles we have learned in our journey of transition to become a mission outpost. After you have inspected each of the principles, prioritize them as they apply to your situation. Number them from 1 to 6 with the most important first step as 1.

____ *Transition must begin with a call of God to change what you are currently doing in order to accomplish what He has called you to do.* Transition must not originate with the desire of a leader or group of leaders to "grow the church" or emulate other church models or church leaders. This principle demands the leader and people spend time prayerfully seeking how to join God in what He is doing in their mission field. You will know your direction when you discern God's mission call on your church. Prayer is your source of direction, passion, and strength to finish what God has called you to become.

____ *Transition must be toward accomplishing this mission, not toward the preferences of a certain style or organization.* The mission is everything in a transition process. The mission to make disciples in your particular mission field must dictate the changes you make. You make changes only as they relate to accomplishing the mission and reaching those in your mission field. The temptation will be to copy what another church or organization is doing rather than take the time to examine whether that same method will be effective with both your members and those you are trying to reach.

____ *Transition will crash under the weight of change if it happens too quickly.* One of our leaders said once that there are two ways to pull off a Band-Aid: quickly or slowly. Both ways involve pain. Both remove hair from your arm. We chose to pull off the Band-Aid slowly. This is why our transition has been over 8 to 10 years rather than 2 or 3. I believe this helped the wounds to heal and keep us together at our core.

Dan Southerland agrees. He offers this mantra: "Repeat after me: I will go slow, I will go slow, I will go slow. It cannot be said often enough: you must go slow when making transitions. If I had to give one overall contributing factor to our success . . . it would be this: we took our sweet time. We actually enjoyed the journey."[22]

Nelson and Appel remind us: "Qualitative time [time ripe for change] varies from church to church. Congregations that are more ready for improvement and have prepared themselves for the new idea are far quicker to adopt the innovation. Stymied churches are more apt to reject the initial idea and may require years to change their self-identity."[23] Patient persistence is better than immediate results in building a lasting movement on mission with Christ.

____ *Transition involves a series of conflicts which will lead to defining moments.* Conflict is the vocabulary word of change. Any church that determines God would have them transition from what they are currently doing to join Him in their mission field must be prepared for conflict. This does not mean putting on a flak jacket. It demands picking up a towel and washbasin.

Know that some conflicts will emerge as defining moments for the life of the church. These become like the twelve stones in the River Jordan when Joshua led the people into the promised land. They become the object lesson to answer the question, "What are those rocks doing there?" (see Josh. 4:1-8). Both Jesus and Paul used conflict as defining moments in their teaching and ministry. We will look more closely at opposition and conflict later in this book.

____ *Transition is best led by a servant leader who has made himself servant to the mission and leads by serving those on mission with him.* Ken Blanchard says there are two kinds of leaders, those who are leaders first and those who are servants first.[24] Only leaders who are servants first can lead the transition process in a healthy manner. Getting your way has no value in servant leadership. Finding the best way to do the mission is a core value in leading through transition. Only those who have given up their rights to be served and find greatness in service to others should lead. A leader in transition serves the mission call of God and leads others to complete that call. Servant leaders are the best guides through transition because the move stays focused on the mission rather than the leader or those following.

____ *Transition is fluid and must adapt to the dynamics of people and circumstances in the change.* Hammering out a predetermined plan without adjusting to the input and feelings of others can be more destructive than helpful. The end picture is the sole objective. Transitioning strategies will vary along the path of change. You cannot force change on people who are not ready for it.

Paul taught his apprentice, Timothy, to learn from the farmer (2 Tim. 2:6). Every time the farmer plants, he becomes dependent on the conditions around the seeds for them to grow. He does his part to respond to environmental and circumstantial realities in order to produce a maximum crop. In the same way, the servant leader in a ministry of transition is dependent on the conditions of the field in which he is trying to plant and grow the seeds of change. Being responsive to changing conditions is the key to producing a bumper crop.

Conflict is the vocabulary word of change. Any church that determines God would have them transition from what they are currently doing to join Him in their mission field must be prepared for conflict.

EXPANDING THE VISION

Key Verse
*Then, after they had
fasted, prayed, and
laid hands on them,
they sent them off.*
—Acts 13:3

The mission call of Christ is on both the church and its servant leaders. This shared calling is the source of unity and the foundation for community. Unity is not that everyone agrees with *what* is being done. Unity comes from a shared belief of *why* things are being done. When you agree on the *why*, the possibilities of *what* soar. Community is the context for discovering and refining your shared calling and vision.

What does genuine community look like? Paul provided a snapshot when he wrote to his closest friends in Philippi. He let them know of his deepest wishes for them: "If then there is any encouragement in Christ, if any consolation of love, if any fellowship with the Spirit, if any affection and mercy, fulfill my joy by thinking the same way, having the same love, sharing the same feelings, focusing on one goal" (Phil. 2:1-2).

Note that the "if" statements describe realities that grow out of a relationship with God, the Father, Son, and Holy Spirit. *Since* (the more accurate translation) these are present in the community of faith, then shared thinking, love, feelings, and a common goal become characteristics of the church. Shared relationship with Christ precedes shared goals.

Hauerwas and Willimon write about community this way: "Christian community, life in the colony, is not primarily about togetherness. It is about the way of Jesus Christ with those whom he calls to himself. It is about disciplining our wants and needs in congruence with a true story, which gives us the resources to lead truthful lives. In living out the story together, togetherness happens, but only as a by-product of the main project of trying to be faithful to Jesus."[25]

Community is the spin-off of seeking to complete the "main project of trying to be faithful to Jesus." Our first project should be making and being apprentices to Jesus. If we will agree on that, community will form around that, and we can move on to reaching those who do not know Him.

Does your church agree on the "why" of its actions? If so, can you state it? This is your mission statement. If not, what are some ways you can communicate it in a heartfelt way?

Community Calls Out Leaders

Barnabas and Saul did not wake up one day and announce to the church that they were ready to leave Antioch in order to evangelize the world or for the church as a body to set them apart for that mission. In the context of worship, the Holy Spirit directed the church to call them out to expand their mission to make disciples of all people. The church in community affirmed their giftedness, passion, and abilities before they sent them off.

Churches support too many so-called missionaries simply because people announced they were called to start or continue a work somewhere in the world. The church does not expand its mission by sending members beyond its immediate mission field on the word of a member alone. Expansion of mission, like community, derives from shared purposes and resources.

The mission to reach the ethnics expanded beyond Antioch when the church shared a similar call that Paul had heard for his life. God places His called among those who can both affirm and expand the mission for their lives.

Read Acts 13:1-3.[26] What was the context of this passage? What was the church told to do? How did the believers respond?

Through the communal habits of worship, fasting, and prayer, the church heard the Holy Spirit's call to send two of its members on mission beyond their fellowship. Acts 13 begins with the church's awareness of the spiritual gifts of those among them. By living and serving together, they knew the "prophets and teachers" in their fellowship. A certain way to know how God has spiritually gifted you is the church's affirmation of your gifts while serving among them.

Some interpret the passage to mean that it was while those whose names were listed "were worshiping" (NIV), the Holy Spirit told the church to set apart Barnabas and Saul. This interpretation would suggest that this smaller group was able intently to seek God's purposes for the church as a whole. They heard in their hearts that God told them to set apart two from the group "for the work to which I have called them" (NIV). God enlisted the called out ones, the church, to set apart His called ones for a special task—expanding the mission beyond the local mission field. "Set apart" meant to set apart for a particular act or function. This was not a change in their status. It was a change in their function to complete the mission.

The company of the called responded to the Holy Spirit's prompting by continuing the spiritual exercises of fasting and prayer and then set Barnabas and Saul apart by the ancient practice of laying hands on them. Then they sent them out. Spiritual disciplines play a role not only in the life of the individual servant leader but also in the life of the mission outpost. These practices prepare the individual and the larger community for the wider influence of His work through them. God often speaks during seasons set apart to pray and fast.

Sending Disciples on Mission

The church's decision to expand its mission by setting apart and sending Barnabas and Saul is the basis of our fourth reality of servant leadership in a ministry of transition.

Reality 4: Servant leaders trust their community of disciples to send them on mission (see Acts 13:1-3).

This reality is essential to a servant leader's call because community is the context for shaping the leader and discerning the fuller meaning of God's calling.

Reggie McNeal warns leaders against living the American myth, the Western, where leaders are portrayed as the good guy who rides in from nowhere, wins the hearts of the locals, defeats the bad guy, and rides off into the sunset. He rightly observes: "Leaders are not shaped in isolation. Leaders are shaped in community. And they are shaped by community. Leaders cannot be separated from the formative processes of community. Despite any claims to the contrary, leaders are not self-made people. There is no such person."[27]

God uses the leader's life in community to form him into the servant leaders He desires them to become. God also

Reality 4: Servant leaders trust their community of disciples to send them on mission.

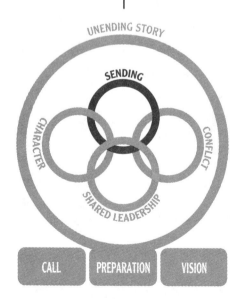

uses the fellowship of the saints to help servant leaders discern God's next steps for their ministry.

Another advantage of living in authentic community is that those in the group keep the servant leader's heart attuned to the hearts of those he leads. Leading alone not only drains the emotional, spiritual, and physical resources of the leader, but it also distances him from the needs of those on mission with him. To lead outside community is to jump into hurricane seas with only a rubber raft.

How connected are you to an authentic community of people? Whom can you talk to when you need to be unguarded? Do those you lead see you as a connected leader?

Who Is Set Apart?

We often refer to the events in the early part of Acts 13 as the basis for ordination. I painfully remember ordination services when I was a child, the hours sitting still on Sunday evenings while men in suits leaned over other men whispering something in their ears. All I knew was that the longer a service went on and the quieter I had to be signaled the more sacred the event. I soon began to equate how I had to act in these services with funerals. As a young boy, I wondered when I would learn the secret rite of what they were doing.

When I was ordained at my home church, I recall the encouragement and blessings I received from the men who huddled over me. I cherish the prayer my father prayed, and I am honored by the names on the certificate that declares my ordination to the gospel ministry. But, as I look back on this and so many of the religious practices of my youth, I realize these were all part of the institution called church expressed in that time in history and in that culture. I came to wonder if what was referred to as my ordination matched the biblical intent of being set apart for mission.

When I began my ministry, I was told that only the ordained could practice the ordinances of the church, baptism and the Lord's Supper. If I was planning to go into the ministry, I must be ordained. So, as soon as I graduated from college, I got married and was ordained. My ministry career had begun. I was part of the ordained clergy now. I could pastor a church.

My first violation of clergy protocol came when I was a youth minister while still in college. I served the Lord's Supper at a retreat without an ordained staff member or deacon present. My reprimand was not serious, but it was clear I had violated a sacred rule, and I was never to perform such unauthorized rites again. I agreed not to do that again, but I did not want to give up the joy of serving and explaining the symbol of the meal to those young believers.

Even when I became a pastor, I continued to wrestle with the clearly defined borders between those who were ordained and those who were not. As a credentialed professional with a terminal degree, I had a place in leadership. My certificates proved it. What about those who were as gifted and capable as me? Why were they not allowed to participate in the joy of sharing the meal and baptizing those they had led to the Lord?

When my theology of the church changed, my theology of ordination changed. I could no longer perpetuate a division between the ordained and the laity when the biblical record offered no division. Yes, different rolls are described for leaders and servants in the Bible. Paul, however, continually exhorted members to "consider others more important" than themselves and everyone—that includes leaders—"should look out not only for his own interests, but also for the interests of others" (Phil. 2:4). Servant leaders in the church should have no distinction from the other members but to be humble servants of Christ.

I have come to believe this: *Churches ordain to an office; they commission for ministry.* This distinction is important because one is the practice of an institution while the other is the practice of a movement. When the church was baptized into the Roman Empire by Emperor Constantine, it became an institution of society. It began to form itself as an organization common to its day. Like the children of Israel adopting the pagan practices of their neighbors in Canaan, the church has been seduced to organize itself like the institutions of its culture throughout history.

Institutions have offices that require personnel. They must have procedures and practices to ensure those personnel are duly credentialed by other accredited institutions. Movements, on the other hand, insist that leaders demonstrate in community their calling and contribution to the mission of the church.

A church working out of an institutional model may incorporate the ecclesiastical practice of ordination (along with its own flavor of theological nuances) to affirm call and set a person apart for "vocational ministry." Such a practice can become exclusively owned by a segment of the church's population which eliminates participation by the body as a whole. In the early church, setting apart members for ministry was part of the ebb and flow of community life among the followers of Jesus.

Churches that live out their call as a mission outpost embrace shared leadership by affirming giftedness and sharing its authority in order to support those on mission. Laying on hands is the physical affirmation of the community to affirm Christ's gifts for service and to identify those in the body who are set apart for different ministries related to its mission.

Describe your church's concept of ordination. The purpose of looking at ordination is not to cause any unsettling in your church. It is simply to clarify how you formally recognize and release leaders in your church. How and when you do this signifies who the church truly recognizes as leaders. Any transitions related to this process should only be addressed after you embrace a shared understanding of the church and church leadership. Be prepared to discuss your description when your mission outpost team gathers.

A Real-Time Example

We first began this practice of laying hands on those on mission because we wanted to demonstrate to Legacy that our small-group leaders were ministers among us. So, after a nine-month season of training, we presented these servant leaders to the gathered church during a worship service. We explained their preparation process and that we wanted to recognize them and set them apart as men and women who would serve the body as its ministers. (By the way, we call our full-time staff "ministry directors" in order not to confuse their role with all the leaders we recognize as ministers.) We asked the small-group leaders to stand where they were in the congregation and asked those around them to place hands on them. We then prayed a prayer of blessing and released them to ministry. We now do this with other ministry leaders.

After this commissioning, two things happened within a couple of months without our planning them. Shifts in ministry occurred spontaneously! They never made the list of what we needed to address to become a more effective mission outpost. One was that small groups began to have the Lord's Supper when they gathered. Gathering around the meal in a living room with others on the journey of faith is different from making it part of the Sunday liturgy. We had trained our leaders in the theology and practice of this ancient meal during our training period. The reports of enhanced community soon came our way.

The second thing that happened was that small-group leaders began to baptize those who through the ministry of the small group had trusted Christ as their Leader and Forgiver. We have two or three "baptism celebrations" throughout the year. During those times we ask new believers who they would like to baptize them and who they would like to stand by them in the water as they make their public confession of trust in Jesus. I am not "Gene, the baptizer" at Legacy. I joyfully share that privilege with others who carry the name of Jesus and serve on mission with me.

We have talked about how leaders see the vision before those they lead, some transitions you may face in your church as you pursue God's vision for your church, and some principles learned from one transitioning experience. We have also observed the roll community plays in expanding the church's mission and knowing whom to set apart for that goal.

In the next session, we will look into the opposition and conflict that are inherent in a ministry of transition.

1. "Make No Little Plans," quoted in *No Little Plans* (Waco, TX: Narrative Publishing, 2000), vii.

2. Dan Southerland, *Transitioning: Leading Your Church Through Change* (Grand Rapids: Zondervan, 1999), 81-82.

3. I have identified 10 characteristics, but space will allow me to describe only 6. We have used these characteristics in our Discover Legacy workshop to illustrate our model for being a mission outpost. See also Ken Hemphill, *The Antioch Effect* (Nashville: Broadman and Holman, 1994).

4. John B. Polhill, *Paul and His Letters* (Nashville: Broadman & Holman, 1999), 73.

5. F. F. Bruce, *Paul: Apostle of the Heart Set Free* (Grand Rapids: Eerdmans, 1977), 132.

6. Brian D. McLaren, *A New Kind of Christian* (Indianapolis, IN: Jossey-Bass, 2001), 39-40.

7. Alan Nelson and Gene Appel, *How to Change Your Church Without Killing It* (Nashville: Word Publishing, 2000), 63.

8. Ibid., 90.

9. Ken Blanchard and Phil Hodges, *The Servant Leader* (Nashville: J. Countryman, 2003), 66-67. The sentences in quotes are from Blanchard and Hodge. The others are my commentary on their insights.

10. C. Gene Wilkes, *Jesus on Leadership* (Nashville: LifeWay, 1996; Carol Stream, IL: Tyndale House Publishers, 1998), 63

11. Most of this content was first published in "An Emerging Church: One Church's Transition from a Local Church to a Mission Outpost," *Growing Churches*, Summer 2001.

12. Bill Easum, *Unfreezing Moves* (Nashville: Abingdon Press, 2001).

13. Southerland, *Transitioning*, 40.

14. I have described the difference between a committee culture and a team culture and how to transition from one to the other in the March-April-May and July-August-September 2001 issues of *Church Administration*.

15. C. Gene Wilkes, *Jesus on Leadership* (Nashville: LifeWay, 1998, rev. ed.), 35-48.

16. Leonard Sweet, *Soul Tsunami* (Grand Rapids: Zondervan, 1999), 92.

17. Brian D. McLaren, *The Church on the Other Side* (Grand Rapids: Zondervan, 2000), 142.

18. Steve Sjogren, *101 Ways to Reach Your Community* (Colorado Springs: Navpress, 2001), See www.servantevangelism.com for current information.

19. Larry Crabb, *Safest Place on Earth* (Nashville: W Publishing Group, 1999), 183.

20. Southerland, *Transitioning*, 40.

21. The first five principles were first published in Wilkes, "An Emerging Church."

22. Southerland, *Transitioning*, 108-9.

23. Nelson and Appel, *How to Change Your Church*, 218.

24. Ken Blanchard, Phil Hodges, and Bill Hybels, *Leadership by the Book* (New York: William Morrow, 1999), 42.

25. Stanley Hauerwas and William H. Willimon, *Resident Aliens* (Nashville: Abingdon, 1989), 78.

26. Another look at this passage is in Wilkes, *Jesus on Leadership* (LifeWay), 40-41.

27. Reggie McNeal, *A Work of Heart* (Indianapolis, IN: Jossey-Bass, 2000), 115, prepublication edition.

OPPOSITION AND CONFLICT

This week you will:

- Learn different causes and responses to opposition toward the mission.
- Learn to handle conflict in community.
- Address the hurt and healing that come from conflict.
- Examine Paul's instructions about spiritual warfare.
- Learn from Paul about conflict resolution.

One day I opened an e-mail from a pastor I had met when I led a conference at his church. He wrote that three longtime members met away from the church and decided that his time as pastor was over. Not wanting to tell my pastor friend to his face what they had decided, they asked a fourth member to do their bidding. This member called the pastor and asked him to come by his office the next day.

When the pastor arrived, this deacon told him what had been decided, asked him to resign, and offered him a severance package. Of course, none of them had the authority to dismiss him, but they had taken it upon themselves to change the leader of *their* church. One of the three was the biggest giver in the church, and the young pastor had not always done what this man wanted. Like too many members who give to their church, the member must have thought, *Hey, I give a lot of money. I should have a say in what goes on around here.* He was having his say.

You can only imagine—unless you have been on that end of such a power move—his shock, fear, and confusion as he left the office. Like an accident victim staggering around the scene of the incident, he didn't know what to do, what to say, or where to go. He decided to e-mail me after he read an article I had written, "Jesus on Conflict."[1] I became angry as soon as I read his message. I had been near these situations too many times. I encouraged him to maintain the integrity of the church's decision-making process while confronting the sin of control that was in the fellowship. He had heard that this was a pattern of behavior for years by these men, but he believed that maybe one of the reasons God had put him there was to bring down this stronghold in the church.

He set out to be honest yet humble. He confronted the sin of control privately and publicly in meetings with church leaders. Everyone knew the church had to make a choice: continue in this dysfunctional way or break the chains of control that were binding them. After several meetings with the deacons—including one he did not attend—he decided to resign. It had become clear that this triumvirate ruled the body, and he no longer had enough support to be an effective leader.

He is no longer a pastor in a local church, yet he continues to serve in a kingdom-related vocation. The church will most likely continue in its usual ways, and God will use them and him. That is the kind of God He is. This incident graphically illustrates, however, how opposition fueled by a need for control can threaten both the leader and the potential success of the mission.

Paul faced opposition from the day he stepped out into the streets of Damascus to tell others Jesus is the Messiah. His opponents dogged him from town to town. Conflict changed his relationship with his closest associate, Barnabas. Paul, the servant leader, modeled for us how to face, overcome, and even excel through opposition and conflict. You can learn much from the apostle to the ethnics; he overcame opposition and navigated through conflict in his ministry of transition.

Day 1

WHEN MISSION MEETS OPPOSITION

Every leader called by God faces resistance. Moses did. David did. Esther did. Jesus did, and Paul did. They faced opposition from their enemies, those they were trying to lead, and among their closest followers. Why would you and those who lead with you expect your situation to be any different? Leading in transition is hard work because you face real resistance.

Several years ago I attended a leadership conference hosted by Robert Schuller at his church in Southern California. At one point in the conference, a panel in which several of the conference leaders, including Schuller and Bill Hybels, fielded questions from participants. A young pastor stood and said something like, "Where you guys have built your churches is easy. There are millions of people, and there is lots of money. But I'm in Nebraska. Can you tell me how to build a church where it is hard?" Stunned silence came from those on the panel. You could hear Dr. Schuller racing through 40 years of creating a church next door to Disneyland and Knott's Berry Farm in a completely secular culture on the edge of Christendom.

Bill Hybels had to be biting his tongue to explain how he and his team struggled to set up every week in a rented theater to "turn irreligious people into fully devoted followers of Christ." He could have told how he lives every day with criticism of their "seeker-driven" strategy from those who have never been to their campus. But both were silent. No one answered. They went on to the next question. Seasoned servant leaders who have led others to create a new reality in the face of opposition kindly move on to the next question when someone implies that their work has been easy. I believe it's one way to heed Jesus' words not to "cast your pearls before swine."

What do you know through experience about opposition to the mission, vision, and transitions you have offered to others? Name leaders you know who have faced opposition because they tried to implement the vision in their ministry. Record in your journal your experiences and why that person stands out in your mind. Be prepared to share your thoughts with your mission outpost team.

Key Verse
But the Jews[2] incited the religious women of high standing and the leading men of the city. They stirred up persecution against Paul and Barnabas and expelled them from their district.
—Acts 13:50

God calls people to join Him in the church, a new creation brought about by His Son, Jesus. Belonging to this new order brings new ways of living, new systems of life, and fresh expressions of relationship. God calls some to lead others out of the old-creation models into these new realities. These are God's servant leaders in the ministry of transition. He calls them out in every age and culture. They lead because they have been taken by the call.

Let's review our pattern for a ministry of transition. Once called, prepared, having seen the end picture, and having launched the mission, we can see that the next reality is opposition and conflict. Here is our overview of the connected realities we observe from Paul's ministry.

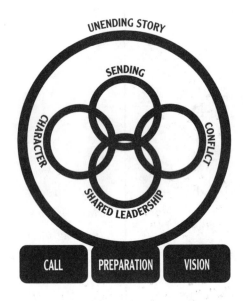

Call requires preparation. Those called must have a clear picture of where they are leading, and once the vision is clear, the mission is launched. Soon after the launch toward the vision, the servant leader faces opposition.

Leadership by its very nature invites opposition and conflict.[3] To lead is to bring change, and change unsettles people's world. The results can range from resistance in the form of passive detachment to aggressive engagement. Someone once said resistance to change proves you are sane! It's normal to resist anything that threatens what you have worked so hard to build and maintain—especially if it is as important as how you live out your faith in God.

The art of servant leadership in a ministry of transition helps people see the reason for the change (the mission), what the change will look like when it is finished (the vision), and the path you will lead them on to get there (the ministry of transition). This can be a dangerous undertaking. Leading others into an uncertain future can cause them to see you as a threat. Heifetz and Linsky describe leadership in transition in this way: "You appear dangerous to people when you question their values, beliefs, or habits of a lifetime. You place yourself on the line when you tell people what they need to hear rather than what they want to hear. Although you may see with clarity and passion a promising future of progress and gain, people will see with equal passion the losses you are asking them to sustain."[4]

God naturally programmed people to fight or flee from perceived or real danger. Leaders enter the danger zone when they challenge people to follow them to a place they would not go on their own.

A Biblical Example

Let's follow Barnabas and Paul as they left Antioch in Syria and launched an extended ministry to the ethnics. They were called. They had seasons of preparation. They had seen the "missional future"[5] through their experiences with pagan ethnics in Antioch. And the community of faith had commissioned them to extend the mission beyond the borders of their city. The story of their first encounters with opposition is recorded in Acts 13–14.

Read Acts 13. As you read the story, take notes of the different opposition Barnabas and Paul face on their trip through Cyprus to Antioch in Pisidia. Record your notes in the margin or in your journal.

The two sent ones first sailed to Barnabas' homeland of Cyprus (Acts 13:4). There spiritual forces opposed them through a sorcerer. We will address the reality of spiritual conflict when completing the mission of God later in this session, but note that the servant leaders confronted this evil spirit and the man became a follower of Jesus (Acts 13:12). Later they sailed to the mainland and came to Antioch of Pisidia. There they presented the message of Jesus to both Jews and ethnics in the city. Acts 13:16-41 is a record of Paul's message in the synagogue. Initially, "Jews and devout proselytes" were interested in the truth of Jesus' identity as the Son of God (Acts 13:43).

When they gathered to hear the message on the next Sabbath, however, the Bible says that the Jews "began to oppose what Paul was saying by insulting him" (Acts 13:45). Insults are often the opposition's only tactic when presented with truth. Paul said that because of their refusal to listen he would turn his attention solely to the ethnics. When the ethnics heard this, they rejoiced because they could become a part of the saving work of Jesus. The Jews did not like it one bit. They "incited" other religious leaders in the city to speak out against these who brought this new message and its implication to their town (our key verse).

Paul and Barnabas "shook the dust off their feet" and headed to the next city. Paul practiced Jesus' words to His disciples to go to those who accept you and "shake the dust off your feet" as you leave those who are not ready to hear (Matt. 10:12-14). What was the mood after having been the objects of persecution? Luke tells us, "And the disciples were filled with joy and the Holy Spirit" (v. 52). Even in the face of opposition, they rejoiced because they knew they were doing what God had called them to do. Joy, unlike happiness, rides above the circumstances of the moment. This opposition in Antioch was a foreshadowing of things to come.

Read Acts 14:1-20. What happened in the city of Iconium? Who instigated the opposition this time? What was the story in Lystra? What did Paul do after he was left for dead outside the city?

The scenarios in both Iconium and Lystra are similar to what happened in Antioch of Pisidia. Both ethnics and Jews initially embraced the message of Jesus. But those who refused to hear the new message from God stirred up the entire city to oppose the two ambassadors of Christ (Acts 14:1-5). When Paul heard about the plot to stone him, he left for the next town, a ploy he had used several years before in Damascus (Acts 9:23-25).

In Lystra the two missionaries performed a miracle of healing. The pagan citizens, led by the priests of Zeus, wanted to worship the two messengers as gods, but the apostles directed their worship to the one true God (Acts 14:11-18). While this scene was playing out, traditionalist leaders from both Antioch and Iconium who had joined forces came to Lystra. Like a hurricane that creates storm surges along the coast, they stirred up enough opposition against Paul and his message to stone Paul and drag him out of town to be left for dead (v. 19). This time, however, Paul did not go to the next city. He got up and walked right back into town, spent the night, and left the next day. No shaking off the dust this time.

Strength to Endure

What gives a servant leader the courage and strength to go back into a situation after he has just been stoned, drug out of town, and left for dead? One resource is personality. Paul was hardwired with a dominant relational style.[6] God chose a man with a personality that had no problem engaging his opposition to lead toward a vision of "one people." This relational style serves well

Even in the face of opposition, they rejoiced because they knew they were doing what God had called them to do. Joy, unlike happiness, rides above the circumstances of the moment.

in a new initiative of transitioning. These leaders actually like the challenge of overcoming their opponents. However, they can come across as arrogant and inflexible without the work of the Holy Spirit in their lives. We will see the downside of this temperament later in this session. Dominance is not always the way to win over the opposition.

Another reason you get up and face your opposition is that sometimes you must let your opponents know their antics to stop your ministry will not work. You must take a stand on principle. They must know this is not about you but about God's call on your life *and theirs.* You are not seeking to win a battle. You are trying to capture their hearts with the purposes of God. Once they have orchestrated their best efforts to discredit you, you must get up and return to the task at hand. Like Paul dragging himself back into Lystra after being stoned, you sometimes must drag yourself back into your office on Monday morning after a four-hour business meeting the night before.

Paul's example teaches those leading in a ministry of transition that sometimes you shake the dust off your feet and leave for the next town. Other times you get up and go back into the town to face those who have stoned you.

Enduring Conflict

A third way the servant leader endures opposition in order to complete his mission is by his passionate commitment to the God-given vision he is leading toward. Once you have said yes to God's call to mission and vision, endurance in the middle of opposition comes from commitment to that call and vision. Temperament and resolve alone are not enough to empower you to endure the harsh opposition you may face. You need a combination of God's presence and an unwavering commitment to what God has called you to do to finish the long run of transitioning.

Reality 5: Servant leaders endure opposition and resolve conflict with a passionate commitment to the vision (see Acts 13–15).

Commitment to God's revealed vision gives the servant leader strength to endure opposition and the patience to resolve conflict. Enduring opposition is part of serving the mission. People oppose change naturally, and every servant leader will encounter the rocky road of opposition.

Consider times you have endured opposition to your leadership in a time of transition. Be prepared to share with your mission outpost team a time when your personality, your principles, or your passionate commitment to the call was a source for enduring opposition.

UNENDING STORY · SENDING · CHARACTER · CONFLICT · SHARED LEADERSHIP · CALL · PREPARATION · VISION

Reality 5: Servant leaders endure opposition and resolve conflict with a passionate commitment to the vision.

CONFLICT IN COMMUNITY

Sometimes issues become so disruptive that they must be addressed in the community of faith. What started as a disagreement over doctrine, method, or direction can spiral into a full-blown tornado of anger and hurt. Personalities, principles, and passions work on both sides of an issue. Some people naturally gravitate toward change. Others resist it in favor of the status quo. Those on either side can refuse to budge based on principle. Add to that a passion for their cause, and you have the ingredients for a chemistry experiment gone bad. An impasse occurs when those on either side of an issue say no to compromise. This is where resolving conflict in the larger community has its place.

Choosing the forum for resolution is critical. Depending on your church's decision-making process, you may not bring an issue to the entire body except as a last resort. Jesus taught His disciples first to handle conflict among themselves. When two individuals cannot solve the issue on their own, they are to bring in another brother or sister in Christ to influence toward reconciliation. If there is no movement toward unity, the disagreeing parties are to bring the matter to the entire church (Matt. 18:15-17). Remember, a hallmark of a people called out by God is how they love one another, not how often they fight.

One other reminder: Don't forget that the size of the church in Jesus' day was much smaller than the hundreds or thousands that gather in buildings on weekends throughout the United States. The average American church of under one hundred in weekly attendance has a better chance of directly transferring Jesus' words into their context, but even small churches deal with the issue of disconnectedness. How you handle discipline in larger organizations is different from the way it can be handled in smaller groups.

The only time you take conflict to the larger community is when it has begun to bring division into the church and to threaten its mission. Conflict is best addressed first between those who hold the differences. When all efforts there have been exhausted, then a gathering of the leaders who represent the body's mission should be consulted. After a decision is made there, the church is then told. This was how it happened when the mission to the ethnics began to jeopardize the unity of the early church.

Acts 15—Anatomy of a Conflict

As Paul and Barnabas returned from their first excursion to evangelize the ethnics, they were met again with opposition. Acts 15 records that conflict and how the church resolved it in community. How this issue was resolved in the early church is not prescriptive for churches today. The scenario, however, provides hints as to how you can deal with conflict related to the mission to make disciples in your mission field. Keep in mind that transitioning to become a mission outpost will bring conflict because your focus changes from maintaining the status quo to reaching the mission field in which you have been planted. The issue of inclusion answers the question, who can be part of Christ's church? The easy answer is "everyone." The hard answer is "the guy who cussed my son out at the baseball game last night but is going

Key Verse
But after Paul and Barnabas had engaged them [their opponents] in serious argument and debate, they arranged for Paul and Barnabas and some others of them to go up to the apostles and elders in Jerusalem concerning this controversy.
—Acts 15:2

through a divorce and has begun to ask eternally significant questions and needs to hear a message of hope."

The anatomy of a conflict recorded in Acts 15 gives seven clues to handle a similar situation in your church.

1. A new reality is introduced into the status quo (Acts 14:27-28). Paul and Barnabas returned to their home church in Antioch of Syria with stories of changed lives. They had seen firsthand how pagan ethnics and hard-core traditionalists had come to be followers of Jesus Christ. They had the proof that the mission they were commissioned to complete was real. They wanted to tell everyone who prayed for them about the success of the ethnic mission. As they returned, they introduced this new reality into the status quo of Jewish men and women who trusted Jesus to be the Messiah.

What new realities have you experienced recently that validate the mission and vision God has called you to complete? What stories are defining moments that you and those you lead are on the right track? When was the last time you gathered the church together to tell them the stories? Be prepared to share your answers with your mission outpost team.

2. Opposition to the new reality comes from traditionalists (Acts 15:1). Those who do not want to change constantly resist new realities. Luke tells us that not only did traditionalists dog Paul and Barnabas throughout their entire journey into southern Galatia, but as soon as the traditionalists in the Jerusalem church heard the missionaries were back in Antioch of Syria, they headed down to make their case. They wanted to make sure the ethnics upheld the orthodox view of becoming a Jew as one became a follower of Jesus (v. 1). Those who oppose your mission are often as passionate and determined as those who own the vision. Their commitment is to orthodoxy while those leading in a ministry of transition are committed to the mission and its vision.

What are some of the most common opposing points of view to the transitions you and your leaders are trying to accomplish? These common views can help you understand the feelings and thinking of the traditionalists in your group. Bring your list to your mission outpost team meeting. Together create a master list you can address later.

3. The issue is sent to those who have the authority to decide (Acts 15:2-6). The issue of inclusion had not been solved since the two missionaries set off on their first trip. It was not solved in the Antioch church when they returned. Someone needed to make the call as to whether ethnics must follow the law to become followers of Jesus. The church in Jerusalem was the seat of authority for the Jesus movement since its inception at Pentecost (Acts 2). Most of the apostles still lived there. Even Paul acknowledged their position of leadership in the church—even if it was a backhanded complement (Gal. 2:9). So, when the question of "What do we do with the new people?" could not be answered among those on the edge of the movement, they carried their case to those in authority to make the call. Observe that "the apostles and the elders" apparently assembled apart from the rest of the church to consider the matter (v. 6).

Who has the authority in your church to handle conflicts decisively? Are they effective? Does the process help the church be healthy, or does it foster divisions in the church?

Notice that the leadership structure in the Jerusalem church was different from democratically led churches today. Comparing your decision-making process with this one described in Acts will raise the core issue of who has the authority to make decisions. You may need to address, affirm, or restructure your decision-making process in order to handle conflict related to transitions in a healthy way.

4. The mission received support from those who shared the same experience (Acts 15:7-11). Peter preceded Paul as an apostle to the ethnics. When Peter stepped across the threshold of Cornelius' house, the world of faith in the one true God shook to its foundation. He followed Jesus into the home of an ethnic whom he had been told his entire life he could not associate with. In Cornelius' living room he saw a movement of the Holy Spirit that was exactly what he and the Jewish followers of Jesus had experienced in the upper room. He could not deny that God had embraced the ethnics with the love and power of his Son, Jesus (Acts 10).

God used this prior experience in Peter's life as a witness to affirm what God was doing among the ethnics evangelized by Paul and Barnabas. He came to the support of his fellow missionaries when he heard the opposition's case (Acts 15:7-11). He personally knew the sting of those who challenged his friends from his report that, just like the Jews, ethnics belonged in the kingdom of God (Acts 11:1-18).

Every servant leader in a ministry of transition needs a person of stature like Peter to carry the banner for the mission with him or her. Who is a Peter in your church or organization who, like you, has experienced the new reality and would stand with you in resolving the issues related to your mission?

Who are the "apostles" among you whose stories about changed lives of those you are trying to reach would help others see the vision more clearly? Write the name(s) here. Collaborate with your mission outpost team at your next meeting to affirm whom you have chosen. Consider appropriate times to share those stories with the church.

5. Leaders retold the stories of changed lives for all to hear (Acts 15:12). After receiving support from Peter, Barnabas and Paul took the platform to tell their stories. Peter's witness silenced the group. He spoke with authority based on his relationship with Jesus and his shared experience with the ethnics. He declared that God made no distinction between Jews and others when it came to salvation by faith (v. 9). He wanted to know why anyone would test God by insisting ethnic disciples adhere to the Law, which they and their forefathers had themselves never been able to keep (v. 10).

The two missionaries followed up his conclusion with stories to support his claims. Life-change stories are the most powerful proof that the mission is effective. With them you can help people join you. Without them you can only argue theories and preferences.

Can you passionately tell the stories of life change that illustrate your mission? Barnabas and Paul both had these stories. You as a servant leader in the ministry of transition should have personal stories that illustrate changed lives based on an innovation or reach initiative into a new people group. Write down some that you have experienced and collect more from your mission outpost team when you meet next.

6. A decision was made by a trusted leader who took input from both sides (Acts 15:13-21). After both cases were made, James stood up and made the call. Peter provided the stories. James provided the Scripture (Acts 15:16-18). Combined they laid a foundation for a clear decision that was not refuted. James found some middle ground that seemed to satisfy everyone. "The righteous shall live by faith" remained the core belief. Guidelines for holy living became a shared practice. James wisely found common ground upon which the mission to make disciples of all people could continue.

What biblical passages are foundational to what you are doing? Do you share them often? Are you careful to ensure that you are not making them say something they are not? What common ground have you found that allows people in conflict to move forward together? Write some examples here.

7. The leaders communicated their decision to the larger community of faith (Acts 15:22-30). The Jerusalem leaders sent representatives with a letter clearly stating the decision they had made. This decision would affect many churches, and they wanted the message to be clear. Another reason for the letter was to state the reality that others had been insisting on practices that were outside the will of their leadership. The leaders took the time and effort to make sure their position was clear to all involved in the conflict.

Communication is always a challenge in changing situations. Hearsay and rumor always fuel the conflict rather than ending it. Do you carefully communicate decisions made by leaders to the church? Are your messages clearly stated, and do those who can answer any questions about the decision go along with them? Do you have an organization that you can use to share decisions with everyone involved?

Resolving conflict is core to successfully leading through transitions. I affirm Nelson and Appel's conclusion that "the single biggest fear and pain that church change produces is conflict."[7] Too many of God's people have been stung by sharp words in meetings. Leaders have been deeply wounded by the actions of those who sense they are losing control. People have been disappointed by a leader's diligence to change without listening to words of caution. Conflict can hurt, but it does not need to be fatal.

As you complete this part of the study, pause and pray for those who may be hurting because of conflict created by the changes to become a mission outpost. Pray for understanding, openness, and agreement on the core issues at hand. Keep this list of names before you this week. Let each person know you are praying for him or her.

Conflict can hurt, but it does not need to be fatal.

CONFLICT THAT HURTS

Matthew (not his real name) sat with his wife across from me in the church conference room. He had called and said they needed to talk with me. Matthew was a friend. We had not only served together at Legacy for several years, but we ran together, shared lunches, training programs, and family events. He was a deacon, and she served faithfully in our children's ministry. They were core people at Legacy.

As I sat and listened, constantly moving my wedding ring from my ring finger to my index finger, he spelled out the reasons it was time for his family to find another church. I had heard the list before—worship style, my teaching style, changes in how we taught children, a spirit of unrest in the body, "not what we're familiar with." What made this more difficult was that true friendship was involved. People choose to leave churches all the time. Some churches grow because of it. Others plateau or die. But the pain of a friend choosing to leave is hard on the one who made the decisions to change.

When Matthew came to the part, "We have decided to start looking for another church," tears began to swell up in his eyes. I did the same. We knew that while we said we would stay in touch, we wouldn't. You can only ask "How's it going?" so many times after you no longer live and serve alongside each other. I told him I understood. We had already talked about how he could stay over the next several weeks, but our mission to reach the unchurched and all that implied did not fit what his family wanted in a church. We prayed and hugged. They left to join another church in the city.

Transitioning from being a local church to becoming a mission outpost creates clashes even among friends. This happens because transitions affect the core of who we are and what we believe. As a servant leader, you must expect and be prepared for conflict that can even separate you from friends.

Have you experienced anything like the story above? If so, you may want to pause and pray for the friend who continues to serve in the kingdom only with another group of disciples. You may want to return to that time of separation and prayerfully ask God to show you what may have prevented it. If you are still hurting from such an encounter, ask your mission outpost team to pray for you at your next meeting.

No "Happily Ever After"

Conflict does not always end cleanly. Godly men and women have differences of opinion, and they disagree. Sometimes those disagreements end without "and they lived happily ever after" as the last sentence of the story. This hurts everyone involved and causes some to wonder where God is in all of it. Some quietly slip out the back door. Others stomp out. Many are left holding the damaged hearts of others in their care.

Separation between friends because of conflict is as ancient as the first mission to the ethnics. Just when it looked like the church had survived the conflict over the inclusion of the ethnics in the church, two of its most visible leaders separated because they could not agree. It is ironic that immediately following the resolution of the potentially most damaging division in the

Key Verse

There was such a sharp disagreement that they parted company, and Barnabas took Mark with him and sailed off to Cyprus. Then Paul chose Silas and departed, after being commended to the grace of the Lord by the brothers.
—*Acts 15:39-40*

church, two core leaders could not find common ground to continue working together.

We know by Paul's personality, passion, and single-focused determination to the mission that he had no sympathy for those who failed the mission. He took his call so seriously that slackers had no place on his team. Quitters were even less valued.

Strong leaders who give their lives to the mission call on their lives find it hard to put up with those who do not share their passion. Committed servant leaders may come across as uncaring and inflexible because they sacrifice so much, endure constant opposition, and plead God's case so many times that if you abandon them, they would as soon write you off as spend the time hearing your reasons for ending your pursuit of the vision. Paul was one of these kinds of leaders.

Read Acts 15:36-40. Describe the conflict between Paul and Barnabas in your own words. What are some reasons you believe these two friends could not resolve their conflict over John Mark? Write your impressions in the margin.

Paul and Barnabas returned with Judas and Silas to Antioch to convey what had been decided in Jerusalem (Acts 15:30-35). They stayed for some time continuing their ministry of preaching and teaching there. Paul sensed a need to return to the churches they had planted on their first trip. Barnabas agreed but wanted to take John Mark with them. Paul refused. John Mark had abandoned the mission on the first trip (Acts 13:13; 15:38). Luke does not tell us why he wanted to go back home when they landed in Pamphylia. Some suggest that the intensity of Paul's near-death stoning, constant public harassment, and battles with evil spirits was more than he was prepared for. Like others who have said, "Sure, I'll join you on the mission field," John Mark may have found the safety of his home church more appealing than frontier living. Many others still do.

Paul apparently believed there was no room for the weak when on mission to bring the good news into new territories. The work was hard. Danger was real. Spiritual warfare was not a fairy tale. When on the front lines, soldiers must be certain their platoon members will not turn tail and run when the enemy begins his charge.

Barnabas was as committed as Paul to reaching the ethnics. He befriended Paul after his conversion and made it possible for him to be accepted by the Jerusalem church. Barnabas had blessed the movement of God in Antioch. He personally went to Tarsus and invited Paul to join him in his ministry there. Both had ministered in victory on their first trip beyond their home church. Barnabas was not a quitter. He actually had more time in the field than Paul. But his personality and priorities included other people—no matter their performance.

Luke tells us that there was "such a sharp disagreement that they parted company" (v. 39). These guys had seen it all. They could count on each other no matter what, but they could not work through this one. So they parted company. Barnabas took John Mark, his cousin, back to their homeland of Cyprus. Paul took Silas, who had come with him from Jerusalem, and they traveled through Syria and Cilicia (v. 40).

Results of an Unhappy Ending

The breakup of this effective evangelistic team may have seemed to some like the end of the mission. God, however, used the separation for His purposes.

One good that came out of this was the creation of two teams where there had been one. Many times the parting of friends creates new relationships that can change the world. Paul and Silas singing at midnight in the Philippian jail never would have happened without this breakup. God can redeem conflict that ends in separation to provide more teams in the field.

Paul may come across as hardhearted in this event. But he was not as uncompromising as he may appear in this story. John Mark eventually became his partner in ministry. Reconciliation did take place. We find Paul in Rome writing to the church in Colosse at the end of his ministry. As he closed his letter to the church, he wrote, "My fellow prisoner greets you, as does Mark, Barnabas' cousin (concerning whom you have received instructions: if he comes to you, welcome him)" (Col. 4:10).

In 2 Timothy 4:11, Paul, at the end of his ministry, asks Timothy to come and see him and then adds, "Bring Mark with you, for he is useful to me in the ministry." Somewhere along the way Paul and John Mark reconciled, and they joined forces to complete the mission to the ethnics. Mark authored the Gospel that carries his name. Mark may have accepted Paul's evaluation of his performance and moved toward him. Or Paul cooled off and reached out to Mark and wrote the incident off as immaturity. The reason for the breakup years before now became a story of reconciliation for the church.

Another positive by-product of conflict in Paul's ministry is the letters he wrote the churches. For example, the Corinthian correspondence was born out of conflict in the church and with Paul himself. Commenting on 2 Corinthians, Polhill writes: "In many ways 2 Corinthians is the most personal of Paul's letters. It was born of a very intense conflict that developed between the apostle and the church after the writing of 1 Corinthians. In the course of events Paul was personally attacked. The very legitimacy of his ministry was called into question. His leadership of the congregation was challenged."[8]

Correspondence born out of conflict gave the church the principles to live by for generations to come. God revealed His Word for all peoples in the crucible of conflict in the church.

Recall some positive outcomes from conflicts you have experienced. Record them in the margin.

oneLegacy

One of the final major conflicts in our ministry of transition at Legacy was updating our constitution and bylaws. We had intentionally not updated them during our 10 years of change. However, when we felt all the pieces were in place and the time was right to make the final formal changes, we would update our guiding documents. We sensed it was time.

If you had told the leadership team, staff, or me that this would bring about another season of serious conflict, we all would have told you that you did not know what you were talking about. But, when you start putting down on paper the transitions you have made over 10 years, you get people's attention. As I have said before, people do not pay attention to change until it affects them directly. Although we had been operating with an annual church conference, church leadership team, and deacons as servant leaders for about five years, and we had introduced being called by another name more than a year before, some people responded like we had made it all up on Saturday and offered it to them on Sunday.

On Sunday, January 12, 2003, we held what we called a TouchPoint, a town-hall type meeting, to answer questions and clearly communicate again the issues we were updating. Five hours after we began, it became clear there was conflict among members that would lead to separation by some. The future was solidified as we wrestled through the implications of change over the past 10 years. The leaders never wavered. The direction was cast in stone for the last time. Over the next weeks people began to vote with their feet and hearts whether they were to be part of that future.

As this began to happen, we saw an opportunity to return to our mission and vision and remind everyone why we were doing what we were doing. We called the campaign oneLegacy. The process was that I would go to more than 20 gatherings in six weeks to recast the vision of becoming a mission outpost in our mission field. Those days were filled with stories of rebuilding relationships, healing hurts, and feeling the passion of those who said, "This is church for my family and me." We continued to see people who were part of our target audience come to trust Jesus as their forgiver and leader.

On Sunday, April 27, of that same year, we baptized 38 people in one service. I was blessed to baptize my neighbors across the street; for seven years we built an intentional relationship that led to their baptism and being part of Legacy. Other adults, teenagers, and children were baptized. It was an incredible affirmation that we were doing what we were supposed to be doing. (By the way, we adopted the updated constitution in June of that same year, and those who chose to leave are involved in other churches.)

I tell you this story because no matter how hot the conflict becomes, God will redeem it for His purposes if you stay faithful to His call for your church and ministry. Never forget Paul's words born out of experience, "We also rejoice in our afflictions, because we know that affliction produces endurance, endurance produces proven character, and proven character produces hope" (Rom. 5:3-4). Like a wise coach God uses trials brought on by being faithful to His call on your life to build endurance into your ministry muscles. This ability to hold up under the strain of conflict results in "proven character" that will give you hope that will never fail you.

If you have experienced conflict in your church and/or ministry, relate to your mission outpost team some of these events. Share stories of affirmation and hope you received through the process. Whom have lost as friends during the process of change? Ask your mission outpost team to join you in prayer for healing your own hurt and to pray for those who are no longer part of your ministry.

You may want to make this leadership prayer by Richard Kriegbaum your own:

The loss we cannot control is bad enough, God, but how I hate it when we do it to ourselves. We try to function like a family, but when family members hurt each other, it is worse than if we did not care about each other at all. . . . We are doing everything we can to cover these human loses, but beyond money and time and kind words, there is still the pain and grief that you must heal. Have mercy on all the hurts and fears among us, including the pain we have inflicted upon ourselves. Oh, God, heal these wounds.[9]

HOPE FOR THE HURTING

Servant leadership is frontline leadership. It performs in the arena of change. It often finds itself patching wounds and covering sores more often than receiving the victor's trophy. Yet a servant leader who has been called by God will not be abandoned by God.

Paul's ministry of transition was played out through conflict, both relational and spiritual. His letters contain instructions on how the church should conduct itself when clashes occur in the fellowship. This advice is not theoretical but comes from real-life experiences. God's Word that comes to us has been hammered out on the anvil of a life submitted totally to Him.

Here are some ways you can find hope and healing in your ministry of transition.

Be humble; look out for others' interests. Paul's letter to the church in Philippi was one of his warmest. You can tell from the tone of the letter that they shared a deep friendship with him. Lydia, a dealer in purple cloth from the city of Thyatira, became a follower of Jesus there. Her home became a center of the missionary movement in that city (Acts 16:12-15). Philippi was where Paul and Silas were miraculously freed from prison while singing songs at midnight. This led to a public apology for the way Paul was treated and an opportunity for him to speak openly about Jesus (Acts 16:25-39).

When Paul wrote back to his friends, he wanted them to keep the fellowship he had known while he served with them. Take his three-point instruction at face value as advice for conducting yourself as a servant leader.

Read Philippians 2:3-4. Fill in the blanks below from the verses you have read.

"Do nothing out of _____ or _____" (v. 3).

Servant leaders in a ministry of transition must always check their pride at the door. To do something in order to win a competition against an opponent has no place in building the kingdom. Conceit is simply self-worship. If pride is my motivation, I will be the cause of conflict every time I make a move toward change. Do nothing, Paul says, that is motivated by these two relationship killers.

"In _____, consider others more _____ than yourselves" (v. 3).

Pride breeds conflict. Humility absorbs it. This hard proverb by Paul is the key to maneuvering through conflict. If you consider others more important than yourself, you will be able to hear them, understand them, and ultimately serve their need. The first principle of servant leadership from the life of Jesus is, "Servant leaders humble themselves and wait for God to exalt them."[10]

"Everyone should look out not only for his own interests, but also for the interests of _____" (v. 4).

Key Verse
*Do nothing out
of rivalry or conceit,
but in humility
consider others
as more important
than yourselves.
Everyone should look
out not only for his
own interests, but
also for the interests
of others.*
—Philippians 2:3-4

Even in the heat of conflict, the servant leader must have a keen sense of what others are wanting. If it's just about me and my stuff, people will not follow. On the other hand, if changes are clearly a response to the call and the leader is aware of the interests of everyone involved, chances for avoiding friendship-splitting conflict are much higher.

Which of the three pieces of instruction best fit your situation? Can these be applied to the church as a whole or to what you personally are experiencing now? When you have chosen one that applies to you or the church, write three things you can do to communicate the message and create its presence in your life.

Lead like a servant of Christ. Servant leaders struggle with the dilemma of when to serve and when to lead. Knowing when to do either one is the art of leading like a servant. Paul led like a servant of Christ. This was not hard for him because his heart had been taken by the love of Christ first. He knew his life was about living out Christ's mission first and then leading others to complete it with him. Paul knew clearly that following Jesus meant giving up social, religious, and intellectual status as valued by the world.

Dying and rising with Christ meant status reversal. In Paul's case, he deliberately stepped down in the world. We must not romanticize this choice. He felt the shame of it among his peers and potential patrons yet held it as a mark of his sincerity. Moreover, it played a critical role in the interplay of his life and thought. Tentmaking was critical, even central, to his life and message. His labor and ministry were mutually explanatory. Yet for most of us, "tentmaking" belongs in the realms of missionary journals and far-flung shores. As a model of ministry in the United States, Britain or Australia, it remains as unseemly to most of us as it did to the Corinthians. At best it is second best.[11]

Leading like a servant in the kingdom is not a trendy concept or an effort to soften definitions of leadership. Leading from a low or no position is the biblical model for how to lead as a follower of Jesus.

Paul's favorite word for his identity was "a slave of Christ" (Gal. 1:10). "Slave" translates the Greek word *doulos,* which was the lowest rung on the social ladder. *Doulos* slaves had no rights or privileges, only the will of their master. Paul was inspired by God to use this culturally relevant image of his day to portray his relationship to Christ and why he did what he did. Nothing else mattered. His position in Christ dictated that his only leadership style could be that of humble servant—humble because he had been bought by Christ and servant because he was given a task to do.

Servant leadership may still be a struggle for you and your team to grasp. Take some time in prayer to ask God to affirm your worth to Him. You have been bought at a high cost, but God has said you are worth it. Then pray again for God to affirm His purposes for you life and ministry. Ask that you lead toward that vision with a servant's heart.

Inspect your heart constantly (2 Cor. 2:4). Paul lived out his ministry from the center of his heart. He kept it sensitive and pliable toward those he served— even when they opposed him. For example, hear his heart when wrote the Corinthians, "For out of an extremely troubled and anguished heart I wrote to you with many tears—not that you should be hurt, but that you should know the abundant love I have for you" (2 Cor. 2:4) They had challenged his motives, his message, and his claim to know Jesus. Yet he remained loving toward them. Paul did not allow his heart to be wounded by their opposition or hardened by the conflicts.

Three things wound your heart if you do not continually listen to it and offer it to the care of others. Each of these enemies of an open, soft heart is a direct result of leading in transition.[12]

Cynicism wounds your heart because you lose your love for the possibilities the vision brings you. Whenever you fail to realize God's vision, you take one step further away from the faith that motivated you. You become caustic about even constructive criticism because it seems everyone criticizes you. Like a veteran police officer who has come to expect the worst in people, you begin to believe people's motives are always evil. You find it hard to trust others. You just tell others you are a realist who expects the best but plans for the worst. You begin to cut others down in order to protect your heart's expectations. You isolate yourself.

Cynicism can be overcome by finding a trusted group of advisors and listening with them to what others are saying. They can protect your heart as they take some of the barbs. Two are better than one when it comes to facing opposition.

Loneliness is a heart killer because you were created for community. I, like you, have heard the stories of leaders who have fallen morally. Several said loneliness was a major factor in their decisions to pursue intimacy with some-one other than their spouse. Leadership is a lonely position at times, but it does not mean you disconnect from people.

Leaders need friends like David needed Jonathan. Friends bring laughter, perspective, spiritual support, encouragement, and escape from the struggles of leading.[13] Friends fill the emptiness of loneliness so leaders can continue to lead.

Hardness kills your heart because a hardened heart in not sensitive to God or people. Experienced leaders call it "thick skin." I have even advised staff members to grow thicker skin to get through the constant complaints from one or two members. Leadership does require a certain amount of tenacity and nerves of steel. But you cannot lead like Jesus with a hardened heart. Empathy is a sign of a great leader. In order to make a wise call, you must empathize with others' feelings with an open heart.

Sometimes you can heal a hard heart with therapy. Healing may result from a sabbatical or counsel from a mentor. Healing a hard heart takes time. Seasons of rest and healing should be part of every servant leader's yearly schedule.

Take some time to inspect your heart. Are there signs of cynicism, loneliness, and hardness? If you need help in this, you may want to risk asking your mission outpost team what they have seen in you through the last meetings. What can you do to heal the hurts in your heart?

Forgive as the Lord forgave you (Col. 3:13). Forgiveness is the first step to healing hurts brought on by conflict. To forgive is to put your pride aside and enter the world of the one who offended you. It means giving up your right to be right. It means living like Jesus. It means washing the feet of the one who has betrayed you. Paul placed a high value on people working out differences among themselves. He believed that from a relationship *in* Christ one could live *like* Christ.

Friends fill the emptiness of loneliness so leaders can continue to lead.

In his letter to the church in Colosse, for example, he told his fellow followers of Jesus to accept and forgive anyone who has a complaint against them (Col. 3:13). Notice he did not say those who physically hit them or threw them in jail. He was talking about the most common reason for broken relationships: complaints against one another. Servant leaders in a ministry of transition have plenty of opportunities to forgive.

What was the benchmark for how to forgive? "Just as the Lord has forgiven you, so also you must forgive," he wrote. The standard for forgiving others is God's forgiveness toward us in Christ Jesus. Jesus set the bar for forgiveness when Peter wanted to know the limits of how many times he must forgive someone. Jesus answered with the multiple of 70 times 7 (Matt. 18:22). There is no end to God's forgiveness toward us; therefore, there should be no end to our forgiveness to others. Only pride prevents us from laying down our grudge against another.

Reggie McNeal observed that "one of the truest evidences of God's heart-shaping activity shows up in the leader during conflict. It is the presence of a forgiving heart." The ability to forgive is evidence that God has done what was necessary to "rid the heart of its cancer pockets of unforgiveness."[14] To lead like Jesus is to forgive those who wound you because you have been forgiven by the One you wounded by your rebellious acts toward Him.

If the Lord's forgiveness of your sins is the standard for how you should forgive others, how are you measuring up in forgiving others? Whom do you still need to forgive so you can be freed to continue to lead? Take time to ask Jesus Christ to penetrate your heart with His forgiveness so you can pass it on to those who have hurt you.

Leaders will be hurt by opponents and those with whom they lead. This is a reality. God has provided a way to heal those who have been hurt so they can continue to pursue the mission he has called them to complete.

AN UNSEEN INFLUENCE

When I get to heaven, one of the things I want to do is check out the DVD (or whatever our histories are stored on there) of my ministry as viewed from God's perspective. I want to see what God saw. I want to watch me like a father watches his son playing soccer in the high school state tournament. I want to see what people did outside the times we gathered in the buildings or in small groups. I want to see the spiritual forces at work on and in Legacy as we worked through the labor of birthing a fresh expression of the body of Christ. I want to do this from the safety of heaven. To see it now would be too over-whelming, or would it? What would it be like to read the motives of people's hearts? How differently would I act if God revealed the spiritual influences on this ministry? Whom would I spend my time with if I could see those who were men and women of integrity, not just who played the game on Sundays.

Servant leadership in a ministry of transition is a spiritual undertaking. If you neglect this truth, all the books and consultants on leading through change mean nothing. To plant or transition to a mission outpost is truly to establish an outpost of light in a world of darkness. You stand against forces of evil that destroy marriages, homes, and friendships. One reason servant leadership in the church is so difficult is that you and I are wrestling for the eternal destiny of people's lives. This isn't wrestling mania on Friday night cable television. It's the real deal. Hauerwas and Willimon exclaimed, "The writer to the Ephesians wrote these words [Eph. 6] 'in chains' (back then, Christians were given jail cells rather than T.V. shows). He told his congregation that, if you plan to follow Jesus, get ready for a real fight."[15]

Servant leaders called by God to transition a local church to a mission outpost must be aware that they interface with spiritual realities, not just orga-nizational ones. Yes, you are leading to change core values, attitudes, struc-tures, and environments, but you are also assailing forces of darkness that do not want your mission to succeed. Any leader who serves in ministry that directly impacts the hearts of people and helps to establish the presence of God in a specific locale enters the arena of spiritual conflict. Few manuals of change in the church address this reality, but it is part of being on mission with Christ.

Paul on Spiritual Conflict

Paul, the apostle, knew he wrestled with spiritual entities, and he led accord-ingly. As you read his letters, you see clearly that Satan was real to him and that he believed the evil one had something to do with many of the struggles he faced to complete his mission. He came face-to-face with evil spirits, rulers, powers, and structures.

Read 2 Corinthians 2:11; 11:14; 12:7; 1 Thessalonians 2:18; and Romans 16:20. Record how Paul describes Satan in each of these references below.

Paul knew his adversary to be one:
• who sought to outwit the children of God in order to prevent restoration in the body (2 Cor. 2:11).

Key Verse

For our battle is not against flesh and blood, but against the rulers, against the authorities, again the world powers of this darkness, against the spiritual forces of evil in the heavens. This is why you must take up your full armor of God.

—*Ephesians 6:12-13*

- who masqueraded as an angel of light (2 Cor. 11:14).
- who sent one of his messengers to physically torment Paul (2 Cor. 12:7).
- who stopped Paul from visiting the church in Thessalonica (1 Thess. 2:18).
- whom the God of peace would crush under the feet of His followers (Rom. 16:20).

Maybe Paul's most famous words about this reality are found in his letter to the Ephesians, where he fought the followers of the goddess Artemis (Acts 19:21-41).

Read Ephesians 1:20-23; 2:6-7; and 6:12. Write in your own words how Paul describes the power of Christ (1:20-23), what it means for you to be "in Christ" (2:6-7), and who are our true enemies (6:12).

Paul, inspired by the Holy Spirit, taught that the resurrected Christ sits in the heavens and is superior to any "ruler and authority, power and dominion, and every title given" (1:21). God has appointed Christ as "head over everything for the church" (1:23). Christ rules supreme over any spiritual entity. "In Christ," the one who trusts Jesus to be who He says He is and stakes his righteousness with God on the work of Christ on the cross, has been raised with Christ, and is "with Him in the heavens" (2:6). You and I who are "in Christ" share the spiritual authority of Christ over the same spiritual entities.

Paul instructed those who experienced the riot against the craftsman's guild with him in Ephesus that the battle is not against people "but against the rulers, against the authorities, against the world powers of this darkness, against the spiritual forces of evil in the heavens" (6:12). This is why, he writes, you must wear spiritual armor when you head into ministry every day.

Paul knew that the riot in Ephesus may have appeared to be against tradesmen who were upset that Paul and his companions may have jeopardized their profits—this is the sociological explanation. But he knew through revelation and experience that a spiritual reality was at work in that town that day. The battle that day was not against Demetrius and his fellow silversmiths. It was against the "world powers of this darkness" that had come over the city through worship to a false god.

What incidents have happened in your life or ministry that you could/do attribute to spiritual influences beyond the usual explanations for the event? Record them in your journal.

Addressing the Powers

My experience and Bible study have combined to show me that the spiritual powers we face as spiritual leaders are real and must be addressed when facing changes among the people of God. The church is as vulnerable to spiritual influence by the "world powers of this darkness" as any other organization. The church, as an organization of people, can be dominated by evil spiritual influences as well as by godly ones. To ignore that the outer expression of the church cannot become the place for evil spiritual entities is to ignore the true nature of what you are as the church.

Building upon the study of Walter Wink on Paul's use of "power" in the New Testament,[16] I have come to the conviction that "ruler and authority, power and dominion, and every title given" are not evil by nature. They are manifestations of spiritual realities and can be ruled by Christ or by evil. Churches, nations, and economies share "inner" and "outer" manifestations of power. Like other organizations, churches manifest their inner spiritual condition in their outer expressions of government and focus. Government is about the power of control or release. Focus is about the power of self-centered or other-centered hearts. A church can either be about controlling people for the interests of maintaining the organization or releasing them for the purposes of God. A church can have its focus on pleasing those who are "in" or serving anyone who has a need.

Wink concludes, "The church's task is to unmask this idolatry [when a particular power places itself above God's purposes for the good of the whole] and recall the Powers to their created purposes in the world—'so that the Sovereignties and Powers should learn only now, through the Church, how comprehensive God's wisdom really is' (Eph. 3:10 JB)." The church is the body of Christ, of which he is the head (Eph. 1:22). But how that church executes its authority to decide and its power to rule differs, depending on the hearts of the people in those positions of power and authority.

Remember the story of the fired pastor at the beginning of this session? When I first read his e-mail, I knew what was going on there was not just three grumpy old men who wanted a new pastor. That church had come to be ruled by "power" that had turned its back on the purposes of God. It had become what some power brokers liked, wanted, and controlled, not what God wanted to accomplish through the called-out ones.

Erwin MacManus had a similar experience when he sat in the office of a chairman of finance who had decided to fire the pastor the week of Christmas. He tried to intervene with Scripture and a heartfelt plea to hear the teachings of Jesus. He directly asked the chairman if he realized that he was consciously opposing the teachings of Jesus. The instigator calmly said, "Yes." Shocked, MacManus asked again, and the man answered that he knew he was disobeying Christ and was preceding with his plans. MacManus concluded, "When those who hold positions of leadership in the church of Jesus Christ stand opposed to the very heart of God and refuse to submit their lives to his Word, it is the death of the life of that church."[17]

John Eldredge tells how you can assess "The Spirit of Religion" in your church: "If it doesn't bring freedom and it doesn't bring life, it's not Christianity. If it doesn't restore the image of God and rejoice in the heart, it's not Christianity."[18]

How would you describe your church? Do people seem to pay more attention to the wants and wishes of a few, or do they exhibit the presence of Christ? Is your church's government about controlling or releasing people to ministry? Is your church's focus inward or outward?

The Resilient Church

Although Satan and his forces seek to stop the movement of Jesus, they will not have the final victory. The enemies of God know their fate, and all they can do is wreak a little havoc now. The day will come when they will be utterly destroyed and the church will reign eternally as the bride of Christ. Every servant leader in the church of the Lord Jesus Christ should serve with the certainty that he or she is on the winning side. The victory of war is certain. But like coalition forces in Iraq after the victory of removing the dictator from power, soldiers are still killed by resistance forces who fight for the days when they were in power.

The church will not fail. No force on earth or heaven can stop its movement as the instrument of God's purposes. We must never forget Jesus'

The church will not fail. No force on earth or heaven can stop its movement as the instrument of God's purposes.

promise to Peter: "I will build My church, and the forces of Hades will not overpower it" (Matt. 16:18). Not even the forces from the headquarters of the evil one can make a dent on the church of Christ. The church is resilient and will not be stopped until its Head returns and establishes His rule.

Paul declared that death itself has no victory over the person "in Christ" (1 Cor. 15:55-57). His doxology in Romans 8 states that no spiritual power, "neither angels nor demons, neither the present nor the future, nor any powers," can come between a follower of Jesus and his love (Rom. 8:38, NIV). These come from a man who had encountered great difficulties and had seen God victorious in every case (2 Cor. 4:8-9).

The church is the bride of Christ, but there will be always be conflict in it. Why? Like a general who gives the opposing military leader his plan of attack, God has given Satan his strategy for reconciling the world to Himself: the church. And like a conniving field marshal, Satan continually attacks and misdirects God's people in order to keep them from accomplishing their mission: being God's instruments to reach the hearts of others. A church without conflict of some kind is a church not impacting the world for Christ. Servant leaders accept this fact and lead accordingly.

What is your confidence level that you and your leaders serve in a spiritual reality that cannot fail if they are in tune with its Leader, Jesus Christ? Do you see yourself and those who serve with you as part of a victorious band of believers whom God has chosen for His purposes?

Journal for the Journey

One morning during a season of conflict, I was reading the Bible's instructions to put on the armor of God (Eph. 6:11). The reason Paul calls Christ's followers to do this is "so that you can stand against the tactics of the Devil." The Greek word for "tactics" here is the word from which we get our English word *methods*. I paused and made a list of the devil's methods I had recently encountered. I entitled the entry, "How Satan Works."

Stabs in the back and runs (Mass distribution e-mail is one way to do this.)
Half-truths (For example, no cross as a piece of furniture in the worship center means Christ is not there.)
Red herrings (If there is no come-down-front invitation, it means the church is not evangelistic.)
Fear of the unknown (Longtime Christians fear lost tradition and loss of reputation among their church friends.)
Distrust bred through falsehoods
Rumors, "Did you know?"
"He said. She said."
Traditions used to limit rather than enhance growth
Constitution and bylaws used to impede effectiveness rather than enhance it

You can certainly add to your own list of tactics. Every one of these "diabolical methods" (another translation of "tactics of the Devil") can be overcome by truth, character, and the powerful presence of Christ in His body, the church. Do not fear, for in the end the church will triumph, and you will stand victorious in the matters of God.

In our next session we will observe the power of shared leadership. We will see how Paul lived in team and how he accomplished his mission by selecting, coaching, and releasing leaders to join him in the mission to make disciples of all people.

1. *Church Administration,* Spring 2003, 10-13.

2. *Jew* is used in this workbook to be consistent with the biblical record. It in no way is intended to be a racial slur to Jews today. Jesus was a Jew. Paul was a Jew. The Jews who opposed the mission to the ethnics could be interpreted as "traditionalists" today. Baptists, Presbyterians, Methodists, and Catholics can be inserted wherever Jews are mentioned in the Acts text as people who oppose God's fresh work among them.

3. I use *opposition* to refer to those who oppose transition from outside the movement. For example, the Jews opposed Paul's insistence on "grace alone" for the ethnics. Conflict here is between those in the movement who war over issues related to the mission. For example, Paul and Barnabas separated as a result of their conflict over taking John Mark on their second trip.

4. Ronald A. Heifetz and Marty Linsky, *Leadership on the Line* (Cambridge: Harvard Business School, 2002), 12.

5. Alan Roxburgh's term, Alan Roxburgh and Mike Regele, *Crossing the Bridge* (Costa Mesa, CA: Precept, 2000).

6. C. Gene Wilkes, *Jesus on Leadership* (Nashville: LifeWay, 1996), 66-67.

7. Alan Nelson and Gene Appel, *How to Change Your Church Without Killing It* (Nashville: Word Publishing, 2000), 227.

8. John B. Polhill, *Paul and His Letters* (Nashville: Broadman & Holman, 1999), 257.

9. Richard Kriegbaum, *Leadership Prayers* (Carol Stream, IL: Tyndale House Publishers, 1998), 34-35.

10. C. Gene Wilkes, *Jesus on Leadership* (Carol Stream, IL: Tyndale House Publishers, 1998), 33.

11. Mark Strom, *Reframing Paul* (Downers Grove, IL: InterVarsity Press, 2000), 17.

12. See Heifetz and Linsky, *Leadership on the Line,* who describe how cynicism, arrogance, and callousness cover the innocence, curiosity, and compassion of a "sacred heart" (226-7).

13. "Healthy Friendships: Life Preservers in the Storm," in *LeaderLife,* Fall 2003.

14. Reggie McNeal, *A Work of Heart* (Indianapolis, IN: Jossey-Bass, 2000), 173.

15. Stanley Hauerwas and William H. Willimon, *Resident Aliens* (Nashville: Abingdon, 1989), 150.

16. Walter Wink, *Naming the Powers* (Minneapolis MN: Fortress Press, 1986), 5; Walter Wink, *Unmasking the Powers* (Minneapolis MN: Fortress Press, 1984); and *Engaging the Powers* (Minneapolis MN: Fortress Press, 1992).

17. Erwin Raphael McManus, *An Unstoppable Force* (Loveland, CO: Group, 2001), 35.

18. John Eldredge, *Waking the Dead: The Glory of a Heart Fully Alive* (Nashville: Thomas Nelson, 2003), 163.

SHARED LEADERSHIP

This week you will:

- Examine the art of shared leadership.
- Be introduced to the sixth reality of servant leadership in a ministry of transition.
- Observe ways to find and keep leaders.
- Examine leadership in Paul's letters.
- Learn about the depth of relationships shared leadership can offer.

A 13-year-old eighth-grader stood before thousands to sing the national anthem. It was before the third game between the Dallas Mavericks and the Portland Blazers in the 2003 NBA's postseason playoffs. Natalie Gilbert from Lake Oswego, Oregon, had won a contest to sing before the sold-out crowd and on national television. She had sung the song at other professional games, and she had never faltered. This day, however, she was singing well into the anthem when she suddenly forgot the words. She tried to start where she left off, but she just couldn't remember the words. Maybe it was because she had the flu and had been sick in bed all day. Maybe it was just stage fright. Whatever the cause, the sold-out Rose Garden arena was awkwardly quiet. She turned to look for her father, but he could do nothing. She stood alone in the spotlight.

The Blazer's coach, Maurice Cheeks, stepped into center court beside her and began to sing. A solo, off-key male voice began to sing the familiar song. Next the thin, soprano teenage voice joined in. Soon the crowd was wailing away, and everyone finished the song together. Wild applause followed. You would have thought it was the greatest rendition of "The Star Spangled Banner" ever.

"I didn't even know if I knew all the words, but as many times as I've heard the national anthem, I just went over and continued to sing," Cheeks told CBS *SportsLine*. "The words started coming back to me, and I just tried to help her out."

"It helped me a lot. It made me feel more comfortable," Gilbert said in a CNN interview. "It was just like having a huge choir of 20,000 people around you just singing a great patriotic song."[1]

Shared leadership saved the day that afternoon in the Portland Rose Garden Arena. Natalie was the positional leader who had been given the task to sing the song, but she faltered. Coach Cheeks did what coaches do: he came alongside a struggling team member and encouraged her by singing along. Cheeks's background was basketball, not singing, but when the need arose, he did what instinctively came to him as a coach. He stepped in and assisted.

Servant leaders in a ministry of transition falter. They forget the words to the vision song. They stand with sweat running down their backs while thousands stand stunned waiting for the next words to come out of their mouths. They need someone to step onto center court with them and prompt their next words. The only way this save will happen is if the servant leader is surrounded by other servant leaders who share the same vision and are willing to step up in a moment of crisis.

Jesus modeled the principle of servant leadership, "Servant leaders multiply their leadership by empowering others to lead."[2] Jesus invested His life into the twelve disciples so that His mission as Suffering Servant Messiah would continue after He ascended into heaven. While he never faltered under pressure, he demonstrated the power of shared leadership to complete the mission. Those who follow Him will lead this way.

Paul, Jesus' apostle, followed his leader's example. Paul always had other servant leaders with him. He survived conflict and expanded the influence of his message and mission through leaders he had appointed and trained. Paul's effectiveness to carry the message of Jesus to the ethnics would not have been what it was without his shared leadership.

Day 1

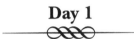

SERVANT LEADERSHIP IS SHARED LEADERSHIP

I received this e-mail from a friend who had served as a pastoral intern at Legacy and now was serving as an associate pastor in another church. He had faced some leadership challenges related to changes the church was facing. He wrote:

> In the process of leading Legacy, has there ever been a time amidst all the second-guessing by others when you started second-guessing your own decisions and even your decision-making process? These were decisions you knew within you were right when you made them. Decisions that were made with all the confidence you had when you started leading. But then . . . as a result of all the questions others had about your leadership and decision-making ability, you began to question your own leadership abilities and decisions?
>
> For the first time in my life (OK so I'm not so old), I have begun questioning my own decisions and my decision-making process. I don't have the same confidence I have had in the past. While this may be where God wants me, this is brand-new territory for me. I'm not sure I know what to do now. I'm not sure about my leadership ability or my decision making. It has created a great deal of anxiety within me. I have never been questioned before, or at least not at the level I am experiencing now.

This is a leader standing in the spotlight not sure he can finish the song he has been asked to sing. His knees are wobbling, and he—like every leader—has come to the place of questioning his ability to lead. Yes, I told him, I had times of second-guessing my decisions and questioning my own leadership abilities and decisions. I welcomed him to the school of servant leadership in a ministry of transition.

Have you ever felt like this ministry leader? When and what were the circumstances? What advice would you give this young leader? Write your advice in the margin. Be prepared to tell your story and share your advice at your next mission outpost team gathering.

Shared Leadership Is the Key

Leading into new territories, constant questions, and open resistance can cause any leader to wonder whether he or she can truly lead. Much of leadership is self-motivation mixed with God-empowered effort, but a leader cannot leverage his greatest influence until he shares his leadership with others. Shared leadership is the key to accomplishing the mission and achieving the vision God has given you.

Paul modeled this reality. If we pick up where we left off following Paul on his mission to the ethnics, we find him returning to the churches he planted on his first trip with Barnabas into southern Galatia. Along the way he added people to his team with whom he shared leadership in the movement.

Read Acts 16:1-3, 11-15, 40. Whom did Paul add to his ministry when he returned to Lystra, the place of his stoning on his first journey? Whom did he add to the local leadership when he came to Philippi?

As Paul began his second trip to visit the churches he had planted with Barnabas, he took with him Silas (Acts 15:40). Silas had come from Jerusalem to carry the decision of the Jerusalem leaders to the church in Antioch. After Paul and Barnabas parted ways, Silas joined Paul as a partner in ministry. Paul intentionally added Timothy to his team when he arrived in Lystra (Acts 16:3). Timothy's heritage as the son of a Jewish mother and Greek father suited this mission to the ethnics well. Paul circumcised him, making his Jewish heritage complete, and made him a member of the traveling team. A result was "so the churches were strengthened in the faith and were increased in number daily" (v. 5).

While in Philippi, Lydia became a follower of Jesus (Acts 16:11-15). Paul did not choose to add her to the team he traveled with, but her home became a primary meeting place for the church there (vv. 15,40).

Paul continually added members to his team and shared his leadership with them. He added Aquila and Priscilla to his team when he was in Corinth (Acts 18:1-4). He took them to Ephesus with him after a season of on-the-job training in the marketplace of Corinth. Paul left them to strengthen the church in this major city as he continued to travel. In Ephesus these two leaders enhanced the ministry of young Apollos by inviting him into their home and "explained the way of God to him more accurately" (Acts 18:26).

Wherever you find Paul, you find a team of leaders who shared the leadership of the mission with him. Read the end of his letters to the churches in Rome, Ephesus, Colosse, and Philippi. Even in his personal letters to Timothy and Titus, he asks his apprentices to greet those in partnership with him. Paul's letters are a catalog of names and stories of people with whom he shared the mission to the ethnics.

Shared Leadership

Paul's example of shared leadership is the basis of our sixth reality of servant leadership in a ministry of transition:

Reality 6: Servant leaders ensure that their God-given mission continues through shared leadership (see Acts 16–21:17).

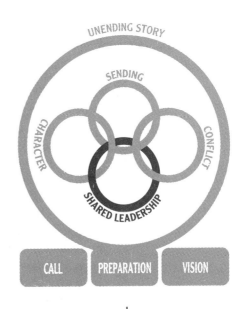

Servant leaders who have made the mission call of God on their lives the primary purpose for all they do share their leadership with others to ensure that the mission will continue even when they are absent. Paul established leadership in every church he started on his journeys. The mission to the ethnics continued even after his death because he planted leaders when he planted churches. Selecting those with whom you share your leadership is crucial.

Team Members That Make a Difference

How do you know with whom to share your leadership? The answer to this question is crucial to your effectiveness in ministry. As you plan to put your team together to accomplish a need or goal related to the mission, remember that Paul was not always 100 percent successful in his selections. Take Demas, for example. In his letter to Philemon regarding his runaway slave, Onesimus, Paul called Demas his "fellow worker" along with Luke (Philem. 24). During his greetings to the churches in Colosse, he simply mentioned Demas with no adjective describing his relationship to Paul (Col. 4:14). In his second letter to Timothy while in Rome, Paul asked his apprentice to come to him quickly "for Demas has deserted me, because he loved this present world" (2 Tim. 4:10). This disciple gradually fell away from the mission he shared with Paul. According to Paul, he was lost to the lure of this age. The mission became too hard for him to handle. He sought safer pastures. We know of at least these two whom Paul chose for his team who abandoned him, John Mark and Demas.

> **Who on your team has either faded away like Demas or simply quit like John Mark? How did it make you feel? What kind of damage did it do to the momentum of your efforts? Write your experience in your journal.**

I have had a lay leader fade away after counseling me to make a change in staff. He encouraged the decision to make the change, but when he saw the pain of the situation and got some opposition from other members, it was not long before he had resigned his leadership position and moved to another church. He was courageous enough to decide but not strong enough to live with the decision. Demas may have been like that.

Bill Hybels has discovered three *C*s of team selection. They are character, competence, and chemistry.[4]

Character we will discuss more fully in the last session of this workbook. For Hybels it means, "I need to have confidence in a person's walk with Jesus Christ. I need to know that they are committed to spiritual disciplines. I need to see evidence of honesty, teachability, humility, reliability, a healthy work ethic, and a willingness to be entreated." When I have followed this advice, I have always found team members who have never failed in character-related matters. On the other hand, if I overlook any of these traits, trouble has followed in small and major ways.

Competence at the highest level is his second *C* of team selection. I discovered several years ago that I tended to hire people who needed Legacy. My personality is to help those who need it, and I often tried to match their

Reality 6: Servant leaders ensure that their God-given mission continues through shared leadership.

needs to ours. I thought I could train them to be high-caliber members of the team. I convinced myself they just needed some guidance and help. Unlike stock performance, when it comes to people, past performance is an indicator of future results. In the high-stakes work to make disciples, on-the-job training is for interns, not team members who share leadership. I always get counsel when seeking to add team members now.

Chemistry for Hybels is "a relational fit with me as well as with other team members."[5] He writes that he never adds a team member who doesn't have a positive emotional effect on him when he or she walks into his office. He has become a "convert" to this advice from a mentor, and it has provided for him team members he loves leading. A major struggle for me on staff teams in particular has been when a team member does not react well with the others on the team. He or she may be more resistant to new ideas than the others or may be more restrained when it comes to open conflict around ideas. Whatever the case, even when one on the team does not match the chemistry of the rest of the team, that team will never reach its full potential.

Hybels' advice matches Nanus and Dodd's instruction that "the fine art of team building requires selecting the right people with the right skills, positioning them so that they can make their greatest contributions, and fostering their sense of mutual responsibility for achieving the organization's mission and vision."[6]

How do your team members measure up to Hybels' three Cs? Pick a team with whom you share your leadership. Assess the character, competence, and chemistry of each team member. You may want to do this in confidence with a trusted leader or keep your assessment to yourself. This will not be new information to you. You have felt this before; you now have a word to go along with what you were feeling. As you assess the team, ask God to guide your emotions and thoughts as you seek ways to have the right people in the right places.

FINDING AND KEEPING LEADERS[7]

Larry and Wendy are the kind of leaders you pray for. They are truly missionaries in the marketplace whose hearts had been captured by God. Larry served as a small group leader and our deacon team leader. Wendy served in our creative arts and children's ministries, and she was a member of our first church leadership team. In the 13 years Larry and Wendy were on mission at Legacy, both proved to be essential leaders.

Larry and Wendy were servant leaders who embodied the mission and vision of Legacy. While they did fill some high-profile leadership positions, their greatest contribution was their behind-the-scenes leadership that provided stability in chaotic times and momentum in days of opportunity. Larry and Wendy were transferred to another mission field. Like Paul and the elders at Ephesus, we cried when we said our good-byes. We had shared something incredible, and we knew things would not be the same again. As they packed and moved on, I knew my leadership was weakened by their absence. My first prayer after they left was, "Lord, where am I to find leaders like that again?"

Good leaders find and keep other leaders. They know that effectiveness in ministry rises and falls on leadership. No matter how well you plan and communicate a new ministry, it will fail without an effective leader in place. Without others leading alongside them, leaders know they will never accomplish the God-sized opportunities offered them. Servant leaders know that to complete the mission they have been given by God they must find mission-driven, vision-drawn leaders like themselves. The process of finding and keeping those men and women is at the heart of leading a church on mission.

Your Best Team

Most of us have played or worked on a team. Some were better than others, but you may have been on a team that really was a team. The people you worked with became more than just fellow workers. They became friends. The work was meaningful, and you wished the experience would never end.

If you have been on such a team, describe that experience in the space below. Describe the purpose or goal of the team. Describe some of the people on the team and why the experience was so special to you. Be prepared to share this with your mission outpost team the next time you meet.

A common question among leaders is, how do you find and keep the leaders you need to accomplish the needs and goals related to your mission? Here are some realities I have discovered in building a leadership base for ministry.

Finding Them

Leaders are doers. They get a jolt out of gathering a group of people to take a hill or create a new ministry to meet the needs of those on their mission field. What do you look for in a leader? Here's a list to begin your search.

Key Verse
*This saying is trustworthy: "If anyone aspires to be an overseer, he desires a noble work."
—1 Timothy 3:1*

"The important thing about being a leader—it's what happens when you are not there."[8]
—Ken Blanchard

Shared vocabulary does not ensure shared mission.

1. Look for a servant heart. Leaders are usually self-motivated people with high expectations and skills to accomplish goals. You want these people on your team—unless they do not have a servant's heart. Ego must be replaced with a love for God and others, or you will spend more time dealing with this leader's pride than those in your care. You want a leader whose heart has been captured by the mission call of God. Observe a potential leader in ministry prior to asking him to lead. Is he a team player? Does he serve those around him in order to make them better leaders? Or does he insist he be the only leader who gets all the credit?

2. Look for shared mission and vision. As you seek leaders to team with, make certain those you invite to join you share your same mission and vision. Your potential leaders must know and share not only the wording of your mission but also its implications. Shared vocabulary does not ensure shared mission. Spend as much time listening to the potential leader's description of your mission as you spend describing it to him. The same is true with vision. Potential leaders cannot lead others to the same future as you if they can't see what you see. Be clear and single in your picture of where you are leading. Otherwise, natural leaders will lead to their own preferred future.

I cannot strongly stress enough how important it is to press down to the potential leader's core perception of what you are trying to accomplish. You can share your leadership with someone over a period of months without knowing they really have something different in mind while they lead. You must spend time up front drilling down into their values, impressions, and personal picture of what you have asked them to do. Otherwise, you will pay the price later on when you have to ask them to relinquish their leadership and rein back the group they were leading.

Passion is the fuel of leadership.

3. Look for passion and giftedness. Passion comes from a commitment to a clear vision. Look for leaders whose eyes light up when they talk about the vision of your church. Passion is the fuel of leadership. Without it leaders waiver and lose their way while others follow. Listen to the increased speed of their words when they talk about what they are passionate about. Watch their facial expressions as they tell you what is written on their hearts. If they are talking about something unrelated to your vision, know you will have trouble changing their passion about what they want to do.

Giftedness is the result of the Holy Spirit empowering people to lead in the body of Christ. Look for people with the spiritual gift of leadership first. Release them into ministries where they can flourish in their giftedness. Seek, too, those who may have supportive gifts that are essential to doing the work of mission. One way to discover this about a potential leader is to complete a SERVE Profile[9] for them.

4. Commit to your leader's success. People will lead if they know they are supported. When you find a leader who matches a need related to the mission and he passionately shares your vision, offer him a clear path for his development and specific avenues of support. Intentional leadership development is required for effective shared leadership. True leaders will insist on resources and support. One way you serve those on mission with you is to support them.

I have committed to my staff that my service to them is to give direction and resources. They will succeed if I provide them with those two things. Without these items the team does not know where the goal line is and will not have necessary resources to get there. My team of ministry directors keeps me accountable to my commitment to them by letting me know if the direction is not clear or if they do not have the resources they need.

Review the four suggestions for finding leaders. Pick a potential leader you have been considering for a place of ministry and assess his or her readiness based on the suggestions above. Does she have a servant's heart? Does she share your mission and vision? What is her passion and giftedness for ministry? Do her passion and giftedness fit what you are asking her to do? What are some ways you can let her know you are committed to her success as a leader?

Keeping Them

When you have leaders who are on mission and are passionately pursuing your shared vision, how do you keep them on your team?

1. Equip them for the initiative they lead. Give your leaders the resources and training they need to be effective. This is the implementation of the promise you made when you recruited them. When they sign up to lead the part of the mission you have offered them, you should be ready to train them in the specific skills they may not have to succeed. Untrained leaders will fall back on their own skill sets to get things done. This can be helpful at times but more often creates haphazard results. Tell them what you need them to do. Teach them how to do it.

2. Help them build a team. Leaders influence others to accomplish goals. A true leader's influence can be multiplied in teams. Working in ministry teams is the most powerful way to do God's work. Be careful to guide those leaders who believe they can go it alone to see the value and practice of team.

This is a constant struggle with highly motivated leaders. They truly do not believe they need a team around them to lead well. This is a misconception on their part. What is needed is a "synergistic leader" who can maximize the assets of the team members to accomplish its mission. Alan Roxburgh reminds us, "The idea of synergistic leadership relates to the functioning of a team of leaders with very different skills working together through the skills of a synergistic leader. . . . The team typology, combining a mixture of leadership qualities, allows the energies and skills of people to be appropriately released and empowered for the transition and transformation of churches."[10]

3. Celebrate, encourage, and say, "Thank you!" Leaders are people, too. They need encouragement and thanks like everyone else. Celebrate their successes in creative ways. Encourage them often, for leadership is a long journey. Always say "thank you" because they are investing themselves in the mission you invited them to live out. You cannot put a price tag on the value of thank you to those with whom you lead. Cheers and applause are appropriate responses to a job well done. Personal pats on the back and a "way to go!" go a long way to encourage volunteer leaders to continue with you.

4. Give leaders a season of rest to recharge. Leaders can't go on forever. While most genuine leaders are self-motivated, they can burn out in the rigors of leading others. Jesus found times to get away. Even the Son of man needed times alone with the Father for prayer and rest from the drain of ministry. Jesus told His disciples to do the same. Such a retreat was the context of feeding the five thousand. Sometimes the demands of the follower means setting aside time for the leader; but that time must come, or you will lose your greatest asset to completing what you have been called to do, a committed leader.

Time away breeds vitality and freshness in leaders. Time away gives them new perspectives to scenery they see week after week. Time away says, "I value you and want you to care for your soul."

A true leader's influence can be multiplied in teams.

109

Which of these four suggestions are you doing to keep the leaders you have? Review the list and rate your self on your effectiveness with each one, with 1 as the lowest level of effectiveness and 5 as the highest.

1 2 3 4 5   1. Equip them for the initiative they lead.
1 2 3 4 5   2. Help them build a team.
1 2 3 4 5   3. Celebrate, encourage and say, "Thank you!"
1 2 3 4 5   4. Give leaders a season of rest to recharge.

Return to the lowest ranked items and write one idea to improve that area of supporting your leaders.

Finding and keeping the right leaders to lead with you in a ministry of transition are essential steps to accomplishing what God has put on your heart to do.

Day 3

THE LEADERSHIP PRINCIPLE

"The day of the professional minister is over. The day of the missionary pastor has come." Callahan's axiom disturbed me. I am a "trained professional" who has invested thousands of dollars to become a certified minister in the local church. My resume reads well for those looking for a seasoned professional to fill executive positions in an institutional church. My educational pedigree plays well in the halls of established churches and religious institutions. If Callahan's prophetic words were true, all that money and work would mean nothing to help me fund my retirement years.

I have come to discover that those who have not been raised in the institutional church or who have left it or who despise it care little if anything about my certification to be a minister of the gospel. They want to know only that I can help them with their life's deepest needs. Most often that begins with serving the needs of life that plague them every day. They know what authoritarian leadership feels like every day in their offices. They sort through enough images and sound bites every nanosecond looking for truth that applies to their lives. They don't want another authority in their lives. They want to know that you care for them and that you believe what you say without blinking. They want to see life change, and they want it for themselves. While it may impress a pulpit search committee, my ability to read the textual apparatus at the bottom of a Greek text means nothing to those seeking help for life's needs from the church. Missionary pastors know this and lead with this reality in mind.

The loss of status by the American pastor/leader outside the church world draws us closer to Paul's experience. The pastors of a generation ago were civic leaders as well as church leaders. They were often the most educated and sophisticated men in the town. Yes, Christians still have celebrities, who are known by those who buy their books and videos and who go on their cruises and to their conferences. You can argue that the American pastor still has status in our culture. I would agree. But few can capture the cultural psyche with books and ideas that speak to a human need or desire.

I also share the belief that God legitimately raises godly pastors to be an influence at a national level for His purposes. Pastors of presidents, corporation leaders, and university campuses still influence people of prominence. God has put these leaders where they are for His purposes. But most pastors in urban centers and the outlands beyond the Bible Belt find themselves less and less influential in their communities. Now I am not crying over the fact that no one pays attention to the paid professional preacher any more. Actually, I like the loss of status. It frees us up to reform who we are and how we are seen among the ethnics where we live and serve. This loss of status puts us closer to how leaders among Christ followers led in the ancient culture of the New Testament.

How have you observed the status of the American pastor or leader changing in your lifetime? What does that signal to you about spiritual leadership in this culture? in the church? Be prepared to share your feelings with your mission outpost team at your next gathering.

Professional Versus No Status

Paul never claimed leadership status for himself. Just the opposite was true. He made sure people knew that he accepted nothing for his efforts, and his highest calling was to be a slave of Jesus Christ. Paul lived in a world where status equaled leadership, and he continually challenged that belief with his writings and example. Mark Strom observed, "While the Corinthians pushed Paul to assume the role and social presence of a leader, he pushed in the opposite direction, making servile labor the dominant image for every expression of talent and role."[11]

Paul downsized his leadership status when he left the ranks of the Pharisees to be a traveling tent maker. His religious peers surely could not have understood such a move and must have added to their frustration of his constant call to service in love. Most leaders move up the ladder of success, not step off it completely like Paul.

Paul baffled his opponents and peers when he claimed, "But *everything* that was gain to me, I have considered to be a loss because of Christ. More than that, I also consider *everything* to be a loss in view of the surpassing value of knowing Christ Jesus my Lord" (Phil. 3:7-8, author's italics). We too often spiritualize Paul's confession, but his losses were real. He took his diplomas off the wall and sold his religious regalia in a garage sale. He severed ties with his professional network. Paul devalued everything that mattered as a leader in the institution of the Jewish faith in order to pursue Christ's calling on his life. And he called others to follow his example.

Read 1 Corinthians 3:5-9. What does Paul call Apollos and himself? How did Paul describe their part in planting the church in Corinth? Write your thoughts in the margin.

The church in Corinth was divided over several issues. One was the issue of leadership. Some said they followed Paul. Others were loyal to the younger pastor Apollos. Still others claimed Peter and Christ were their leaders (1 Cor. 1:12; 3:4). This same reason for divisions still exists in churches today. Paul, however, explained that leaders in the church were simply "servants through whom" people trusted Christ (1 Cor. 3:5, NIV).

Each leader had specific roles in helping to plant and to grow the church.

Paul planted and Apollos watered. But God was the one who caused them to grow (v. 6). Paul shared servant leadership with the young, fiery Apollos. He saw Apollos and Peter as "co-workers" (v. 9), not rival leaders like the people in the church saw them.

Paul named his coworkers, the *sunergoi* of his ministry, in several of his letters. Priscilla and Aquila were "co-workers in Christ Jesus" (Rom. 16:3). John Mark and Justus were also among Paul's band of *sunergoi* (Col. 4:11). These who "worked together" shared victory, loss, and pain of leading people to know Christ and to grow into His likeness. They shared servant leadership to accomplish the mission to the ethnics.

Name two coworkers in your ministry. Describe why you consider them to be coworkers. Tell your mission outpost team.

Leadership in Paul's Churches

"Paul's letters provide no model of church structure or lines of authority. He has no 'doctrine' of church or leadership."[12] Alan Roxburgh observed that "in these early years of the church's development, diverse leadership roles were in operation. These roles seemed to be highly flexible and situational. They were not so much formalized identities within a well-defined organization, as functions that operated in order to facilitate and move forward the mission of the church. . . . Some were operative through a single person, but most spread through an array of vivid and varied personalities."[13]

What can we glean from Paul's letters that would comprise "Paul on leadership"? Here are some—not exclusive—major emphases throughout his writings that help us see the nature of leadership he modeled and taught.

Christ is head of the church. You start and end here when you describe leadership in the church. No person, group, or organization is head of Christ's body, the church. Christ alone is head (Col. 1:18). The implication of this truth is that any leader among God's people must submit to Christ in order to lead in the right direction and with the right set of values. No servant leader would ever act or speak in contradiction to Christ's teachings and actions.

Multiple leaders lead. Paul recognized a plurality of leaders in the church. His lists are always plural unless he addresses one as part of the whole. He claimed that apostles, prophets, evangelists, pastors, and teachers were to equip members of the body for works of service (Eph. 4:11). Elders were to "direct the affairs of the church" (1 Tim. 5:17, NIV) and be held to standards of character (Titus 1:6), but Paul did not consider these in a position of status. He saw them serving in functional roles to build up and serve the body. Shared leadership among multiple leaders is Paul's preference. All are equal (1 Cor. 3:8).

Giftedness is the basis for any role in the church. Paul placed his highest value on giftedness from the Holy Spirit as the basis for one's place in the church. He carefully outlined for the arguing Christians in Corinth how spiritual giftedness was the way people found their functional role in the church. God appointed in the church apostles, prophets, teachers, and others to serve the body through the Holy Spirit's work of gifting (1 Cor. 12). There was no hierarchy of positions, but spiritually gifted people serving out of their giftedness for the common good of the body.

Authority is from Christ Jesus, the head of the church. Paul's authority was from Christ and Christ alone. He argued passionately that his authority did not come from any other person or group of people recognized as leaders (Gal. 1:15-24). This authority apart from others did not give him license to rule over others. In the defense of his apostleship, he wrote, "So 'the one who boasts must boast in the Lord.' For it is not the one commending himself who is approved, but the one the Lord commends" (2 Cor. 10:17-18). The "name of Jesus" was all the authority any disciple needed to be on mission with Christ who called him.

Character, godliness, and evidence of the presence of the Spirit are marks of leadership. Paul provided lists of characteristics of servants and leaders in the church so his apprentices would know the kind of people with whom to share their leadership (for example, 1 Tim. 3:1-7). These lists are not exhaustive, nor were they intended to be legalistic ledgers of piety. They are portraits of people to whom the church could point and say, "That person is what we are talking about when we talk about being a follower of Jesus." Servants and leaders among God's people are to be people of godly character and have evidence of the Holy Spirit working through their lives.

Which of these descriptions from Paul's letters fit your church's model of leadership? Which ones challenge the matrix of your church's leadership? List those in the margin.

Why, Then, a Leadership Team?

At Legacy, we struggled like many other churches to reconcile our decision-making processes with the biblical record. We tried to think biblically rather than to allow conventional thinking to guide our direction. This was not easy. As we wrestled to work out the model that met our needs and did not conflict with the biblical record, we carved out Legacy's church leadership team. This model is best for us at this time.

Governance is a tricky issue. We must admit that it is too often influenced by the culture rather than by the bits and pieces of information given to us in the Bible. American church members use concepts like "checks and balances" and "representation" as if the church were founded on the U.S. Constitution. Every generation in countries where the church is an accepted institution must struggle to ensure it governs itself by biblical guidelines rather than by cultural ones.

One example of how this struggle reveals itself in many churches is in the use of *Robert's Rules of Order.* I believe this nonbiblical reference for conducting business has more authority in some churches than the Bible. American congress and Baptist business meetings may be the last bastions of such "order." When we were updating our constitution, we sought counsel from a law firm who worked almost exclusively with churches in such matters. Their recommendation was to leave all references to *Robert's Rules* out of our constitution and bylaws because they had found that the little book of rules was used more often to stop decisions rather than to help make them. We knew this from experience. *Robert's Rules* had been invoked to halt the revision process we were in at the time!

How do you address the governance issue in a mission outpost? How do you implement shared leadership into the task of leading people on mission?

We chose a shared leadership model at Legacy. The church leadership team has a practical and biblical reason for being. Practically, as we grew, fewer people were needed to make more informed and timely decisions in order to seize opportunities of growth and meet the needs of those related to the mission. As we grew larger, the number of our decision makers grew smaller. Those who controlled the church's progress by voting did not like this direction and tried to get a vote together to stop it.

Biblically, we observed that while multiple leaders shared the responsibility and authority of leadership, congregational voting to make decisions was absent in the biblical record. We also experienced that a 51 percent vote on a subject did not foster unity. More often it cemented the line of separation among the people. We vote only as a way to choose members of our leadership team and for corporate actions listed in the bylaws that require a vote from the membership. Votes on these actions are taken at our annual church conference.

Here is the language we use in our bylaws to describe the biblical basis for how we govern ourselves. We recognize that in Scripture there is a leadership principle, an equipping principle, and a servant principle. The leadership principle is the rationale behind our leadership team. The functions of the team are in a separate section of the document.

> ***The Leadership Principle***—This principle correlates to the early church leaders who were referred to as bishops (*episkopos*—overseers, 1 Tim. 3:1-7) and elders (*presbuteros*—those trusted to be the spiritual leaders of the church, Titus 1:5-6; 1 Tim. 5:17). These terms were used interchangeably throughout the New Testament; however, they always referred to those entrusted to lead emerging congregations in worship, ministry, and spiritual direction. We acknowledge that the biblical model of leadership is multiple, shared leadership.

We believe that our church leadership team provides multiple roles for shared leadership with a servant leader leading them and that this is the best model for us to accomplish our mission to make disciples. It is not, however, the only way to address the issue of how leaders lead in a mission outpost. You may find other models more helpful in your situation.

Describe the leadership structure in your church. Evaluate how it serves your mission to make disciples. In a spirit of humility and with a servant's heart, what are some things you and your mission outpost team could address to allow those gifted and set apart to lead in your church more effectively? Share your ideas at your next meeting.

HOW SHARED LEADERSHIP WORKS

Shared leadership works itself out best in team. This concept has been a prevailing value in business and ministry for some time.[15] But being a team is hard work. Spirited leaders think working in team slows things down. Disengaged members of teams cause dysfunction and prevent the team from reaching its goals. Teams turn into committees when goals and accountability are set aside.

I had coffee once with the person leading our leadership team selection process. He had asked me to meet him to discuss what made our team work so well and how could we find people to replace those rolling off who will not jeopardize the dynamics of the team.

I told my friend that several factors made a team like the one we currently had an effective one. Here's my short list:

Everyone on the team is completely sold out to the mission and vision of the church and the implications of that mission and vision. I have found that people can ascend to a certain set of words and beliefs, but when it comes to laying down one's preferences for the implementation of mission and vision, only true servant leaders can do that. Teams who have circled up and said, "This is what God wants us to do; we will do it until God tells us not to any more," are teams who will do great things for God.

Everyone on the team has experienced the struggles firsthand of transitioning the church to a mission outpost. So you won't have team members like John Mark who cut out after his first firefight on mission, teams should be made up of seasoned (not bitter and bleeding) troops who can stand the tests of opposition to change. In one sense, everyone on the team has been given a purple heart which carries with it not only the pride of service but also the scars of sacrifice.

No one on the team has personal agendas for being on the team. Early in my ministry I would put everyone on teams who asked to be on them. I found out the hard way that some people want to be part of certain teams to push a personal agenda for the church. Team members who lay down personal preference for shared values make the best team members.

Everyone on the team has a heart for serving one another, staff, and the people of the church. Philippians 2:1-4 describes these team members' hearts. It's not about them. It's about serving the interests and needs of others in the context of the church's mission.

We talked for more than an hour about this topic and spent many more in conversations with potential team members to hear their heart on these matters. God led us to the leaders for the next season of growth in our church.

Evaluate yourself as a team member by the short list of characteristics above. Which are most like you? Which are the ones you must work on?

Team Behavior

We have used Patrick Lencioni's *The Five Dysfunctions of a Team* to build our ministry directors team. It has proven to be a valuable resource to help expose

Key Verse
When they had appointed elders in every church and prayed with fasting, they committed them to the Lord in whom they had believed.
—Acts 14:23

"The leader is one who mobilizes others toward a goal shared by leaders and followers. . . . . Leaders, followers and goals make up the three equally necessary supports for leadership."[14]
—Gary Wills

those unseen aspects of human behavior that prevent teams from functioning well. Lencioni has articulated each dysfunction positively to describe how members of truly cohesive teams behave.[16] Each one serves as a basis for the next.

1. They trust one another. Lencioni means by this that members of the team are willing to be vulnerable within the group. I have found this to be a difficult step for some team members to take. Trusting team members can shed tears together, and they can openly share their unguarded feelings with the group.

2. They engage in unfiltered conflict around ideas. Lencioni says that if trust is not built among team members a fear of conflict sets upon the team and they cannot enter into passionate debate about a topic. You can get red in the face over an idea if you trust those in the room will still honor you when the debate has ended.

3. They commit to decisions and plans of action. Lencioni has observed that without healthy conflict no one can commit to plans of action because some have reservations about them. Truly cohesive teams have fought through decisions, adopted viable plans, and commit to seeing them completed.

4. They hold one another accountable for delivering against those plans. Without commitment to decisions and plans born out of conflict based on trust, Lencioni teaches that accountability is not possible. Without it a team will never accomplish their goals.

5. They focus on the achievement of collective results. Lencioni says that "inattention to results occurs when team members put their individual needs . . . or even the needs of their divisions above the collective goals of the team."[17]

Use the Team Assessment in Lencioni's book to get the truest look at your team's condition. Without it, however, you can go back through the above list and assess your team's health. Record your evaluations in your journal.

The Importance of Multiple Leaders

The conflict brought on by the ethnic mission created a chance for the church to change. This conflict was resolved because of an interaction between multiple leaders with multiple leadership styles. The dispute was not a theological one but one in which the existing members had to decide whether they would embrace new brothers and sisters in Christ who were not of their same faith background. Erwin McManus reminds us that the results of this gathering "unleashed the church to become the pliable and adaptive movement that has radically impacted the world in the past two thousand years. The church is a paradox of unchanging convictions grounded in God's truth and the incarnational expression of every culture and people who respond to the God of grace."[18]

Return to the events recorded in Acts 15 after Paul and Barnabas' first journey on mission to the ethnics. We observed some characteristics of how change came about in that situation, but we did not examine the role each leader played in resolving the issue of inclusion. Shared leadership among a multiplicity of leaders guided the church through one of its most critical conflicts.

Five kinds of leaders interacted in the Acts 15 scenario. Each one played a crucial part in resolving the conflict. Each one held a shared leadership role that was necessary to bring an innovation to the group, get perspective, and make a call that all could move forward together. There is a season for every type of leadership, and every leader may find himself or herself acting as one of these types some time in a ministry of transition.

Every movement has a catalytic leader who pioneers change.

Paul, the catalytic leader—Every movement has a catalytic leader who pioneers change. Paul was the catalyst for change in the makeup of who would be part of the church. He boldly called for radical inclusiveness and insisted things change to make room for the new brothers and sisters in Christ. Paul pressed the issue until conflict arose. Catalytic leaders do that.

In my context of ministry, I often serve as a catalytic leader. I am not wired that way in personality like Paul, but if an innovation is clearly necessary to keep on mission, I will be the catalyst to implement it. Catalytic leadership is essential to introducing change to a static or unhealthy situation. God uses these leaders to stir up dying fires and to ignite new ones like lightning striking a forest.

Peter, the bridge leader—Groups need leaders who stand as a bridge between the old realty and the new one. Peter was the bridge leader in this conflict who straddled the shared past of the Jewish followers of Jesus and the new ethnic followers. He could relate to the fears of lost tradition, but he had experienced the fresh wind and fire of the Holy Spirit falling on an ethnic household. His speech to the leaders in Jerusalem bridged Paul's innovation to their respected past and made a way for the traditionalists to get to the new shore.

Transitioning requires bridge leaders. You need those who honor the past but who have experienced or seen the future and are willing to build a bridge of transition to it. Senior members of a congregation or staff members with long tenures can be bridge builders in seasons of change. While bridges can be crossed both ways, true bridge leaders construct one-way passages to the future which are anchored to the solid rock of the past.

James, the consensus leader—James made the call related to Paul's innovation. He did so in a way that brought elements from the past to merge with the realities of the present. His decision included general, time-honored principles that could be translated into any culture with the radical, new covenant truth of justification with God through Christ alone. His decision created a consensus that allowed both groups to move forward together.

Consensus can sometimes be dangerous to the church's mission. You can compromise a catalytic concept with too much consensus building. On the other hand, without some consensus the catalyst can cause an explosion in the laboratory that could burn the place down. Consensus leadership combines the past with the future to create a present alive with possibilities.

Barnabas, the supportive leader—Barnabas tells his part of the story in the Acts 15 record. He is not a prominent player at this meeting, but he is present. He was a supporting cast member in the movement of God among the ethnics. Everyone in the Jerusalem church knew him from their first days after Pentecost. He was a charter member whom the church often called upon to inspect the working of God around the epicenter of the church. In Acts 11:20-24, when the church at Antioch started growing by presenting the gospel to the Gentiles, Barnabas was sent to Antioch by the church at Jerusalem to check it out. He was chosen because he was a good man, full of the Holy Spirit and faith. He was also known among the Christians in Antioch as a supporter of God's work. They, too, called upon him to pioneer Christ's work among the ethnics. At the gathering in Jerusalem, he simply told his stories and stood beside the catalytic leader as a sign of support.

Supportive leadership is necessary in seasons of transition. Every catalytic leader needs a supportive leader who can tell similar stories. Every bridge builder needs this leader to gain support for the far side where the bridge she constructs will end. Supportive leaders are quietly present in the chaos

While bridges can be crossed both ways, true bridge leaders construct one-way passages to the future which are anchored to the solid rock of the past.

117

of change to encourage the other leaders and act in concert with them.

The traditionalist, the status quo leader—In Acts 15, the status quo leaders met Paul and Barnabas in Antioch and caused such a disturbance it became headlines. Both the catalytic leader and the status-quo leader refused to budge from their positions, so they took the fight to Jerusalem. The status-quo leaders refused to accept the innovation brought by the missionaries and resolved to stop it before it went any further. In Jerusalem they led other traditionalists to stand against the inclusion of the ethnics without first conforming to their interpretation of the Scriptures.

I tend to paint these leaders with dark hues. As a servant leader in the ministry of transition, these leaders often lead against the new work of God. Traditionalists, however, have a role to play in transition. They always make sure you know where you have come from and what the rules of the game are. Their tendency to be uncompromising insists that catalytic leaders provide solid evidence and heart-deep resolve for the innovation they bring. These leaders are the weights you press against to build leadership muscle. Status-quo leaders can help hone the sharpness of a vision, but they must not stand in the way of on-mission leaders and followers.

First, go through this list of leaders and identify the one most like you. When you have done that, write down some instances in which you have served the body as that kind of leader. When you have finished with that, go through the list and write names of people in your church who serve in the different roles of leadership. This list can be helpful as you choose leaders and as you introduce change into the body.

Day 5

THE DEPTH OF SHARED LEADERSHIP

At the end of the 2001 ministry year, the leadership team with whom I had served gathered to give me my annual review. Anyone who constantly goes through this exercise knows the anxiety of such a situation—even when you know and trust those who are evaluating you. The team gathered in our conference room, and Tom, the designated leader that evening, sat what looked like a treasure box on the table. He began to tell the story that when he was a boy his grandfather would bring out a "wonder box" and let him pick anything out of it for his own. The toys were mostly trinkets, but to a boy, they were gold. He said the wonder box had become to him a symbol of treasures that he looked forward to choosing from any time his grandfather would take it from the shelf.

Tom read from a sheet he later gave to me: "As a team, it is our sincere desire to impart to you a comprehensive set of wonderful, highly valuable tools that will serve as compass points, or perhaps road markers, to lead your journey. We expect that keeping these tools readily available, at your right hand, safe in a 'wonder box' is sure to meet many an unexpected need."

Then each member of the team took a turn to take an object from the wonder box and explain its meaning to me. Patsy gave me a pen and ink pot and reminded me of "the value of a well-placed word." Randall gave me a framed print of an old man drawing on a dock and reminded me of "the value of experience." Mark handed me a worn wooden chisel and pointed my attention to "the value of the simplicity of faith." He prayed God would chisel away everything that would limit my faith. Tom, who had introduced the wonder box, handed me an ornamental cross and reminded me of "the value of tenacity." "Like the leaders of the early church, tenacity—enduring leadership—is what God has called you to be about," he wrote on the card.

Wendy placed before me a mirror with the 23rd Psalm printed on it and spoke of "the value of spiritual sensitivity." Greg then handed me a copy of *Driving Mr. Albert: A Trip Across America with Einstein's Brain*, and taught me again "the value of intellectual levity." Finally, the other Tom on the team pulled a clock from the wonder box and reminded me of "the value of a well-timed message." The team then gathered around me, placed their hands on me, and prayed for me and my ministry. I have not been as moved in my heart since that evening. When they had finished and we had used up all the tissues in the room, we walked through the leadership opportunities they foresaw for me in the next 12 months.

I tell you that story because it epitomizes for me the meaning of authentic community in team. Shared leadership is only shared tasks unless it is done in community.

When in your experience as a leader has a team come around you to affirm your gifts and strengths? When have you orchestrated a similar event to affirm others? Be prepared to tell your mission outpost team of your experience.

Key Verse
He knelt down and prayed with all of them. There was a great deal of weeping by everyone. And embracing Paul, they kissed him, grieving most of all over his statement that they would never see his face again.
—*Acts 20:36-38*

Authentic Community

The very nature of God is community. It should then follow that His servant leaders experience it and even be agents who create it.

It is no accident that the community of the Antioch church birthed the team of Barnabas and Saul. We should not be surprised that the crisis of inclusion described in Acts 15 was resolved in community. We should not wonder that the metaphor of belonging to "God's household" or the "family of God" was core to the early church's perception of itself (1 Tim. 3:15; Gal. 6:10; 1 Pet. 4:17). Each team on mission with Paul grew out of life spent together in homes, the synagogue, and the marketplace.

Paul did not carry out God's mission for his life alone. From his ministry in Antioch, which began in partnership with Barnabas, until he landed in Rome, he was with at least one other person. Teams function best in the atmosphere of community. Like the plants that could not survive in the terrarium you made in elementary school unless there was an ecological balance in the closed system, teams cannot function unless they breathe the oxygen of community in the system of doing mission.

The Bible describes the church as family and a fellowship of Jesus' followers. Those are two tightly knit groups. Change can threaten them. For change to happen in any form, a sense of community must exist among the people. Another reason for building community is that the first characteristic of a ministry team is "togetherness."[19] Community creates this feeling of togetherness. Teams thrive when there is genuine care and common experiences among the people.[20]

> **Ask yourself these questions: Can my church be described as a community of believers who care for one another and share common goals toward our mission? Is our church emotionally healthy enough to weather the storms of change? Can the sense of community sustain the momentum of change?**

Community Builders

Building community with those with whom you share leadership is foundational to keeping your team healthy. It does not just happen. Like creating an environment for a good marriage, you must lovingly offer opportunities that enhance the growth of community among your team members. Here are some ideas.

Play together. Once we went to lunch and then to an indoor go-cart racing facility. You can learn a lot about team members by racing with them and observing their behavior with a clock running and horsepower under them. Depending on the makeup of the team, we have played golf together and gone to professional sporting events. Getting away together helped create opportunities to share life without sharing work.

Pray together. I remember one day during a ministry director's weekly meeting that one of the ministry directors began to share his fears about his ministry. He allowed himself to cry in front of us. We instinctively stood, gathered around him, and prayed that his fears would not immobilize him. We also committed to address those fears with him.

Bill Hybels suggests "community exercises" like "the hot seat," where each member of the team sits in a chair in the middle of the group and answers questions posed by other team members. These questions give the person in the hot seat a platform to be vulnerable with the group. Another exercise he calls, "What do you want on your tombstone?" A member of the team was asked to leave the room. While they were outside, the other members created

---

Teams function best in the atmosphere of community.

an epitaph that captured the essence of the person. On another retreat, the church's executive pastor asked everyone to paint a picture of his or her soul and then to shares its meaning with the group. My favorite is Hybels' suggestion to wash one another's feet to serve those on the team.[21]

Which of the exercises listed above can you use with your team? What kinds of exercises have you used to build community in your teams in the past? Which ones worked well? Which ones would you use again?

A Sign of Community

When leaders must separate because of relocation or end of tenure, the depth of that team's community is exposed. Watch leaders say good-bye and you will see whether their lives have been melded together through sharing ministry and life together. One of the most moving stories that illustrates the depth of shared leadership in team is found in Acts 20. It is Paul's farewell to the elders in Ephesus.

Read Acts 20:17–21:1. What were the circumstances around the scene? What were some words or actions that show the closeness of Paul and the elders? Why do you believe they shared this closeness? Describe what you believe the emotions of both Paul and the elders were that day. Write your answers in the margin.

Describe a similar emotional farewell you have experienced in your life or ministry. How was your farewell like that of Paul to the elders in Ephesus?

What an incredible picture of friendship and shared ministry! Look at Luke's description of the scene: "When he had said this, he knelt down with all of them and prayed. They all wept as they embraced him and kissed him" (Acts 20:36-37, NIV). That's genuine caring for one another. They knew that they might never see Paul again because he had committed to go to Jerusalem, and there the opposition authorities would surely capture and arrest him. The elders knew him well enough to know that if he said he would go, he would go, regardless of the danger that faced him.

Note the events and experiences that had molded them to share such deep relationships.

Verses 17-21 tell us that he served with them to bring the news to all people. He lived with them "house to house." You build community when you spend time in people's homes. One of the downsides to church buildings is the tendency to meet in corporate-style rooms on the church's campus. I prefer living rooms to board rooms. Paul did too.

In verses 22-24, Paul shared the honest truth about the dangers that lay before him in Jerusalem. From his call to his death, he faced "chains and afflictions." The leaders in Ephesus shared some of that affliction with him. Together they knew the onslaught of evil and the opposition brought on by enemies. Paul shared his personal resolve to complete what they had been part of. He wanted to finish the race. Leaders in community can share their fears without feeling weak or that they will not be trusted afterward.

In verses 25-31, Paul explained his behavior, reminded them of his love for them, and gave them personal instructions—the hard facts of what they would face when he left. You can tell they had faced these forces together before. Shared leadership in community can be honest about the dangers that lie ahead.

Verses 32-35 tell of Paul's desire for their continued growth in the Lord. He reminded them of his example not to take any payment from them. He recalled Jesus' words that it is more blessed to give than to receive, a saying he lived by every day he was with them. Leaders in community model the group's core values.

The thought of never seeing their friend and fellow worker again grieved them to tears (v. 38). The loss was almost too great to bear. Teams who thrive in community treat the loss of a team member as a death. So much has been shared. Who will you trust like that again? Can you ever find a replacement? What will we do without his skill set? These are all questions you ask when a true team member is taken from the group.

Luke begins chapter 21 of Acts with, "After we had torn ourselves away from them" (NIV). "Torn ourselves away from them," he wrote. Like spouses making themselves release their embrace because one has to go away, Paul and his friends separated to continue the mission to make disciples. This separation was real, tender, painful because they had connected at the deepest part of their lives: shared leadership in a mission that impacts the eternal destiny of people's lives. You don't hear that kind of language about people leaving because they got a better offer somewhere else. You don't see this demonstration of emotion when someone leaves for a promotion. Luke's choice words describe people who genuinely loved and cared for one another.

As I write, we are going through the process of selecting new members for the church leadership team. I have caught myself longing for that team in 2001 to come back. But it can't be. Wendy and Greg have moved. Wonder box Tom stepped off. The other Tom, Patsy, Mark, and Randall have been joined by Ken, but he and Randall roll off this year, and Mark is now on our staff as director of discipleship ministries. Tom and Patsy will be all who are left from that original team who gave me the wonder box. But like taking the field with a well-worn glove, I have confidence those relationships will deepen even more.

Rather than mourn the loss of "the good old team," I am anticipating whom God will gather together to share the journey of mission and vision with me in this next season of growth. I look forward to the high-fives to celebrate big wins and tear-filled meetings when we confess our fatigue and fears. I am already hungry for the laughter and thirsty for the challenge. I can't wait to see what God has written on the depths of the new members' hearts and how God will use them to mold me and lead the church into its God-ordained future. No, I'm not sad to lose the past. I am pumped to know the God who put that group together is the same God who will put the next one together to accomplish His eternal purposes through us.

1. Report on American Online, 28 April 2003. The event was on 25 April 2003.

2. C. Gene Wilkes, *Jesus on Leadership* (Carol Stream, IL: Tyndale House Publishers, 1998), 214.

3. Alan Roxburgh and Mike Regele, *Crossing the Bridge* (Costa Mesa, CA: Precept, 2000), 121.

4. Bill Hybels, *Courageous Leadership* (Grand Rapids: Zondervan, 2002), 80-85.

5. Ibid., 84.

6. Burt Nanus and Stephen M. Dobbs, *Leaders Who Make a Difference* (Indianapolis, IN: Jossey-Bass, 1999), 149.

7. Adapted from article by the same name originally published in *LeaderLife*.

8. Ken Blanchard, Phil Hodges, and Bill Hybels, *Leadership by the Book* (New York: William Morrow, 1999), 142.

9. C. Gene Wilkes, *Jesus on Leadership* (Nashville: LifeWay, 1996), 84.

10. Roxburgh and Regele, *Crossing the Bridge*, 146.

11. Mark Strom, *Reframing Paul* (Downers Grove, IL: InterVarsity Press, 2000), 178.

12. Ibid., 179.

13. Roxburgh and Regele, *Crossing the Bridge*, 111.

14. Gary Wills, *Certain Trumpets: The Call of Leaders* (Carmichael, CA: Touchstone Books, 1995).

15. George Barna, *The Power of Team Leadership: Finding Strength in Shared Responsibility* (New York: Waterbrook Press, 2001). Wayne Cordeiro, *Doing Church as a Team* (Ventura, CA: Gospel Light, 2001). Dale Galloway, *Building Teams in Ministry* (Kansas City, MO: Beacon Hill Press of Kansas City, 2000). Kenneth Gangel, *Coaching Ministry Teams: Leadership and Management in Christian Organizations* (Nashville: W Publishing Group, 2000). Pat McMillan, *The Performance Factor: Unlocking the Secrets of Teamwork* (Nashville: Broadman & Holman Publishers, 2001).

16. Patrick Lencioni, *The Five Dysfunctions of a Team* (Indianapolis, IN: Jossey-Bass, 2002), 189-90. He has provided an assessment tool in the book to help identify "dysfunctions" at work in your team.

17. Ibid., 189.

18. Erwin Raphael McManus, *An Unstoppable Force* (Loveland, CO: Group, 2001), 87-8.

19. Wilkes, *Jesus on Leadership* (LifeWay), 104-8; (Tyndale, 1999), 219-24.

20. Adapted from, C. Gene Wilkes, "So You Want to Transition from Committees to Teams? Here's How," *Church Administration,* Summer 2001.

21. Hybels, *Courageous Leadership,* 87-9.

MESSAGE, CHARACTER, AND THE UNENDING STORY

This week you will:

- Examine the message of your call.
- Observe characteristics of mission outpost preaching and teaching.
- Review the importance and development of character.
- See ways to finish well.
- Observe the value of knowing you are part of an eternal story in which you are a significant character.

You have been challenged to enter the ministry of transition in week 1. You have observed the importance of call and preparation, seeing the vision and expanding the mission in weeks 2 and 3. You have been given tools to face opposition and win through conflict in week 4, and you have seen that shared leadership is the key to completing the mission in the last session. In this session you will examine the message of the mission, the character of the messenger, and the unending story of Christ's Great Commission. Our ministry of transition graphic is complete with this session.

This ministry of transition is an "unending story." This is because God continues to work in His creation and among His people. Until He returns as "a thief in the night," He will continue to offer opportunities for the faithful to respond to His presence in His world. Our response will usher in seasons of transition and change. This is how God has worked in history from the beginning of time.

The mission has a message modeled and communicated by a person of character who knows he or she is part of an unending story called eternity. Servant leaders in a ministry of transition

UNENDING STORY
SENDING
CHARACTER
CONFLICT
SHARED LEADERSHIP
CALL   PREPARATION   VISION

carry the message of their call to those they have been sent to serve. This is their life message, and they can speak of nothing else. They sing its lyrics like a child who has learned a new song.

I have heard Leonard Sweet say that leadership is giving people a song to sing. That song is the song of the servant leader on mission with God. Like Paul who could sing about nothing but "a righteousness that comes from God through faith in Jesus Christ" and that "you are all one in Christ Jesus," the servant leader hums and sings the melody God has written on his heart. He has done his job when choirs of singers surround him on the stage of life.

Character carries the message. A message without a messenger of character is muddled at best. People cannot hear a leader they do not respect. On the other hand, consistent character exhibited through the torrent of transition amplifies the voice of the messenger. Character comes over a long season of testing and trial. It develops as the servant leader is challenged and opposed. While the process is painful, the tests of transition create a crucible for godly character.

Finally, you and I are part of the unending story of God's eternal love. Trust in this fact gives us the eternal perspective that what we face here in this life is only a breath compared to time in eternity with the One who sent us. Knowing we are part of an eternal saga for people's souls gives significance to what we do. Being players in God's redemptive history motivates us to press on to the high calling that awaits us in heaven. Hope comes from trusting what you do contributes in some way to what God is doing to "bring all people to Himself through Christ Jesus."

The mission has a message modeled and communicated by a person of character who knows he or she is part of an unending story called eternity.

THE MISSION HAS A MESSAGE

Brian McClaren, pastor and author of *The Church on the Other Side,* challenges the church to stop thinking of theology as "a matter of technical training" and to revive it through "a quest for truth and beauty." He continues:

> To say that the church on the other side needs a new theology is not to suggest heresy. It is simply to distinguish between the message (God's truth, revelation, action, and expression) and theology (our task, our work, our language, our search to understand and articulate God's message). . . . In the new church we will try harder to remember that God is God and we are mere creatures, and that our attempts to understand and articulate his message and truth are always approximations.[1]

When a servant leader makes engaging the mission field a priority over maintaining a local church, how you say what you have always said becomes a key issue. Building bridges from the Word to the target culture calls for new ways of presenting God to others. When you walk up Mars Hills to address the Areopagus, you cling to the essentials of your faith but test new strategies of speaking the message into the lives of those who await your words. Paul was a master at adapting how he presented his core message of salvation. His message never changed. He adapted it to each situation so it could be heard.

Every servant leader has a message. The message flows from the mission. It is the source of courage to face an uncertain future, and it is also the source of the message. For Paul, the call to mission contained the content of his message. Jesus called him "to carry My name" to the ethnics (Acts 9:15): "[I] appoint you as a servant and as a witness of what you have seen of me and of what I will show you. . . . I am sending you to them to open their eyes and turn them from darkness to light . . . so that they may receive forgiveness of sins and a place among those who are sanctified by faith in me" (Acts 26:16-18, NIV). His call to go to the ethnics contained the message that in Jesus they could turn from darkness to light.

Call compels a message. It tells you not only what to do but also what to say. Paul cried out, "For if I preach the gospel, I have no reason to boast, because an obligation is placed on me. And woe to me if I do not preach the gospel!" (1 Cor. 9:16 [15-18]). He sensed that telling others about Jesus was an obligation God placed on him. All he could do was tell others of Jesus' "dying and rising." God called Paul to carry the gospel to the ethnics. This mission drove what he did and to whom he went and what he said.

Our Core Message

Every leader has a core message. I have discovered my life message is servant leadership after the model and teaching of Jesus. But servant leadership is only a single aspect of the larger message I share with all people on mission with Jesus.

Can you write your life's core message? If you have come to discover what God has written on your heart, write it in the margin and share it with your mission outreach team when you meet. If not, ask your team to begin praying with you so that God will reveal it to you.

Paul spelled out his life's core message in the opening paragraphs of his letter to the Romans. Here it is: "[This wonderful good news of God] It's news I'm most proud to proclaim, this extraordinary Message of God's powerful plan to rescue everyone who trusts him, starting with Jews and then right on to everyone else! God's way of putting people right shows up in the acts of faith, confirming what Scripture has said all along: 'The person in right standing before God by trusting him really lives'" (Rom. 1:16-17, *The Message*).

His core message was that God has a plan to rescue everyone who trusts Him—everyone, Jews and ethnics alike. The way people get right with God is through trusting God, and when they do, they really experience life! This is his "gospel," the good news he wanted everyone to have. Like a doctor with the cure for cancer, he gave his life to making sure everyone had an opportunity to accept the cure God had revealed to him.

Christlike Character

A lasting message stands on the shoulders of godly character. When there is no character, the message is never heard. Those who lead in a ministry of transition soon discover that character, tested in the fires of conflict, is often the only voice they have to tell their story. People watch the messenger to see if he or she truly believes the message. Character offers the basis for trust that allows risk in those who follow.

This truth is the basis of our seventh reality of servant leadership in a ministry of transition.

Reality 7: Servant leaders lead with a clear message and Christlike Character (see 2 Cor. 4:5).

Read 2 Corinthians 4:5. What is Paul's message? How does he describe himself to his readers? Write your answers in the margin.

Paul declared to his Corinthian audience, "For we are not proclaiming ourselves but Jesus Christ as Lord, and ourselves as your slaves because of Jesus" (2 Cor. 4:5). This declaration tells us his message was not about him. His message was that Jesus, the risen Messiah, is Lord of all. The first confession of faith was "Jesus is Lord" (Rom. 10:9). This was in stark contrast to the world's confession, "Caesar is Lord." Paul shared a clear, yet dangerous message. To speak it could cost him his life. Self was not the focus in his preaching. Jesus Christ as Lord of all was his message.

He not only declared his message; he also described the character of the messenger. He was "your slave because of Jesus." Paul used his favorite term for his position in Christ and ministry, *doulos.* This time, however, because of Jesus' leadership in his life, he had become a *doulos,* a slave to the Corinthians. Paul humbly demonstrated his love for the Corinthians by taking the position of a slave to serve them in Christ. He had already told them,

A lasting message stands on the shoulders of godly character.

Reality 7: Servant leaders lead with a clear message and Christlike character.

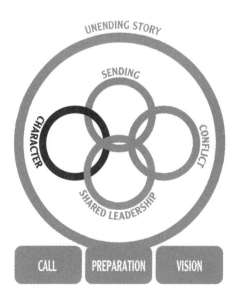

"My message and my preaching were not with wise and persuasive words, but with a demonstration of the Spirit's power, so that your faith might not rest on men's wisdom, but on God's power" (1 Cor. 2:4-5, NIV). He did not come with "wise and persuasive words," which they would expect from a leader. He came quietly with the "demonstration of the Spirit's power." The result? His desire was that their trust not be on his smooth words or skillful argument but on the power of God to change lives.

Paul's Clarion Call to Follow Jesus

Paul faced the same gulf between language, image, and story in the Old Covenant and the new expressions of God in Christ Jesus that we do. He stood with one foot in his religious past and the other in his relational future. Rituals, right thinking, and conformity to tradition framed his pre-Christ message. Grace, freedom, and having a relationship with the living Son of God were the colors he painted with after encountering Christ. Paul sought to convey a message of hope in a dark, hurting world that had convinced itself of its wisdom and power. He pointed to idols, quoted poets, philosophers, and prophets in order to build bridges from where people listened into the adventure of faith he knew. He told the Jesus story over and over. He shared it in private conversations and in formal presentations. He spoke to individuals in the marketplace, small groups in houses, and large groups in forums and other public gathering places. He would speak with whomever would listen wherever they gathered.

Paul trumpeted a clear call to follow Christ. He consistently called people to hear the core story of Jesus and to trust Him as rescuer and leader of their lives. Here are some characteristics of his call to follow Jesus.

It is all about Jesus. End of sentence. Close the book. If you want to know the center of Paul's message, it was all about the one who died in his place; rose on the third day and sits at the right hand of the Father; and who called him and empowered him to mission. Everything he wrote and spoke flowed out of who Jesus, the Christ, is. He was preoccupied by "Christ's dying and rising."[2] Paul had one message and said it in many ways, "Jesus Christ, and Him crucified" (1 Cor. 2:2), "Jesus Christ as Lord" (2 Cor. 4:5).

What is at the core of your lesson or message? Do you seek to impress your listeners with your knowledge and insight, or do you put your best efforts into helping them know Jesus? Do you teach more about right doctrine or to enhance people's relationship with God?

People are the reason for the message. Paul rubbed shoulders with people like pedestrians during rush hour on Fifth Avenue in New York City. After Jesus knocked him off his high horse on his way to Damascus, he never considered himself better than anyone else. He saw himself as obligated to ethnic and Jew to tell them the story of Jesus (Rom. 1:14). So he left the sacred halls of the temple in Jerusalem to work in the streets of Corinth and Ephesus. He packed up his pharisaical garb and put on the clothes of a traveling businessman. He refused pay for his professional skills but collected funds for the poor in the church in Jerusalem. Paul "engaged the world rather than retreating into an intellectual or religious ghetto."[3] People were the reason for his message. His audiences included pious people (Jews in the synagogue), nonreligious people (pagans in Athens), and followers of Jesus (the church).

Teachers and preachers sometime feel challenged to bring messages no one has ever heard before, a new insight on a familiar passage or story.

Paul had one message and said it in many ways, "Jesus Christ, and Him crucified."

I have come to believe that those who have grown up in the church and who want something "deep" are actually saying, "Tell me something I haven't heard before." They are seeking secret knowledge like the Gnostics Paul battled in Colosse.

Ask yourself, "Am I trying to impart secret knowledge or am I seeking to help others know Jesus?" Who are the targeted audiences you prepare to talk with each week? Is building people's faith or demonstrating your perceptive skills the motive for what you choose to teach?

The message reached the lost and built up the church. Paul constantly reached out to those who did not trust Jesus as Forgiver and Leader. He longed for everyone, ethnic and Jew, to know Christ. He spent many hours and pages explaining who Jesus is in the context of his listener's world. He also sought to build up the church. His letters began with an explanation of who Jesus is, and they ended with how to apply who He is to how people lived. He built up the church by addressing issues like marriage, lawsuits, parenting, and how to treat people within the cultural structures of his day. He taught his friends how to pray, live like Jesus, care for the poor and hurting, and love one another.

Paul chose a variety of venues to teach and preach. He went to places of worship (synagogues and temple). He waited in the marketplace. He went into the public square to make his case for Christ—for example, the hall of Tyrannus in Ephesus (Acts 19:9). He moved among private homes to share his message (Acts 20:20). He went to where both the lost and the disciples lived and worked.

The balance between reaching out to those who don't know Jesus and those who have had Him around their entire life is tricky at times. Mission outpost preachers and leaders seek to find the balance between explaining Jesus to the lost and building up the church.

How would you rate yourself as to the balance of your message? Do you lean too much on one audience or the other? Do you expect both the lost and the believers to come to you for answers, or do you move through a variety of venues like Paul to get the word out?

Servant leaders in a ministry of transition lead with a clear message and Christlike character. Let's look next at what preaching and teaching may look like in a mission outpost.

> Servant leaders in a ministry of transition lead with a clear message and Christlike character.

MISSION OUTPOST PREACHING AND TEACHING

Key Verse

Again, if the trumpet does not sound a clear call, who will get ready for battle? So it is with you. Unless you speak intelligible words with your tongue, how will anyone know what you are saying? You will just be speaking into air.
—1 Corinthians 14:8-9, NIV

Much of what you do as a speaker for the mission is vision casting. You constantly call people to follow Jesus (personal vision) and invite them to join you on the mission to make disciples of others (church mission and vision). In order for all to have an opportunity to hear, you must offer your message in a variety of forms.

One Sunday during a season of helping people to see the visionscape of our future, I chose to draw some images on a flip chart. We also prepared a video of me telling the story from the rooftop of our buildings, and I taught from Scripture. Monday morning I received this email (names are changed):

I wanted you to know that I thought the job you did yesterday communicating the vision for the church was excellent. You said the same things you've been saying for years, but you made it even more visible. Your presentation really connected with Laurie, and I think she *really* "gets it" now. In fact, she wondered why you hadn't said all those things before when we were going through all that "stuff" [earlier in the year]. I reminded her that you did—just in a different way.

Here's the lesson for me in all this. Everybody learns differently, and different ways of communicating will speak to different people. For instance, Kim tells the story that your description of our mission as going out after sheep on a hillside rather than sheep already in other pens helped her "get it." For me, your mini-lesson on the Acts 11 church that you presented to the deacons helped me "get it." Yesterday, your picture drawing helped Laurie "get it." The more repetition and the more different ways of communicating will help more and more people "get it." Seems like Jesus also understood this about people and thus provided many different ways for people to "get it."

The purpose of mission-outpost preaching and teaching is helping people "get it." How do we do that? Like Paul, we make our message clear and intelligible so that people will know what we are saying. We do not want to be accused of "just speaking into the air." We want people not only to hear the Jesus story but to get it and conform their lives to it.

What are some different ways you have communicated your mission and vision? What are some ways you have seen others communicate that helped you "get it"? Write your ideas in your journal.

A Clarion Call for All

As mission outpost people we are to sound a clear call for others to trust Christ and join Him on mission. That call is found in the word: the Word, Jesus Christ; the word, the Bible; and the message of our mission. Jesus is the

130

Word whom we tell about whenever and however we can (John 1:1-3). Paul wrote, "Before you trust, you have to listen. But unless Christ's Word is preached, there is nothing to listen to" (Rom. 10:17, *The Message*). The world listens for a clear message. But our call to follow Jesus is often so garbled, like the cacophony of tongues in the Corinthian church, that people cannot understand a word we say, even though we look sincere when we say it. The world listens for the call. We are the ones to sound it. However, that call must be clear, or those who hear it will not know whether to prepare for battle or retreat.

We who follow Jesus do not worship images and idols. However, we live in a world of sound bites, images, and mass communication. You and I form opinions about people and reality based on 20-second video clips and sound bites every day. The danger is that there is no context for what we see and hear. We will not sit through an entire news conference, so we let a sound editor pick out a snippet here and there to form our opinion of what was said. Video editors can make an isolated incident look like an ongoing war. We don't have time to listen, but we want to hear what's going on, so we find ourselves depending on pieces of data and edited images rather than complex stories to understand our world.

Many who come to our services each week—both followers and seekers of Jesus—want our message to be packaged like fast food. They don't have enough time to read and know the words of revelation, so they want us to cut it into portions they can digest, to put it in images they can see. Our temptation as mission storytellers is to cater to their image/sound bite-driven reasoning and their thirst for fast-food packaging.

Mission outpost preachers and teachers have a message to proclaim, a story to tell, a clear call to sound. That is why you are on-site and working. But we must be careful to ensure that the core message of Jesus is our call to others. We must correctly handle the word of truth (see 2 Tim. 2:15). Truth, not personal opinion or popular practice, is the center of our messages. We cannot simply pick and choose words and phrases that match our theme or outline just because they came up in a word search. Context changes perspective. Connection to mission is essential. Original meanings matter. Without the message of Christ in our speeches, we end up getting in line to be another Dr. Phil or Oprah.

To make Christ central to our message is essential, but how we communicate that message will change according to our cultural context. This means the methods of telling His story will change from the last generation of preachers and evangelists. Like effective missionaries in a mission field, native images and idioms become bridges from one culture to a new one formed by Christ. Mission outpost preachers and teachers do not insist those in the mission field learn the archaic language of a religious system in order to know the ancient truths of God. No, mission-field Christ-tellers listen for the songs and stories that are familiar to native ears and use them to create fresh paths to Jesus. The art of mission outpost storytelling is different from the science of preaching and teaching in the local church. This is the challenge and adventure we face today.

What do you resonate with in the section above? What causes some concern? Be prepared to share your thoughts with your mission outpost team when they gather next.

Mission-field Christ-tellers listen for the songs and stories that are familiar to native ears and use them to create fresh paths to Jesus.

Speaking to the Locals

Missionaries who work out of a mission outpost learn the language of the locals. The missionary learns the language of the mission field in order to communicate to those who live there rather than insisting that the locals learn the language of the missionary before the message can be heard. Preaching and teaching must follow the same direction of learning. Be aware that those in the local church may mistake the language of the locals as slang or unsophisticated. They may demand you use the king's English when speaking of holy things. But the missionary must decide which is his target group when choosing the words and ways to tell her story. Language is a barrier on any mission field.

If you commit to speaking the local language, how do you go about learning it? One way to learn to speak to the locals is to know their culture and language. Studies like *The Clustered World: How We Live, What We Buy, and What It All Means About Who We Are* by Michael J. Weiss give insight to the "Young Influentials," "Kids and Cul-de-Sacs," and "Executive Suites" who live in our neighborhoods. General characteristics of these cluster groups can help you assess whether you are connecting with those around you.

Technical assistance can be helpful in learning the local language, but the best way is to hang out with the locals—those who are not already immersed in local church culture. My whole use of language and presentation forms changed when I began to learn the language of those in our mission field. The lessons came at soccer games, in father-daughter organizations, and when meeting parents of my daughters' friends. Talking with my neighbors who were not churched helped me know what they were interested in and the needs they faced each day. They taught me to translate the language of God to those in the streets.

Mission outpost preaching and teaching must be in forms and words that those in the mission field can understand. These forms must become bridges for the message and fit the character of the messenger. Bill Easum insists: "The time has come when we must experience the convergence of the oral story, the beat of sound, and the visual. Indigenous preaching no longer can be done with three points and a poem. Today's audience requires more than just words. As a result, pastors no longer preach an essay. Instead they, along with a team of people, create an experience in which people are transformed by the sum of the elements of the experience."[4]

The locals hear enough words every day. Religious experts do not impress them any more. They want to experience the holy, to sense God's presence. The locals live in a multisensory world, and they wonder why church folk limit their senses to hearing alone. Why do secular media do a better job of telling their story than those who have the life-saving message of Jesus?

I was taught in seminary to be a preacher who presents a message, not a worshiper who leads people into the presence of God. My models for speaking were monologues of carefully crafted tomes. But as I listen to the locals, I discover that story is how you share our message with them. I do not do a narrative message every week, but my message finds its home in the redemptive story of God's love. Curtis and Eldredge remind us, "Life is not a list of propositions, it is a series of dramatic scenes. . . . Story is the language of the heart. Our souls speak not in the naked facts of mathematics or the abstract propositions of systematic theology; they speak in the images and emotions of story."[5] Lessons framed in the story of life help local listeners hear the clear call to follow Jesus.

Michael Slaughter calls us to unlearn what we know about offering our message to the world by telling us, "Being created in God's image makes us

Message plus shared life equals authentic ministry.

132

multisensory beings. People learn best when all their senses are engaged. The next generation of churches will avoid the stiff and cerebral and will offer people a multisensory experience of God."[6]

How well do you know the language of the locals? Respond to the quotes of Easum, Curtis and Eldredge, and Slaughter. What is one thing you can do to present your message in ways so the locals can "get it"?

Legacy is committed to telling the story of Jesus in a way that engages all the senses. Our creative arts team incorporates dancers, artists, vocalists, and instrumentalists to lead people in worship. Like the Levites of old, they circle the worshipers and guide them into the presence of God. They serve in team with me to present the theme of the worship experience. My message is only one part of the entire experience. I use video clips produced in house or from films, faith stories by those with changed lives, dramas and interviews to help tell the story. Movement, light, sound, and creativity become bridges for the "ancient future" story of Jesus to find its way into the hearts of the locals so they, too, can know what we have experienced by trusting him.

Being a mission outpost in our mission field means capturing the arts and all art forms to communicate the message that Jesus Christ is Lord.

Day 3

CHARACTER MATTERS

Few manuals on transitioning discuss the character of the leader during the seasons of change. I believe, however, that the leader's character is a key to help people move through the apparent chaos of leaving the past and orchestrating the future. The character of the leader can help or hinder hearing the message. Faulty character can damage progress made toward the vision. The character of the leader is where God's work in the leader's life is most evident.

When people observe the leader, they should see a humble heart, pure motives, and actions that are not self-serving. Followers engage the mission and pursue the vision when these character traits are present in their leader. Businesses, schools, and communities have begun to emphasize character development as part of what they produce. Faith-based groups like Character First offer training and resources in this area of personal development.[7]

Paul staked his ministry on his character. His enemies argued with his methodology and even his theology, but they could not assail his character. He guarded it jealously and referred to it as a defense against those who slandered him. Throughout his letters he insisted that how he acted with those he wrote told of his love, anger, patience, and care for them.

Read 1 Thessalonians 2:5-10. How did Paul describe his ministry among them? What did this say about his character?

Paul reminded his readers that when he came to them his motives were pure. He "never used flattery," nor did he "put on a mask to cover up greed"

Key Verse
You are witnesses, and so is God, of how devoutly, righteously, and blamelessly we conducted ourselves with you believers.
1 Thessalonians 2:10

"Mature ministry flows from a mature character."
—J. Robert Clinton

(v. 5, NIV). God was his witness to how he conducted himself among them. He not only shared his message, "the gospel of God," but he shared his life with them as well (v. 8). Message plus shared life equals authentic ministry. Paul refused to make his message the only focus of his ministry. He cared for them enough to share his life with them. Finally, he was able to point to his behavior as indication of his pure motive and desire to serve them. He challenged them to remember "how devoutly, righteously, and blamelessly" he conducted himself among them.

Servant leaders live lives that can be described as "devout, righteous, and blameless." These are not signs of perfection but of the pursuit of holiness. A leader is devout when she honors the things of God above all other values. A leader is righteous when she chooses the right over the easy and benchmarks her choice against the righteousness of God. She is blameless when her actions are unassailable by critics and accountability partners alike.

Paul instilled these values in his apprentice, Timothy. He told him not to let anyone look down on him for his youth but to be an example for those in his care "in speech, in conduct, in faith, in purity" (1 Tim. 4:12). Character is exposed in our speech, how we act, in whom we put our trust, and whether our lives are pure in the things of the Lord. We do not want to be seen as "whitewashed tombs, which appear beautiful on the outside, but inside . . . full of hypocrisy and lawlessness" (Matt. 23:27-28). Servant leaders want to be "pure and blameless until the day of Christ" (Phil. 1:10, NIV).

Paul insisted that his motive to serve grew solely out of an "obligation to preach." He was not self-serving in any way. He acknowledged that some preach out of "envy and strife, but others out of good will." Some speak "out of rivalry." Others preach "out of false motives or true" (Phil. 1:15-18). He brought his message because of his call, not out of his need to compete with others or from motives that were not true to his mission.

A primary tenet of Paul's defense of his character was that he vowed he did "not peddle the word of God" (2 Cor. 2:17, NIV). He had an intense commitment to present the gospel without compensation, which in his day was his "right" as an itinerant teacher. He intentionally gave that up to be free to say what needed to be said. He argued with those who assailed his character in Corinth that he did not use his "right" to be supported by them. He said he used "none of these rights," but his "boast" was to "preach the gospel and offer it free of charge" (1 Cor. 9:12-18).

In the margin write a description of Paul's character in your own words based on the passages discussed? What claims did he make that you can make about your character? Ask your mission outpost team to help you assess those claims.

The Crucible of Character

Character shows itself as consistent behavior under pressure. Behavior is what people see, and it is the clearest indicator of your character. J. Robert Clinton has identified how God uses isolation, conflict, and life crises as tools to develop a mature character. He concluded, "Mature ministry flows from a mature character, formed in the graduate school of life."[8] We have seen how God used the "silent years" of Paul's ministry to prepare him for his mission. This period of isolation was part of God's development of his character.

Hard times create character. Hard times also expose character. Conflict and opposition to the mission can create a crucible of character development. Character is created by the yes and no you choose everyday in the

Character shows itself as consistent behavior under pressure.

context of conflict. Paul taught from his personal experience that "affliction produces endurance," and it is endurance that produces "proven character" (Rom. 5:3-4). Character proven over time and tested in tough times is what produces hope in those who trust Jesus (Rom. 5:5). That kind of hope never fails. Like a runner training for a marathon, the "affliction" of training produces the endurance necessary to carry the athlete through to the end of the race. That endurance, when maintained, results in proven results race after race.

Paul paradoxically boasted of his weakness that came from trials. His confession became that when he was weak, Christ was strong. He would boast in his weaknesses rather than his strengths because when he was helpless Christ's character shone through his (2 Cor. 12:10). He came to know that the "treasure" of salvation was held in fragile "clay jars" (2 Cor. 4:7). Hard times created a humble heart in the apostle. He claimed Christ's success through his life was a result of the difficulties he faced. Strom observed, "What is clear is that Paul understood the success of his ministry not to have come in spite of his hardships and vulnerability, but precisely because of and through these."[9]

Paul asked for prayer to be bold in whatever situation he found himself, not to be released from it (Eph. 6:18-20). He also told the Corinthians to stay in the situation they were in when Christ found them (1 Cor. 7). Changing settings does not make you bold; boldness comes from accepting your situation and being on the same mission wherever you are. This is why Paul was happy to be "an ambassador in chains" (Eph. 6:20), an odd title for leaders in American Christianity today.

How has God used hard times in your life to develop your character? What are some confessions you stand upon that have come from those times of testing? Write you thoughts in your journal.

Character is also the basis for spiritual authority. It is a by-product of a mature character developed through a maturing process.[10] Servant leaders who serve the mission and lead by serving those on mission with them exhibit mature character and discover they have an authority they did not set out to gain. Authority to lead in a ministry of transition flows from a daily pursuit of God. Experiencing God, not seeking a position, is the path to authority in servant leadership. Spiritual authority flows out of character that has been influenced by the Spirit of God in a personal, daily relationship with him.

Another by-product of character born out of adversity is an open heart. Trials can cause the leader to encase his or her heart in an iron box where no one can see the wounds and pain. This iron-boxed condition of the heart keeps the leader from empathizing with the loss of others. They develop a "just get over it" attitude toward those who are struggling through changes. When the heart is hardened, the message is hard to hear. Busting through barriers becomes the pattern of change. People's feelings don't matter much to the one who has lost them himself.

Adversity can also result in an open heart. Character based on this is transparent, vulnerable, and willing to step into the world of the hurting ones. Heifetz and Linsky point out the virtue of an open, or sacred heart:

A sacred heart means you may feel tortured and betrayed, powerless and hopeless, and yet stay open. It's the capacity to encompass the entire range of your human experience without hardening or closing

Authority to lead in a ministry of transition flows from a daily pursuit of God.

135

yourself. It means that even in the midst of disappointment and defeat, you remain connected to people and to the sources of your most profound purposes. . . . A sacred heart is an antidote to one of the most common and destructive "solutions" to the challenges of modern life: numbing oneself.[11]

Many servant leaders in a ministry of transition are tempted to survive a situation in a numbed state. Rather than connecting to people, you withdraw to doctor your wounds. An open heart allows the adversities you experience to train you in godliness and mold your character into the likeness of Christ.

What is the path to character that allows the message to be heard and the mission to be central? It is service to God's mission call on your life. A servant's heart is at the core of a leader's character who makes a difference in the kingdom of God. Service is the path to become like Jesus, our mentor and friend. Service is the test of character as well as the path to Christlike character. To refuse to serve the mission for the sake of those you lead is to expose a pride-filled heart. It is no longer about the call. It is about you, and that is the beginning of the end of your ministry.

Service is also the path to healing the hurts that come from leading through transitions. Erwin McManus summarizes the power of service to heal: "This is the way of God. There is healing in service. It resonates with the human soul. This path is not only a promise of adventure; it is a promise of wholeness. When we choose this journey, from the first step forward, we grow in the image of God. Each step shapes us to look more like him."[12]

Character formed out of adversity, service, and experiencing God is the foundation upon which the servant leader presents the message of mission and leads people into God's future for them.

Let's look now at a ministry of transition that finishes well.

Service is the path to become like Jesus, our mentor and friend.

Day 4

FINISHING WELL

I enjoy providing peer learning groups for church leaders. It has provided community for those in a ministry of transition where they can share their hopes and hurts. Some of those friendships last until today. I received an e-mail from one of the members of a group who had been trying to transition his church for almost two years. Here's his message. I edited it for use here.

> Things here at . . . are better in some ways and worse in others. We have a solid group of supporters who will stand with us and believe that what we are doing is important. In all, we lost about one-third of our attendance (about 100 people). Some of them are still trying to pull others away and harm our reputation in the community. I have never seen such vicious actions on the part of former members. We have been accused of everything except the September 11 attacks!
>
> We have two seemingly insurmountable problems as I see it: (1) About 80 percent of our income goes to keep us afloat. We do well just to pay the bills and keep payroll current. There is no money to do the things that will help us grow—not to mention even making a missional impact! (2) The other thing is even more unsettling. Our message is not being received as well as we had hoped. We get a lot of people here to see what we are doing, but they don't like it. I have come to see that [this part of the country] is so bound in religious tradition that anything contemporary or different is viewed with terrible skepticism. Our "slice" of the marketplace is so thin, growth is negligible. The people who are here are happy and excited—there just aren't enough of them.
>
> In short, *I am beginning to think we have done the right thing in the wrong place* [author's italics]. We have made a near complete transition to a purpose-driven model that I believed would make a huge impact, and it has not. Maybe it just hasn't had enough time. But now that is running out.
>
> I believe our team is going to have to break up and go our separate ways soon. We just can't sustain our current payroll much longer. Keep us in your prayers. And if you hear from some search committee, don't be alarmed.[13]

Finishing well in a ministry of transition can be as hard as the ministry itself. People are the unpredictable variable in change. Their choices, attitudes, and actions can make a well-thought-out strategy plan look like a preschooler's drawing of the universe. You can do the right thing but be in the wrong place when you do it because those you seek to lead refuse to follow. Finishing well is part of the art of servant leadership in a ministry of transition.

You are in good company with the Apostle Paul when you find yourself wondering if you "have done the right thing in the wrong place." He had to have wondered the same thing as he left cities like Corinth and Athens. Does an e-mail message like this one or Paul's realization that it could appear to some that he has failed in some way (2 Cor. 13:6-8) mean the servant leader is a failure? Not in any way! Servant leaders finish well when they are faithful to their call until God says stop or move on. The question of success for the

Key Verse

I have fought the good fight, I have finished the race, I have kept the faith.
—2 Timothy 4:7

"Remember, Jesus went all the way, and that meant patience, and that meant suffering."
—Brian D. McLaren

servant leader in the ministry of transition is, have I been faithful to my call, and has God used that faithfulness in some way to further His kingdom?

What are some times when you have thought you may be doing the right thing in the wrong place? How did you respond to that thought?

Paul was in prison in Rome toward the end of his ministry when he wrote to his apprentice Timothy. He had been faithful to his call, and he had seen God do miraculous things through him. He had also felt the stones of opposition and strategies to stop him. How did he summarize his work?

Read 2 Timothy 4:6-7. How did Paul describe his life? In the margin write verse 7 in your own words. What does this confession say about Paul's assessment of his ministry?

Paul used the language of the temple worship to describe his life as he sat in prison in Rome. He was "being poured out as a drink offering," and he was sure "the time for his departure" was close at hand (2 Tim. 4:6). But he was not despondent or discouraged knowing that his ministry was drawing to its end. He made three declarative statements that reveal he knew he was finishing well. Like a bruised and bloody fighter, he had "fought the good fight." Like a tired but victorious runner, he had "finished the race." As a persecuted leader in a mission outpost, he had "kept the faith."

Paul assessed his ministry of transition in response to Christ's call on his life by drawing from real-life metaphors everyone could understand. Notice the maturity of his statements. He was not declaring victory over all others. He did not claim to be successful in every battle. He humbly confessed he had done his part in bringing Jesus to the ethnics.

To "fight the good fight" is not to knock the guy out in the first round. The image implies going the distance; and whether victory is won, the fighter would be remembered as hanging in there, taking punches, and throwing some of his own. To go the distance takes discipline, training, and a heart to keep going after the first effective blow is struck.

To "finish the race" means more the older you are. Winning is everything in youth. Young, talented runners don't even think about whether they will finish the race. They plan and train to win the races they enter. At 50, my goal is simply to finish the marathons, ultramarathons, and triathlons I enter. I was never a gifted runner, but I have only one DNF (did not finish) in my limited running experience. I am usually in the middle of the finishers in my age group and am happy to have my name posted among those who completed the race. To finish the race of transition is to say a lot. Since the ministry of transition is an ultramarathon and not a sprint triathlon, finishing is a huge accomplishment. Paul knew this, too.

To "keep the faith" is never to waiver from your convictions or purpose. You finish well when you can say, "I never sold out to convenience," or, "I never denied my faith in Christ's call on my life to do this." Keeping the faith is being challenged by everything from teaching a feel-good gospel to watering down the deep truths of Scripture and continuing to proclaim a clear call to follow Jesus. Keeping the faith is pursuing call over career and risking your pension plan to follow Jesus wherever He leads.

Which of the three examples for finishing well best describes your heart? Be prepared to share this with your mission outpost team.

The question of success for the servant leader in the ministry of transition is, have I been faithful to my call, and has God used that faith- fulness in some way to further His kingdom?

Finishing Well

Paul's confession in his letter to Timothy is the basis for our final reality of servant leadership in a ministry of transition:

Reality 8: Servant leaders finish well (see 2 Tim. 4:7).

Servant leaders finish well because they are committed to their call and care enough for their people not to leave until their work is done. They may not win a prize for being the first to finish or being the best at their trade. They will win the prize from their Leader if they fight a good fight, finish the race, and keep the faith.

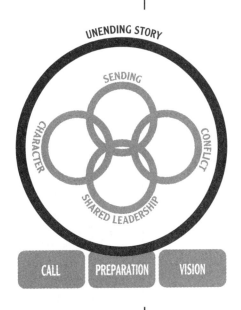

Why Some Leaders Fail

Some leaders do not finish the race of transition. There are many reasons for this, but one is that the leader becomes more committed to pleasing people than to completing the mission. Pleasing people, I believe, stops more transitions than any other reason. A person is not a leader when, as soon as he is opposed, he turns back from where he was leading. The mission is jeopardized when leaders fail to follow through.

A biblical example of this failure to move forward because peer pressure was too great was when Peter pulled back from participating with the ethnic followers of Jesus when traditionalists came from Jerusalem to Antioch. Paul confronted Peter for his giving into peer pressure to maintain the status quo.

Read Galatians 2:11-14. Why did Paul say he "opposed" Peter? What was the result of Peter's actions? Write your response in the margin.

Paul "opposed [Peter] to his face" because he believed he had compromised his commitment to the shared mission to reach ethnics for Christ. Peter had joined Paul in eating and associating openly with ethnics when they were together. However, when some Jewish followers of Jesus showed up from Jerusalem, Peter would no longer associate with the ethnics. Paul called this hypocrisy (v. 13).

I call this the "weak-kneed Peter" syndrome. Leaders face it all the time. A pastor, for example, begins a new work, but as soon as a disgruntled donor or dissatisfied influencer begins to resist, he returns to the status quo. The pastor may have added staff to start the new initiative, and when the leader retreats, the staff member is left hanging out to dry—confused and frustrated now that he must maintain what he or she was told to change. When this happens, those who came to the church in response to the new initiative become confused and uncertain about the true identity of the church. They wonder what really drives the church on mission. They guess correctly that there are powers at work they do not see. This is why some people say, "I just want to attend worship and be in a small group. I don't want to get involved in the politics of the church. I've seen that before, and it's not pretty."

Accommodation to resistance is the enemy of endurance that is necessary to finish well. Pleasing power brokers rather than "keeping the faith" will destroy the leader and that which he leads. It will keep him from finishing well. I am not saying, "Don't listen to people's thoughts and feelings." Good

Reality 8: Servant leaders finish well.

139

leaders seek and accept honest input from those they lead. They make adjustments related to that input, but they do not turn back from the direction set by the mission simply because they get negative input or threats to stop funds.

The mission is everything for the servant leader. Once committed to the mission, a servant leader in a ministry of transition does not step away from its implications—even when influential people threaten to withdraw support. You can't have it both ways.

Where are you on the people pleasing meter? Do people's opinions sway your thinking and even commitment to the call to become a mission outpost?

Signs of Finishing Well

One indicator that a pastor, for example, has finished well is that when called to another mission field, members do not look for your alter ego. Too many churches experience whiplash when your opposite shows up six months after your departure. This happens when the people say, "He was a great pastor, but we really need a preacher." Or, "Boy could he preach, but he never went to the hospital." If you have not established the mission and vision as the basis for choosing leaders, you have not finished well. You have left the majority who outlasted you to bring the church back to their likes.

When you depart, those in your ministry should say, "He brought us this far on our mission. Praise God. Now who does God have for us to take us closer to completing it?" My prayer is that if or when I am called to another ministry, the leaders who select my replacement will evaluate my effectiveness as a servant leader who led them to a certain place. They will know the progress we have made toward the vision God showed us, and they will prayerfully seek a leader who is a better leader than me to move them closer to the vision. Servant leaders don't have to be the best leader among the portraits that hang on the foyer wall. Each must be the leader who did his part in moving people closer to God's call on their lives at that specific time in the life of the church.

What kind of leader do you sense your church would choose if you were to leave your position of leadership? This applies to staff and ministry leadership positions. Is the mission and vision so much a part of the church's culture that they would want a leader who can build on what you did? Or would they simply seek out the kind of leader they want for themselves?

Another indicator that you have finished well is when you leave your ministry as a baton to pass to the next leader rather than a mess for a cleanup crew to fix. Too many leaders leave the church they served with more problems than when they came. If you are going to enter the ministry of transition, care enough to stay until the church is healthy enough to receive a new servant leader. Several times through my tenure of transition I have been tempted to leave. But that usually came when there were no other options but to continue the "good fight." Seeing only conflict and opposition can send even the strongest leader to update his resume or look for calmer waters.

Finishing well means you pass the baton of mission, vision, core values, and a passion for God and people to the next leader. Serving in a mission outpost is a relay race. Each leg is run by an individual leader who does his or her best to run that leg to the best of his or her ability. The success of the race falls on the team of runners, not one person. Finishing poorly means that when you leave, a disaster cleanup crew is the only option for the next season of leadership. While disasters happen in transitions, a servant leader who loves the people will help clean up the mess before he goes to another ministry.

Is your ministry currently a baton or a mess? What is the state of your ministry if you left today?

Leave a Legacy

Nanus and Dobbs state that "a long-term perspective is important if one is to think about, at the appropriate time down the road, bequeathing a legacy, handing over the past to the future."[14] To leave a legacy that lasts, leaders will:

Prepare others to be leaders—This is a way to allow someone in the organization the leader has built to succeed the outgoing leader. Leadership development is key to passing leadership on to someone else in the organization.

Know when to leave—Leaders leave for various reasons. They have completed the job they were called to complete. They long for new challenges. They sense God has another venue for their leadership. Voluntary departures allow the leader to give his reasons for leaving and "to shape that event and even their legacy."

Face the music—Even great leaders can stay too long. My greatest fear is someone saying, "I wish Gene would go ahead and leave. He's just waiting around to retire, and we need to get on with it." Servant leaders must take an honest assessment of their ministry to know when its time to go. Nanus and Dobbs conclude, "It is not easy for anyone to face the fact that a time may come when the best option is a definite but dignified exit."[15]

Finishing well and leaving a legacy is a servant leader's opportunity to bless those with whom he served and led. Don't be the one not to complete what God has called you to do, but if you are done, finish in a way that honors God and blesses the people.

Richard Kriegbaum offers this prayer for those who may be his successors: "Protect me from preserving my own position or power or perspectives at the expense of future leaders. When they point out where I have not led well, shut my mouth and open my heart. Help me make it safe for them to try new things. Let me touch the spirit of those who possess the heart of a servant. I want to know them and love them and watch their energy flow into others around them. I want to claim them for this work and pray them into my place."[16]

Finishing well and leaving a legacy is a servant leader's opportunity to bless those with whom he has served and led.

141

THE UNENDING STORY

Key Verse

Then he stayed two whole years in his own rented house. And he welcomed all who visited him, proclaiming the kingdom of God and teaching the things concerning the Lord Jesus Christ with full boldness and without hindrance.
—Acts 28:30-31

The last words in the Book of Acts are "without hindrance." Luke intentionally coined the last sentence of his record of the Acts of the Apostles to reflect that what was started by God at Pentecost continued to flourish unhindered around the world. Like the ending to a magnificent novel that makes you want to read the sequel or enter into the adventure of the characters you have learned to love, this ending to Acts draws true followers of Jesus into the adventure of leading people on mission. The church, which "the forces of Hades will not overpower" (Matt. 16:18), grows as an unstoppable force to the ends of the earth.

Servant leaders in a ministry of transition are part of that same story. The saga of Acts is open-ended. There is no conclusion because there is no ending until the Author and Finisher puts down his pen and closes the book of history. We who serve in a mission outpost are part of that unending story. What we do now echoes in eternity and impacts the lives of people's eternal destinies. We want to be in the race, in the fight, to remain faithful to play a part of this eternal struggle for the hearts of people.

What does this "unending story" provide for the servant leader?

1. It gives us an eternal perspective to our troubles compared to his riches in glory. Eternity is the punch line to life's joke. It lets us put things in perspective. Eternity and our union with Christ in heaven help us survive the struggles on this side.

2. This unending story is the source of our hope. When the servant leader faces conflict and opposition or when she is about to throw in the towel, the story of others who have gone before and faced greater odds and worse afflictions give her hope to continue on.

3. In the unending story of eternity, we will find our Leader's pleasure for our faithfulness. Every servant leader longs to here his Leader say, "Well done, good and faithful servant" (Matt. 25:21). It is the pleasure of the one who called him, not the applause of people, that motivates the servant leader to join the ranks in the story of eternity.

4. It motivates us to "press on to take hold of that for which Christ Jesus took hold of [us]" (Phil. 3:12, NIV). Servant leaders in mission outposts have been "taken" by Christ and sent on an adventure like no other. Being convinced you are part of the same story that did not end in the Book of Acts causes you to "press on to take hold" of the One who called you and gave His life for you.

5. This eternal story lets us forget what is behind us and "strain toward what is ahead" (Phil. 3:13, NIV). The unending story dims the hurt of the past and brightens the hope for the future. We have a "heavenward" calling that we do not want to squander on earth. We press on like pioneers seeking safe passage through the Rockies. We have read about an ocean, and we want to seek it. No majestic mountain range with all of its beauty and danger will keep us from seeing the ocean of God's love for us.

The mission to make disciples will continue until the One who sent us calls us home. We will always know at the end of day that our God has not called us to fail but to contribute. He who suffered loss on the cross will suffer with us. He who promised His presence to empower us for the mission will fill us with power to face whatever the natural or spiritual world throws at us. We continue because we are not yet home.

Servant leaders in a ministry of transition are characters in the unending story of God's love for all peoples. Convinced of this, they boldly serve the mission and lead people toward God's vision.

I like the way John Eldridge ends his book *Wild at Heart*: "Now, reader, it's your turn to write—venture forth with God. Remember, don't ask yourself what the world needs."[17] Ask yourself what makes you come alive, and go do that, because what the world needs is people who have some alive.

It's your turn, servant leader. "Venture forth with God."

1. Brian D. McLaren, *The Church on the Other Side* (Grand Rapids: Zondervan, 2000), 65.

2. Mark Strom, *Reframing Paul* (Downers Grove, IL: InterVarsity Press, 2000), 182.

3. Ibid., 186.

4. Bill Easum, *Unfreezing Moves* (Nashville: Abingdon Press, 2001), 100.

5. Brent Curtis and John Eldredge, *The Sacred Romance* (Nashville: Thomas Nelson, 1997), 39.

6. Michael Slaughter, *unLearning Church* (Loveland, CO: Group, 2002), 62.

7. Suzanne Mickelson, a Legacy member and corporate leadership trainer at a major corporation in our area, pointed me to this group. She described it as a company that provides training to businesses, schools, and communities based on 49 character qualities. Go to http://www.characterfirst.com/ for more information. Their primary resource is *Achieving True Success*. It introduces the concept of character development within the family. Another superb resource on character is Os Guinness, *When No One Sees, The Importance of Character in an Age of Image* (Colorado Springs: NavPress, 2000).

8. J. Robert Clinton, *The Making of a Leader* (Colorado Springs: Navpress, 1988), 167.

9. Strom, *Reframing Paul*, 111.

10. Clinton, *The Making of a Leader*, 167.

11. Ronald A. Heifetz and Marty Linsky, *Leadership on the Line* (Cambridge: Harvard Business School, 2002), 230.

12. Erwin McManus, *Uprising: A Revolution of the Soul* (Nashville: Thomas Nelson, 2003), 252.

13. I heard from him at the writing of this workbook that peace had come to the church and it was growing some. He was still looking for the right place to do what he was called to do.

14. Burt Nanus and Stephen M. Dobbs, *Leaders Who Make a Difference* (Indianapolis, IN: Jossey-Bass, 1999), 240.

15. Ibid., 249.

16. Richard Kriegbaum, *Leadership Prayers* (Carol Stream, IL: Tyndale House Publishers, 1998), 38.

17. John Eldredge, *Wild at Heart* (Nashville: Thomas Nelson, 2001), 220, 200.

LEADER'S GUIDE

General Instructions

The following information will guide you as the leader of this study. Feel free to adapt the suggestions to fit the needs and goals of those you are facilitating. After answering a few general questions, we will provide guidelines for each of the seven meetings you will facilitate as the leader.

Who is this study for? This study is for those who sense change is necessary in their ministry or church in order to pursue God's call to engage the mission field around them. It is for those who have seen God at work through other churches and desire to be part of what God is doing to revive and reform the church and to be more effective in reaching people for Christ. This workbook is for anyone seeking to gain insight into the ministry of Paul, the apostle, who brought the message of Jesus to the ethnics. His ministry of transition is an example and model for any servant leader wanting to be obedient to God's call on his or her life.

This book is for pastors, staff, and leaders of ministries in or alongside the church. Most churches entrust leadership to these people and groups, and they should be the first in the church to complete the workbook. Each leader should have a group around him or her who will be a key to any changes that come within the organization. Groups or teams around these leaders should be included in the early uses of this workbook. This workbook can be a guide for an entire congregation or organization to enter a ministry of transition.

This workbook is for any follower of Jesus who has sensed a clear call to take the message of Jesus into the mission field around him or her. God has chosen a single person many times to do His work among a people. Simply by going through this study with an open heart could lead to finding what God desires for you to do for Him where He has planted you.

How can I use this study in my church? If you lead a ministry, you can walk through this study on your own. You can expect God to speak to you as you study the Bible and the ministry of Paul, the one sent to the ethnics. If you are planning to lead a group through this process, you are encouraged to do the entire workbook yourself before leading the group.

This book can be used as a Bible study as part of a Sunday School ministry, a workbook for Discipleship Training, or as an individual study for those seeking deeper knowledge about the Bible and God's work with and through people. Ministry teams, deacons, and small groups can benefit from this study. It is best used as a primer to transition any ministry or church to become what God has called it to become.

Your Mission Outpost Team and Journal

The contents of this workbook are most effective when completed and shared with a small group of people. The leader is encouraged to recruit a mission outpost team to go through the study with him or her. We call this team after the biblical model of the mission outpost church that originated in Antioch described in Acts 11. This team may be key leaders in your church or ministry who you must include in any transition issues you face or perceive you must face. The members of your mission outpost team may be potential leaders in your ministry whom you are seeking to recruit to aid you in a season of transition. The team members may be friends who have the same sense you do about following Jesus into your mission field, and together you want to explore what God may be calling you to do.

This team will gather once a week. During the small group meeting, members of the group will be asked to share thoughts, insights, and feelings from the previous week's study. "Be prepared to share your answer with your mission outpost team at your next meeting" will be part of each week's discussion. Completing these items will ensure the team time will be most productive.

Journaling is a way to record your feelings and insights as you walk through the ministry of transition. Each person on the mission outpost team is encouraged to purchase a personal journal. Instructions will be given throughout the workbook to record thoughts, insights, and prayers during the study and/or through the duration of transition. This can provide a record of God's work to complete His call on your life. The author has included some of his own journal entries to encourage you.

How long is the study? How often do we meet? *Paul on Leadership* is a six-week, five-day-a-week study. Each week's study will cover one topic in five daily lessons. Review the table of contents for the topics and progression of the study. Plan at least 30 minutes to complete each daily study. This time will vary according to each participant's desire and ability to complete the work. Some people work faster than others, so do not discourage those who may take more or less time to finish each day's lesson. Do not wait until the night before your mission outpost meeting to complete the week's work! You will miss the impact of each day's study if you do.

You will meet seven times as a small group to process what was learned in the daily studies. For continuity, it is best to meet for seven consecutive weeks. Plan on about an hour for each group meeting. (Instructions for each meeting follow.) If you meet in a home and provide snacks and a time of worship, plan for an hour and a half to two hours for your meetings.

What do I need to lead a mission outpost group meeting? You are the leader of this study in your church because you are in a leadership position or someone asked you to lead. Do not be concerned that you must know all the biblical passages and principles in this workbook before you lead the group. (We recommend that you complete the entire study on your own before leading a group.) As the leader, you are simply the facilitator of each week's meeting. Follow the instructions in this leader guide, and it will provide the questions to answers and the comments to make. Participants will provide answers and insights from their personal studies during the week.

You will need a Bible—the HCSB is the primary version used for the study—and a workbook for each participant for each meeting. Journals are optional. You can also make copies of the worksheets provided at the end of this leader's guide for those in the group.

You will also want to choose an appropriate meeting place to hold your group meetings. You can meet in a classroom at the church's facilities or in an office or home. Choose a place that best meets the needs of the group and your church's goals for offering this study. Notify those participating in the group prior to your first meeting where you are planning to meet. At the first meeting you can decide if that is the best setting for the group. You may want to rotate where you meet among the homes or offices of the members.

You will need an open and compassionate heart as you lead. Each participant will come with his or her own needs and expectations for the study. Most will be in leadership and therefore will want to have influence upon the group and the process of transition. You are a mentor to the group—not the answer person. Plan to spend any extra time outside the mission outpost team meetings to nurture those in the group who may need your influence. Your purpose as the leader is to help people know and live out God's calling on their lives and to learn how that fits into God's plan for the church or ministry.

What does a typical group meeting look like? While each meeting can be customized to fit the needs and goals of your group, a typical meeting will follow this format:

Opening Prayer	5 minutes
Group Interaction Activity	10–15 minutes
Group Sharing *(what they learned during the week's study)*	45–60 minutes
Closing Prayer Time *(prayer for specific needs in the group)*	10–15 minutes

Most of the time will be spent answering questions from the workbook study during the previous week. As mentioned earlier, the goal is not to get all the answers right but to lead people to a deeper understanding of who they are in Christ and how to live like Him in their daily lives. Participation in the sharing time is for personal growth, not to fill in all the blanks.

How do I get people to join me in this study? People have limited time, and most are not looking for something else to do. However, when God begins to stir in the hearts of leaders and participants that there is something they must do to be on mission, people must respond. Recruit with urgency if that is so. Recruit with a call to see what God may want your church or ministry to become. Invite people to learn more about the servant leader, Paul, who left the comfort and status of organized religion to join a movement of God.

Most churches need four to six weeks of publicity prior to the first meeting in order for the membership to know and register for the study. This time frame is for publicity after the staff or church leadership team has adopted the study as part of their ongoing ministry. You can use your church newsletter, the local newspaper, and/or specialty publications to announce the study. Another way to encourage people to enroll in the study is to have someone (maybe yourself) give a testimony in a worship service as to what the study has done and can do to help users understand their identity in Christ. Have a sign-up sheet ready for people to enroll in the study at the end of the service.

Mission Outpost Team Meeting 1

Goal—To introduce participants to one another and to the overall direction of the study.

Opening prayer—Pray that members will allow God to guide them as they seek to see their mission field and church as God sees them. Pray, too, that they will be sensitive to God's Spirit leading them to be more like His servant Paul in their ministry and faith.

Group interaction activity—Since this is your first meeting, you may want to spend more time in this activity than in the weeks ahead. Ask participants to introduce themselves and to tell about a time in their life when they had to make a change because of a decision they made or circumstances around them. Ask them to share their feelings about the change, the struggles related to the change, and how their lives were different after the change. Examples can include anything from losing weight to making a career change.

You begin with your story of change. When you have finished, say, "We will spend the next seven weeks studying the leadership and ministry of Paul. His ministry was one of transition from old to new ways of relating to God. We will spend our time examining the Bible and hearing how God is calling each of you to participate in His purposes to reach all people for Him. Let's begin to look at the need for change in our church/ministry."

Group sharing—You have recruited this team as either a study group or a potential team that will enter with you into a ministry of transition. Ask each member to describe his or her place of ministry. Ask them the tenure of their ministry and what changes they have seen take place while they were there. Ask them, too, to describe some change they have led while in ministry and what that experience was like.

Distribute workbooks to each participant. Read the opening story in week 1 together. After reading the story, ask them to share their initial feelings about the story of Jefferson. After they have shared, say, "The author wrote, 'My fear was that our church would become such a place if we let 'progress upstream' or 'dependence on doing what we've always done' take away our opportunity to be effective for God. I didn't want Legacy Drive Baptist Church to become another 'museum to missed opportunity.'" Ask them to turn to the section "Is Your Church Jefferson?" and ask them to take a few minutes to write their first impressions to the questions asked there.

After they have finished writing their answers, allow time for each one to respond to the questions. As the facilitator, make sure everyone participates and that no one dominates the group. This is not a time to air a personal agenda or to criticize leaders. It is the beginning of a journey you will all take together as you complete the workbook. When you finish, say, "Next week will go further into this session, and we will share what we will learn about Paul and his ministry to the ethnics. Make time to do the assignments we are about to review, and come ready to discuss what you are learning."

Review "This Week's Assignments.

Closing prayer time (prayer for specific needs in the group)—Have the group stand in a circle and hold hands, if you feel this is appropriate for your group. Ask members to say a sentence prayer asking God to begin to guide their thinking and knit their hearts together in unity as they pursue God's mission and vision for their ministry/church.

This Week's Assignments

1. Ask each member to memorize this week's key verse, Ephesians 3:7-8 (day 1).
2. Ask them to complete week 1 of the study. Give them the hint that anywhere in the workbook the instructions say, "Be prepared to share your answer with your mission outpost team at your next meeting," that will be part of each week's discussion. Completing these items will ensure the team time will be most productive.
3. Tell the group, "The mission outpost team time will be based on your responses to the interactive parts of the workbook and the personal review statements and questions. Be sure to complete the whole day's lesson in order to participate in the interaction of the team at its next meeting."
4. Leader: Contact each participant before the next meeting. Thank them for joining the group and offer your prayers and support throughout the study. Remind of the time and location for the next meeting.

Mission Outpost Team Meeting 2

Goal—To introduce participants to the need for change and to Paul, the apostle, as a servant leader.

Opening prayer—Pray that each member will allow God to guide them as they look at the need for change in order to respond to their changing mission field and God's call on their lives to make disciples. Ask that God speak clearly through the group to discern his desires for each person in the group and for the ministry/church in which they serve.

Group interaction activity—Just for fun, ask group members (if they are married) to describe their most memorable anniversary. If someone is not married, ask him or her to describe the most memorable date or birthday party that someone planned for them. Allow time for those who want to share to do so. Remind each one of the importance of showing others how much they are loved by the things we do for them.

Group sharing—Ask members to recite the key verse, Ephesians 3:7-8.

Ask the group to turn to the reflection section at the end of day 1. Ask them to share what they wrote in response to the directions that begin, "Here is the list of Callahan's three observations."

At the end of day 2, participants were asked, "What is the scope of your influence? Do you have an 'ends of the earth' perception of what God can do with your witness of words and actions? Or do you see your influence only to those who show up in the church's buildings? Are you telling your Christ story to those in your home and hometown?" Ask the members of your group to share their answers with one another.

In day 3 you were asked to interact with the list of shifts in Paul's ministry. Ask members of your mission outpost team to turn to the worksheet in the leader guide (p. 154). Ask them to record the impressions of all team members. This collection from the team can give an indication of what the team may want or need to address in your ministry.

Ask the group, "Do you believe that our church is mission-driven as Paul was?" Wait for answers. When the group has responded, ask, "Do you believe we are a vision-drawn ministry/church?" If the answer is yes, ask them to describe that vision. If the answer is no, you have an opportunity to facilitate that process by beginning the vision quest as mentioned in day the reflection on day 4, or do a more extensive quest after this study.

Day 5 opened with a story about Tom and how he mentored high school students in his garage. Do you have a person like Tom in your ministry/church? If so, describe that person to the group and how he or she contributes to your mission to make disciples.

Review "This Week's Assignments."

Closing prayer time (prayer for specific needs in the group)—Take time to list any personal needs of members in their personal, family or work life. Pause and pray for a particular need if you feel led. Close the time praying that God will reveal to each individual in the group His clear call on their life and ministry.

This Week's Assignments

1. Ask each member to memorize this week's key verse, 1 Corinthians 4:1 (day 2). You may want to have them turn to that page and put a star by the verse to remind them.
2. Ask them to complete the study for week 2. Tell them that this week is important to them personally. It is about knowing and being obedient to God's call on their lives and their ministries.
3. Ask members to pray for one another as they seek to understand their calling in Christ.
4. Consider finding an object like the ones described in week 2 that symbolize the commitment of the team to one another. Either prepare to give that symbol to the group at the next meeting or come with ideas for the group.

Mission Outpost Team Meeting 3

Goal—To introduce participants to God's call to join Him on mission and how God may prepare them to carry out that mission.

Opening prayer—Pray that as the group considers God's call to join Him on mission they will discern the true nature and implications of that call. Also pray that they will be willing to allow God to do whatever is necessary to prepare them for that mission.

Group interaction activity—The opening story to week 2 is about Doug, who found his ministry in the marketplace. Ask the group to tell about a person they may know who has faced similar circumstances. Ask them to describe what the interim time between jobs was like. Did the person find a similar job or a different place to live out his or her calling? Say, "This week's session was about God's calling affecting everything you do. Let's look at how calling affected Paul and how God prepared him to live out that calling."

Group sharing—Ask members to recite the memory verse for this week, 1 Corinthians 4:1 (day 2).

Ask members to share their answers to the question, "What are some ideas, ways of doing church or beliefs about God that have changed from your childhood to now?" in day 1's material.

At the end of day 2 is a personal/group reflection activity. Ask each member to share his or her personal answers. When everyone has finished sharing the answers about themselves, ask them how they answered in relation to their ministry/church.

Day 4 begins a section on preparation for mission. Ask members to turn to the opening section of day 4's material. Read, "You may be or have been on a team that shared something to signify their commitment to one another and to the mission they had been given to complete. Write a description of that symbol and what it meant to you and your team." Ask them to share that description with the group. Ask them if there is a symbol you, as a current group, could share to signal your commitment to one another.

In day 5 is the section "Five Questions Your Church Must Answer." Review these questions on page 53. Record the answers from each team member on page 155, and then come to consensus as to the primary direction the group should take in relation to their answers.

Review "This Week's Assignments."

Closing prayer time (prayer for specific needs in the group)—Take time to pray for any personal items the members are facing in their personal, family, or work life. Pause and pray for a particular need if you feel led. Close the time praying that each member will open his or her heart to the actions that God could use to prepare them for His purposes in the days ahead.

This Week's Assignments

1. Ask each member to memorize this week's key verse, Galatians 3:27-28 (day 4). You may want to have them turn to that page and put a star by the verse to remind them that it is the memory verse.

2. Ask them to complete week 3 of the study. Tell them that this week is about seeing their mission field as God sees it and discerning when to expand the mission beyond their current situation.

3. Tell them to complete the daily lessons, including personal review sections.

4. Ask members to pray for one another individually as they seek to understand the realities and principles associated with leading the church through change.

Mission Outpost Team Meeting 4

Goal—To introduce participants to the realities and principles associated with a ministry of transition and to discover ways God would have you expand the mission.

Opening prayer—Pray that God will show them the pieces of this session that apply directly to their lives and the ministries they share together. Pray that God will reveal to them those who would be set apart to expand the mission to make disciples of all people. Pray for God's protection of their ministry/church during days of change and transition.

Group interaction activity—Ask the group to share their answers to the questions at the beginning of day 2, "What are some transitions you have experienced in your personal, family, or business life?" Pick one of those transitions and describe how that season of transition affected you emotionally, spiritually, or physically.

Group sharing—Ask members to recite the memory verse for this week, Galatians 3:27-28 (day 4).

Begin the group sharing time by turning to page 156, "The Antioch Mission Outpost Model and My Ministry/Church." Ask them to record other members' answers and to share their own answers. After everyone has shared, ask the group to answer the question, "How do we rate as a model of a mission outpost like the one in Antioch?"

In day 3 you reviewed some "shifts in ministry" you may face as a ministry/church. At the end of that day's materials, you were asked to identify the transitions you may need to address immediately and to state what is the priority transition. Ask each member to tell which transition he or she chose.

Day 4 introduced you to six principles of transition. Which one did you identify as the most needed in your ministry/church? Ask each member to share his or her answer with the group.

In day 5 the section "Who Is Set Apart?" raises the issue of ordination and commissioning of people for ministry. In the reflection section, the instructions that begin, "Describe your church's concept of ordination." Invite member to share their answers with the group.

Review "This Week's Assignments."

Closing prayer time (prayer for specific needs in the group)—Pray for any needs members are facing in their personal, family, or work life. Pause and pray for a particular need if you feel led. Close the time by praying that each member will be boldly obedient to what God has led them to address related to completing the mission He has called them to complete. Pray that the mission call of God will burn in each heart and that God will empower them to step out in faith to make the changes necessary to do His will.

This Week's Assignments

1. Ask each member to memorize this week's key verse, Philippians 2:3-4 (day 4). You may want to have them turn to that page and put a star by the verse to remind them that is the memory verse.
2. Ask them to complete their study of week 4. Tell them this week is about facing opposition and enduring conflict in the ministry of transition.
3. Tell them to complete the daily lessons including the personal review sections.
4. Ask members to pray for one another as they consider the opposition and conflicts they may face as they lead in a ministry of transition.

Mission Outpost Team Meeting 5

Goal—To introduce participants to possible opposition and conflict that arise as a result of implementing transitions toward the vision God has called your ministry/church to become.

Opening prayer—Pray that members will be sensitive to the hurts and wounds that other members may have in their lives because of conflict. Ask God to reveal to each member what he or she must do to right any wrong in relationship with others as a result of this time together. Pray that God will continue to mold the group into a team of Christ followers who want nothing more than to see God's vision for the ministry/church come into being.

Group interaction activity—Session 4 begins with a story about a young pastor who was asked to resign by a small group of members in the church. Ask the members of the team if they have experienced anything like that personally. This could have happened in a job firing or in their church or ministry. Be sensitive to the emotions that may surface during this time of sharing. Pause and pray for others' hurts if you feel the need to do so.

Group sharing—Ask members to recite the memory verse for this week, Philippians 2:3-4 (day 4).

Day 1 walks through the conflict over including ethnics into the Jesus movement as recorded in Acts 15. Turn to page 157, "Anatomy of a Conflict." Ask them to record one another's answers. After everyone has finished sharing, compile the information into a single sheet as a way to communicate what they have experienced to others.

Ask members to share their responses to the reflection section in day 3 that begins, "If you have experienced conflict in your church and/or ministry, tell your mission outpost team the good things that have resulted from these tough times."

In day 4, the blanks are filled with the following words from Philippians 2:3-4. "Do nothing out of rivalry or conceit" (v. 3). "In humility, consider others more important than yourselves." "Everyone should look out not only for his own interests, but also for the interests of others" (v. 4). Ask members which of Paul's instructions apply to their lives at this time.

Day 5 addresses the spiritual influences that can cause conflict in a ministry of transition. Ask members to answer the following questions from their workbook, "How would you describe your church? Do people seem to pay more attention to the wants and wishes of a few, or do they exhibit the presence of Christ? Is your church's government about controlling or releasing people to ministry? Is your church's focus inward or outward?"

Review "This Week's Assignments."

Closing prayer time (prayer for specific needs in the group)—Take time to pray for those who may be hurting because of conflict in their lives. Ask the group members to mention the names of people with whom they have had conflict. Pray for each person and the situation. Ask God to heal broken relationships and move the ministry forward. Also take time to pray like Paul against any evil influences that may infect the ministry or church. Claim Jesus' promise that the church will be resilient through any conflict or opposition.

This Week's Assignments

1. Ask each member to memorize this week's key verse, 1 Corinthians 3:6-8 (day 3). You may want to have them turn to that page and put a star by the verse to remind them that it is the memory verse.
2. Ask them to complete week 5. Tell them that it is about the importance of shared leadership in a ministry of transition. We will observe how Paul

shared his leadership through effective ministry teams and their leaders.

3. Tell them to complete each of the daily lessons including the personal review sections.

4. Ask members to pray for one another individually as they seek to expand the mission by sharing their leadership with others.

Mission Outpost Team Meeting 6

Goal—To introduce participants to the art of shared leadership and how to find and keep leaders.

Opening prayer—Pray that members will be open to including others in leadership related to accomplishing God's purposes in their ministry/church. Pray that each member will have a servant's heart and the desire to equip others for ministry with them.

Group interaction activity—Week 5, day 1 begins with an e-mail message from a young leader who wondered if the author had ever second-guessed his decisions. The study asked, "Have you ever felt like this staff member? When and what were the circumstances around it? What advice would you give this young leader?" Invite members to share their similar feelings and the advice they would give this leader.

Group sharing—Ask members to recite the memory verse for this week, 1 Corinthians 3:6-8 (day 3).

In day 2, the participant is asked to share his or her experience with "my best team." Ask them to share that experience now.

Ask members to share their answers to the questions in day 3, "Name two coworkers in your ministry. Describe why you consider them to be coworkers."

Day 4 addresses the effectiveness of multiple leaders in conflict. Have members turn to page 158, "Multiple Leaders Make a Difference." Read the instructions to the group. They will share their answers from their work during the week prior to the meeting. Say, "Here is a group of leaders that God has placed among us to accomplish His call on our ministry/church. If we are willing to share our leadership with them, God can do greater things through and with us."

In day 5 the author tells about the time his leadership team affirmed him by giving him gifts with a message. Ask, "When in your experience as a leader has a team come around you to affirm your gifts and strengths? When have you orchestrated a similar event to affirm others?"

Review "This Week's Assignments."

Closing prayer time (prayer for specific needs in the group)—Take time to pray that each member of the team will seek out others to share leadership. Thank God for the multiple leaders in this group and in the ministry/church. Pray that the group can grow closer together as a team to do the work God called them to do.

This Week's Assignments

1. Ask each member to memorize this week's key verse, 2 Corinthians 4:5 (day 1). You may want to have them turn to that page and put a star by the verse to remind them that it is the memory verse.

2. Ask them to complete week 6 of the Study. Tell them that this week is about the message of mission and how to most effectively communicate it. They will also observe how Paul finished well.

3. Tell them to be sure to complete each of the daily lessons including the personal review sections.

4. Ask members to pray for one another individually as they seek to complete

the study and continue to wrestle with the issues facing them in their ministry of transition.

Mission Outpost Team Meeting 7

Goal—To introduce participants to the message of the mission and how to communicate it to their mission field and to introduce them to the importance of character in the leader of a ministry of transition.

Opening prayer—Pray that as the group addresses how to communicate the message of the mission to their mission field God will reveal the most effective ways to proceed. Pray that as the group speaks to character issues everyone will be open and vulnerable to the Spirit's leadership.

Group interaction activity—Have members turn to page 159, "My Core Message." Read the instructions to the group and then ask them to share. Take time to affirm each core message. Ask for ways the group can help other members share that message effectively.

Group sharing—Ask members to recite the memory verse for this week, 2 Corinthians 4:5 (day 1).

In day 2 the author spoke to having a "clear call" where Christ is center to all we say. Say: "You were asked to answer the following questions, 'What do you resonate with in the section above? What causes some concern?' Share your answers with the group.

Day 3 addressed the issue of the leader's character. The participant took time to assess how Paul described his actions among the Thessalonians. Ask members to share their answers to the following instructions, "Write a description of Paul's character in your own words. What claims did he make that you can make about your character? Ask your mission outpost team to help you assess those claims."

Paul described how he was ending his ministry in 2 Timothy 4:6-7, day 4 of session 6. He used three images to tell Timothy how he felt about how he was finishing. Ask members to share their answers to the question, "Which of the three examples for finishing well best describes your heart?"

Day 5 ends with providing ways for the servant leader to feel a part of the "unending story." Turn to that list and ask the members to share which of the five suggestions help them most in their ministry of transition.

Closing prayer time (prayer for specific needs in the group)—Form a circle and hold hands. Thank the group for their participation and faithfulness to the study and to the group. Take time to pray that each member of the group will live out his or her life message in both character and actions. Thank God that each one is part of the "unending story" of salvation for all people and that God has invited them to participate in it.

Shifts in Ministry

Use the worksheet below to collect the answers from your mission outpost team as they share in the group time. This can give you a sense of where you are as a group in assessing these shifts in ministry.

Foundation for being made right with God:

Target group:

Leadership in the movement:

Strategy for reaching your mission field:

Base of operations:

Span of effort:

The goal of your life's work:

5 Questions Your Church Must Answer

The answers to these questions will tell you whether you are ready to begin the adventure of becoming a mission outpost.

1. Why has God placed us in this mission field? The answer to this question is your purpose or mission.

2. If we say we know why we are here, is everything we are currently doing contributing to that reason for being on mission? If so, how are we enhancing that ministry's effectiveness? If not, are we willing to change or remove those things that are not contributing to our mission? The answers to these questions guide your initial decisions for change.

3. What is God's picture of what we should become? Can we paint that picture in 25 words or less or in a drawing or picture? The answers to these questions provide a simple picture of your future. This God-inspired image is what you transition toward.

4. Have the core leaders prayerfully accepted the mission as God's call on the church body as a whole? If so, are they willing to put into practice the implications of that call? If not, what issues need to be addressed before there is agreement about the implications of the call? The answers to these questions will help you discover who will be the leaders of the transition and those you need to continue to serve as you lead them into God's future for your church.

5. What essential changes do we need to make to become what God has called us to be? The answers to this question begin the detailed process of strategic decision-making to become what God has called you to do and become.

The Antioch Mission Outpost Model

Record the answers from the other members of the group on the "score card" below.

T / F   "My church is intentionally mission-driven. All we do serves our mission to make disciples of all people."

_____   On a scale of 1 to 10 (10 being most like your church), rate your church's willingness to speak to lost people as evidence of their desire to share the message of Jesus with people unlike themselves.

T / F   "People are continually recruited to join us in our ministry of making disciples, to serve the needs of those brought into the family of God through the work of God's Spirit."

How well does your church train believers to become maturing disciples of Christ? Circle the description that best describes your church.
Very well   OK   Not very well

Do you believe your church members have a positive reputation as Christians in your community?

Rate your church's generosity toward sharing with other churches and meeting needs of those in your community.
Very generous   Generous   Not very generous

Explain your answer.

T / F   "My church sends a proportionate number of our members out on mission to tell others about Jesus through their actions and words."

An Anatomy of a Conflict

Use this sheet to record the answers of those on your team.

1. A new reality is introduced into the status quo (Acts 14:27-28).
   What new realities have you experienced recently that affirm the mission and vision God has called you to complete are valid?

2. Opposition to the new reality comes from traditionalists (Acts 15:1).
   What are some of the most common opposing points of view to the transitions you and your leaders are trying to accomplish?

3. The issue is sent to those who have the authority to decide (Acts 15:2-6).
   Who has the authority in your church to handle conflicts decisively?
   Are they effective? Does the process help the church be healthy, or does it foster divisions in the church?

4. The mission received support from those who shared the same experience (Acts 15:7-11).
   Who is a Peter in your church or organization who has experienced the new reality like you and would stand with you in resolving the issues related to your mission? Who are the apostles among you whose stories about changed lives of those you are trying to reach would help others see the vision more clearly?

5. The point leaders retold the stories of changed lives for all to hear (Acts 15:12).
   Can you passionately tell the stories of life change that illustrate your mission?

6. A decision was made by a trusted leader who took input from both sides (Acts 15:13-21).
   What biblical passages are foundational to what you are doing? Do you share them often? Are you careful to ensure you do not make them say something they are not? What common ground have you found that allows people in conflict to move forward together?

7. The leaders communicated their decision to the larger community of faith (Acts 15:22-30).
   Do you carefully communicate decisions made by the leaders to the church? Are your messages clearly stated, and do those who can answer any questions about the decision go with them? Do you have an organization you can use to share decisions with everyone involved?

Multiple Leaders Make a Difference

From this list of leaders, identify and circle the one most like you. Then go through the list and write the names of people in your church who serve in leadership roles. Record names from others in the group as they share. This list can help you choose leaders as you introduce change into the body.

Catalytic Leader (Paul)

Bridge Leader (Peter)

Consensus Leader (James)

Supportive Leader (Barnabas)

The Status Quo Leader (The Traditionalists)

My Core Message

In Session 6 of *Paul on Leadership* you were asked to write your life's core message and to be prepared to share it with your mission outpost team. Write your life's core message here.

Write the names of the other members of the team in the space below and record their life messages as they share them with the group. Pray that this core message will be reflected in their character and actions.

CHRISTIAN GROWTH STUDY PLAN

In the **Christian Growth Study Plan (formerly Church Study Course),** this book *Paul on Leadership: Servant Leadership in a Ministry of Transition* is a resource for course credit in Leadership and Skill Development plans. To receive credit, read the book, complete the learning activities, show your work to your pastor, a staff member or church leader, then complete the following information. This page may be duplicated. Send the completed page to:

**Christian Growth Study Plan
One LifeWay Plaza
Nashville, TN 37234-0117
FAX: (615)251-5067
Email: cgspnet@lifeway.com**

For information about the Christian Growth Study Plan, refer to the Christian Growth Study Plan Catalog. It is located online at www.lifeway.com/cgsp. If you do not have access to the Internet, contact the Christian Growth Study Plan office (1.800.968.5519) for the specific plan you need for your ministry.

COURSE CREDIT INFORMATION

Please check the appropriate box indicating the plan you want to apply this credit. You may check more than one.

❑ Leadership Development: for all church leaders (LS-0001)
❑ Church Leadership: for Discipleship Training directors, pastors, church staff, and other DT leaders (LS-0047)
❑ Associational Leadership: for Discipleship Training directors and other associational DT leaders (LS-0068)
❑ Men's Ministry, Family Ministry, Women's E Ministry (LS-0037)
❑ Church Growth Ministry (CG-1038)

PARTICIPANT INFORMATION

Social Security Number (USA ONLY-optional)	Personal CGSP Number*	Date of Birth (MONTH, DAY, YEAR)

Name (First, Middle, Last)	Home Phone

Address (Street, Route, or P.O. Box)	City, State, or Province	Zip/Postal Code

Please check appropriate box: ❑ Resource purchased by self ❑ Resource purchased by church ❑ Other

CHURCH INFORMATION

Church Name

Address (Street, Route, or P.O. Box)	City, State, or Province	Zip/Postal Code

CHANGE REQUEST ONLY

☐ Former Name

☐ Former Address	City, State, or Province	Zip/Postal Code

☐ Former Church	City, State, or Province	Zip/Postal Code

Signature of Pastor, Conference Leader, or Other Church Leader	Date

*New participants are requested but not required to give SS# and date of birth. Existing participants, please give CGSP# when using SS# for the first time. Thereafter, only one ID# is required. **Mail to:** Christian Growth Study Plan, One LifeWay Plaza, Nashville, TN 37234-0117. Fax: (615)251-5067.

Rev. 3-03